T0355532

James Hankins, General Editor

MARRASIO

ANGELINETUM AND OTHER POEMS

ITRL 73

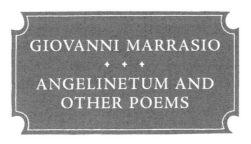

GIOVANNI MARRASIO
♦ ♦ ♦
ANGELINETUM AND OTHER POEMS

TRANSLATED BY

MARY P. CHATFIELD

THE I TATTI RENAISSANCE LIBRARY

HARVARD UNIVERSITY PRESS

CAMBRIDGE, MASSACHUSETTS

LONDON, ENGLAND

2016

Series design by Dean Bornstein

Library of Congress Cataloging-in-Publication Data

Names: Marrasio, Giovanni, approximately 1404–1452, author. |
Chatfield, Mary P., translator.
Title: Angelinetum and other poems / Giovanni Marrasio ; translated by
Mary P. Chatfield.
Other titles: I Tatti Renaissance library ; 73.
Description: Cambridge, Massachusetts : Harvard University Press, 2016. |
Series: The I Tatti Renaissance library ; 73 |
English translations on rectos with Latin originals on versos.
Identifiers: LCCN 2015037320 | ISBN 9780674545021 (alk. paper)
Classification: LCC PA8547.M5376 A2 2016 |
DDC 871/.04 — dc23
LC record available at http://lccn.loc.gov/2015037320

Contents

༄༅༅

Introduction

֍֍֍

Begin to love the men of Sicily.

Carmina Varia XVII.56

Ordinarily, when one sets out to describe the life of a writer, there are numerous sources beyond the writer's own works from which to glean all the important facts. With Giovanni Marrasio that is not the case. Although a few poems and letters from his contemporaries exist, most of what we know about him — and that is not much — comes from his poetry.[1] He has been esteemed as the first poet to revive the Latin love elegy since the fall of Rome, and his poetry achieved a measure of popularity in the last age of the manuscript book.[2]

Yet Giovanni Marrasio accounted himself a failure. A sympathetic reader could easily conclude, to the contrary, it was not he who failed, but his teachers, his quondam friends, and the social mores of the Italian peninsula that failed him. A young man of sound education, extraordinary talent, and warm disposition, Marrasio was doomed, as an avant-garde Sicilian in northern Italy, never to find a patron and never to have a fulfilling position. In the end he came almost to discount the talent he possessed and to despise the gifts that had at one time earned him unqualified praise. His poems — in the *Angelinetum* and in the collection now called the *Carmina Varia* — tell the story of a person continually hoping against hope, and the reader can only mourn for him, old before his time and dying full of regrets.[3]

In his late fifteenth-century book of three hundred short biographies, *Vite di uomini illustri del secolo XV*, Vespasiano da Bisticci describes Marrasio (whom he calls "Malraso the Sicilian") as an exceptional poet, but one perhaps too modern for his time, intensely devoted to a manner of writing—imitation of the classical elegiac poets—that would not come into vogue until the middle decades of the fifteenth century.[4] Bisticci's intimation is that being ahead of his time, not serious enough, un-Ciceronian one might say, made Marrasio underappreciated. A modern biographer, Gianvito Resta, seems to share that feeling, suggesting that Marrasio's seriousness of purpose vanished as he began to experience the thoughtless and irreverent life ("l'ambiente spensierato e goliardico") of the university students of Siena. As one follows the course of Marrasio's life through his poetry and the few extant letters, the reader may draw a slightly different and sadder conclusion.

Marrasio was born in Noto in southeastern Sicily (A VII.33) sometime between 1400 and 1404. Of his parents we know only his father's first name, Guglielmo, given on a diploma Marrasio witnessed from the Studio at Ferrara, and the fact that he presents himself in A VII.9–10 as

> not sprung from obscure parentage:
> My mother had an illustrious name, as did my father.

He seems to have had a fine education in the grammar school of Noto, one that nourished his scholarly and literary ambitions, as it did those of other Sicilian scholars, including Giovanni Aurispa, Antonio Cassarino, and Giovanni Campiano, for each of the latter went on to higher studies and to fortune in the cities of northern Italy.

When the young Marrasio arrived at the Studio in Siena is uncertain, because the exact year of his birth is uncertain, but we can surmise that he was there by 1424, for we know that he was about twenty years old when he first caught sight of Angela Piccolomini. In A VII.33–34 he says that

For twenty years I remained a body without a heart:
  Angela alone gave me life, talent, and feeling.

And we know, too, from a poem to one of his friends (CV VI)
that he was in Siena at the time of the plague of 1424, choosing
not to flee the city as that friend and others did.

The Siena of that moment was a university town at the height
of its fame, with an eager group of students centering their out-
door life around the elegant Fonte Gaia and competing through
poetry for the attention of their teachers and with each other in
their love affairs. Marrasio quickly came to think of Siena as his
second birthplace, as he writes in lines (A VII.28–30) that recall
the famous epitaph on Vergil's tomb:

  Noto bore me, Siena bore me.
  Who would believe such marvels, that in our time Marrasio
    Was begotten twice—in his Sicilian home and then in
      Tuscany?

He set about making himself a lively member of the student fel-
lowship, even falling wildly and desperately in love with the daugh-
ter of one of Siena's most aristocratic families, the Piccolomini.
Whether he was overstepping the bounds when he did so is hard
to determine. Among the *Carmina Varia* is a chatty poem to Enea
Silvio Piccolomini, the future Pope Pius II. He numbered Tom-
maso Piccolomini among his student friends, even including a
poem addressed to him in the *Angelinetum*; and his contemporaries
seemed to find his love-affair-in-verse a matter of affectionate
amusement (CV A, B). But in the torrent of his protestations of
overmastering love, he has little moments of worry about being
unfit, as a Sicilian, to look for love in return. In the middle of the
poems comprising the *Angelinetum* is one, not to his beloved, but
to a friend, Giovanni da Prato, suggesting that Giovanni has been
begging

> . . . the gods that Angelina should shrink
> From me, a Sicilian, that she should shrink from my face.
> (A V.26–27)

And he is comforted by another friend, Maffeo Vegio, who — writing as if he were Angelina herself — says of Marrasio

> Fine manners, lively virtue, the glory and honor
> Of high nobility distinguish you.

Therefore

> As once his charming Licoris pleased Gallus,
> And Lesbia, they say, pleased you, Catullus . . .
> So I, Angelina, will be exalted by Marrasio Siculo.
> (CV C.63–64, 89–90, 93)

He is reassured and can write to Vegio in return that he is able to imagine Angelina repeating Vegio's words, with a hopeful addition.

> She spoke your song, such as it was, with which in my love
> You consoled me: "I want to be a Sicilian woman."
> (CV I.17–18)

The Fonte Gaia, the exquisitely carved white marble fountain of Jacopo della Quercia (1419) that stands at the top of the Piazza del Campo in Siena, figures heavily in the *Angelinetum* and its associated poems. It was both the actual and the symbolic heart of university life, a gathering place whose waters had a mythic history and a present-day reality of refreshment and reinvigoration. To Marrasio's poetic mind, its waters can restore one to youth; to its waters as to an Italian Castalian spring, he attributes his poetic gift; from beside its waters, he can see Angelina's window; in its waters, dyed red from his blood, she will see his body when he kills himself for love. Even his imagined sorrows are full of a hopeful and passionate life; for the Muses of the Fonte Gaia, the Latin Camenae, seem almost real, and he writes as if he can summon them at any time for inspiration.

By the time the group of poems comprising the *Angelinetum* was complete in the late summer of 1429, Marrasio seemed to have finished, abandoned is perhaps a better word, his studies at Siena and moved on to the Studium in Florence, where he already had a number of friends both in the student body and among the leading professors. That the dedicatory poems at the beginning and the end of the *Angelinetum* are to Leonardo Bruni, the greatest Italian humanist of the day, suggests that Marrasio was already known among the Arno city's humanists as an up-and-coming poet; and Bruni's lavish praise for Marrasio's work likewise attests to the latter's comfortable status among his most eager followers.

It is not known for certain what course of study Marrasio was pursuing either in Siena or in Florence. Among the most famous professors in Siena in the 1420s was the Sicilian jurist Niccolò de' Tudeschi (or Tedeschi), a great authority on canon law, and it may have been his reputation in his homeland that first drew Marrasio and his Sicilian companions to that city.[5] Vespasiano says that while in Florence Marrasio studied canon law, but if that is so, he left in 1430 without a degree and moved on to Padua to study medicine. What we do know for certain is that those six years in Siena and Florence turned out to be the happiest time of his life. The general lightheartedness of that time in Siena and Florence is attested to, not only by the *Angelinetum*, but by the first group of poems in the *Carmina Varia*, which include not only poems about his fellow students falling in and out of love but delighted poetic responses (CV II and III) to words of praise by two of the greatest Florentine intellectuals: Leonardo Bruni and Carlo Marsuppini. Bruni called Marrasio "a brilliant youth" and wrote him that he "should be ranked with poets like Ovid and Propertius and Tibullus, for these are thought to have written elegy the most faultlessly and elegantly of all" (CV D); while the great Carlo Marsuppini, the revered "universal professor" who taught rhetoric, poetry, Greek and Latin philosophy, saw fit to send Marrasio a copy of his translation of the *Batrachomyomachia*, accompanied by a letter, which ended with this fulsome praise:

> we send this little work, as though it were by Homer, to you, glory of the Muses, who have achieved so much in song that you seem to be numbered among those like Tibullus, Propertius, and Gallus. (CV E)

Such encomia must have lifted his heart to the heavens and filled him with the hope of finding a position of service and honor with one of the important families or cities of Tuscany. When he received them he was just twenty-five.

The next we know of Marrasio for certain is that he has left Florence — the plague was raging in that city again — and has taken up the study of medicine in Padua, where he is at first discontented and then deeply unhappy. In a moving letter to his friend Antonio Beccadelli, known as Panormita, he asks why his erstwhile friend has not written to him and calls Padua "the filthiest of towns and the shit of city-states" (Appendix I.4). At the same period he writes to his friend Francesco Tallone, describing himself at the outset of the poem as "without inspiration or Muses or love" (CV XIV.2). The rest of the poem is a record of all that has made him unhappy in Padua. Though he says that he has worked at his medical studies and "willingly learned to bring help to the sick" (CV XIV.8), "no love warmed [his] heart" and "now [he is] afraid of the cold and slimy swamps, / the pathless fens, and altogether lifeless lakes" (CV XIV.9, 11–12).

Discouraged, lonely, oppressed by the place and its weather, Marrasio left Padua in the early spring of 1432 and made his way to Ferrara, a move that brought hope to his heart and a corresponding lift to his spirits. Here, as he tells Tallone, he begs his friend to

> . . . choose for me a comely nymph
> From these vales to sing of often in my tunes.
> (CV XIV.25–26)

And he must have found one such, for in his very next poem he is complaining about "the transmutation and toilsome life of lovers" (CV XV) in language reminiscent of Tibullus' first poems to Delia.

Ferrara, under its ruler Niccolò III d'Este, was one of the liveliest and most renowned centers of culture in Italy. Niccolò's court circle included the famous humanist and teacher Guarino Veronese and Marrasio's older friend and fellow townsman Giovanni Aurispa Piciunerio, known simply as Aurispa; and it is easy to see in the work he produced in the year and a half that we know he was living in Ferrara that Marrasio, buoyed by the scholarly and literary activity he encountered, hoped through friendship and his skill as a poet to find a permanent post there. After all, Panormita, his companion from university days, was already in service at the court of the Visconti in Pavia. Why not Ferrara for him?

To this end, in 1433 he threw himself into the composition and presentation of a masque to be given to an assembly of notables gathered in Ferrara for the celebration of a treaty of peace signed on April 26, 1433. That the masque seemed to have been extremely elaborate we know not only from Marrasio's description (CV XVII) but also from a contemporary letter describing the delight and amazement with which it was received by the spectators (Appendix II.2). The masque involved a huge and motley cast of mythological characters, including Mars and Bellona, Aesculapius, Mercury, Priapus, Venus and Cupid, Vertumnus, Proteus, Hercules, Cerberus, the Furies, and the Fates. In a poem addressed to Niccolò III (*CV* XVII), Marrasio greets the marquis on behalf of the maskers and urges him to allow them to bring joy to his city. Marrasio then boldly puts himself forward as a possible court poet:

> If you so command, I shall lead the Muses from the Fonte
> > Gaia
> > To the long reaches of the glorious Po.
> > > (*CV* XVII.47–48)

The *titulum* of this poem, which announces that it is written by Marrasio on behalf of Sozzino Benzi, whose father was the most famous professor of medicine in Italy, suggests the nagging anxiety that underlay his bravura, as does its final line (*CV* XVII.56),

> Begin to love the men of Sicily.

Whatever hopes Marrasio may have had about a future in Ferrara were dashed by receiving, as an answer to both the masque and his poem of presentation, a poem written by Guarino Veronese on the marquis' behalf that compares the brief life of a masked character to the brief life of a human and urges "distinguished Sozzino, with the poet Marrasio," to live it up while they are young:

> While time permits, while your age decently allows,
> > Seize delight to the full with joyful breast.
> > > (*CV* F.41–42)

Even though this response seems to throw cold water on all his hopes,[6] Marrasio replies with a poem in praise of Guarino's poetry, and we feel him holding back all disappointment in order to put on a brave face. The epigraph at the end of the poem says that the poem concerns the "birth, death and life of masques"

(CV XVIII), and Marrasio writes abstractly about the nature of masques, almost as if he had not received any discouraging word at all from Guarino. Is there a deeper meaning here?

Although there is no record of other performances, Marrasio seems to have written more than one masque, because he makes mention, in the poem to Cyriac of Ancona immediately following, of a group of new masques, which he begs Cyriac, an amateur classical archeologist then resident in Ferrara, to "receive his new masques" and improve them (CV XIX.8, 11). Here he seems to be grasping at the final straw that Ferrara might hold out for him of possible preferment in the work he loves. Nothing came of it. Records are too scarce to tell us much of what Marrasio did with himself during the years between the end of 1433 and 1440. He completed his medical studies in August of 1433, and probably remained in the town seeking a position; but fortune was not as kind to him in Ferrara as it was to his hometown friend, Aurispa.

An event that suggests Marrasio's presence in the area during those years was the appearance of Marrasio's name in a list of candidates for the office of chancellor of the Commune of Perugia, following the death of Matteo Vanoli, the previous holder of that office. The list included such distinguished men as Filelfo and Aurispa, which suggests how well Marrasio was thought of, but the position went to Tommaso Pontano, and once again Marrasio's hopes were dashed.

That he continued to stay in Ferrara despite his disappointment is suggested by Poem XVI in the *Carmina Varia*, addressed to Leonello d'Este, son of Niccolò, upon his succession to his father as marquis of Ferrara. This poem, though written in late 1441 or early 1442, is placed ahead of the earlier "Ferrara poems," and its placement serves only to underscore the weight of silent frustration Marrasio must have suffered there. It praises Leonello for the peace that he and his father had brought to northern Italy, for his love and patronage of the arts, and for his political wisdom, and it hesitatingly suggests that Marrasio would love to be called on to write more "of you and your house" (CV XVI.36). But to no avail. Hence, after a brief sojourn in Genoa, he traveled homeward toward Sicily, leaving behind the second city where he had dreamed of securing a position worthy of his poetic talents.

Yet Marrasio was not without hope as he went, for in June of 1442, Alfonso V "the Magnanimous," a great and generous patron of the arts, had just conquered Naples and integrated it into the Aragonese Empire that dominated the Western Mediterranean. Foremost among the men of letters in his entourage was Panormita, Marrasio's old schoolmate and the scapegrace author of *Hermaphroditus*, who had moved on from Pavia in 1434 to join the Aragonese court. Marrasio stopped in Naples long enough to receive a sizable benefice, then went back to Sicily. There he almost immediately married a young woman half his age and fathered two daughters. Archival records show that he practiced medicine on the island and was, between September 1443 and August 1446, in the pay of the *universitas* of Palermo. He seems to have spent time also in his native city of Noto, for in September of 1447 he was given the title *patrizio* (patrician) of Noto and thus became a town dignitary.

Two short poems from this period—CV XLIII and XLIV— suggest Marrasio's participation in the modest cultural life of the island, and we know from the collected letters of other humanists that he continued to maintain a correspondence with his friends on the mainland, where the *Angelinetum* was much admired and copied. (Nearly seventy-five copies survive, a remarkable figure in the last age of the manuscript book.) But the bulk of his poetic output in the years between 1443 and 1452 is addressed to Tommaso Parentucelli, Pope Nicholas V; to his friend, Alfonso di Cuevasruvias, the archbishop of Monreale; or to King Alfonso V. With the latter two he almost assumes the role of court poet,

deploring a disaster, drafting several versions of an epitaph, prais-
ing a mistress, sending a gift. While the poems to the pope assume
more of a familiarity than may have actually existed between the
two men, they also show a knowledge of current events and an
enormous appreciation for the work of building the Vatican Li-
brary, translating Greek literature into Latin, and rebuilding rav-
aged Rome—all hallmarks of Nicholas' papacy. Nicholas, by re-
plying to one of Marrasio's epigrams with an epigram of his own
(*CV* XXVI), shows more kindness to the no-longer-hopeful poet
than any of those to whom he had turned earlier in his life—at
least if the poem is what it purports to be.[7]

Of the poems written for the two Alfonsos, king and arch-
bishop, the one describing the death of the archbishop's brother
(*CV* XXXVI) is of particular interest, for in that poem Marrasio's
talent as a poet and his profession as a doctor unite to provide the
first (perhaps the only) description of a trepanning in verse. The
careful description of the entire hunting disaster and its aftermath
suggests that Marrasio was present both as participant and as
medical man, attesting to a certain closeness between the poet and
the archbishop. The four reworkings of an epitaph for Garcias de
Cuevasruvias suggest to this closeness as well; and we know from
documents that Marrasio maintained a house in Palermo even af-
ter he ceased working for the city as a medical man.

The poems addressed to King Alfonso V are more obviously
those of someone wishing to ingratiate himself with a prince.
They derive from the year 1451, when he made a frightening sea
voyage to Naples, which he describes with great vividness in *CV*
XXXIII, and where, having lost his young wife and a daughter to
the plague (*CV* XXXII.7–17), he decided to embrace the religious
life, took holy orders, and began, in hope of a more secure posi-
tion, to look for an ecclesiastical benefice. It was in his old friend
Panormita as well as his new friend, the archbishop Alfonso, that
he placed his hopes.

Besides the emotional pain from the losses of these years, Marrasio also suffered physically—from a fall from his mule, which seriously injured his kidneys, and from repeated attacks of quartan fever, which seemed to have laid him low for months at a time and brought on a severe depression. The central poem in the latter half of the *Carmina Varia* and by far the longest is an anguished plea to God to be given respite from illness and time for repentance. Drawing on arguments from Aquinas and examples of suffering from the Bible, especially those of Jonah, and quoting whole lines from many of the classical poets, particularly Ovid, Marrasio describes his illnesses in minute detail and begs for time to repent and, if it is God's will, to go to Rome and see the pope. He declares his sorrow for having written

> . . . fictions . . . [that] have not made men blessed,
> Nor have they taught us about our eternal home.
>   (CV XXX.229–30)

If the poem about his illness is long and morose, the poem about his cure, which follows it, addressed to Pope Nicholas, is short and full of cheer. But then another blow strikes, this time a long bout with quartan fever, a type of malaria that recurs every seventy-two hours, with which Marrasio was laid up for many months and which ended only on Easter Day 1452. In April of 1452 he journeyed to Rome, as he had fervently desired, and was able to see the pope and make an offering of his poems. He then went back to Sicily, but his years of illness had taken their toll, and he died on September 12, 1452, shortly after his return, not having yet reached the age of fifty.

In 1429, in the springtime of his hopes, in the poem with which he presented his *Angelinetum* to Bruni, Marrasio, like the best of the ancient poets, called his elegies *nugae*, or trifles (A IX.17), meaning in effect that they were anything but. He was dedicating his poems to the most prominent humanist of his time, in the sure and certain expectation that they would be received with congratulations. In the spring of 1452, Marrasio, ill and discouraged, presented his poems to Nicholas V once again as *nugae*, this time likening them to "humble spinach" (*CV* XLVI.50) and wishing no more than to give an overburdened leader a few moments of pleasure. A lifetime of disappointment lay between those years.

Professor Luke Roman read the manuscript of my translation and suggested many improvements. I offer this book in gratitude to Professor Walter Kaiser and Professor James Hankins, the former my old teacher, an indefatigable fund-raiser, and friend, the latter a most generous and deeply committed General Editor. Without them this series would not exist.

NOTES

1. For what can be gleaned about Marrasio's life and career, see the biographical sketch, with ample bibliography, by A. Tramontana in *DBI* 70 (2008), online at www.treccani.it/enciclopedia. Further information can be found in the Notes to the Translations.

2. For Marrasio's position in the history of the Latin love elegy, see Jozef Ijsewijn with Dirk Sacré, *Companion to Neo-Latin Studies*, Part II: *Literary, Linguistic, Philological and Editorial Questions*, 2nd ed. (Leuven, 1998), 81.

3. See *CV* XXXII.125–26. Note that the title *Carmina Varia* is a modern title invented by Gianvito Resta, editor of Marrasio's poetic works, to distinguish the Latin poetry not included in the *Angelinetum*. They form part of a longer anthology of Marrasio's poetry, in many manuscripts called the *Poematum et prosarum liber*; it is possible that the latter title descends from Marrasio himself. References to the two parts of Marrasio's oeuvre in this introduction and elsewhere are abbreviated as follows: *A* = *Angelinetum*, *CV* = *Carmina Varia*.

4. Vespasiano Bisticci, *Le vite*, ed. Aulo Greco, 2 vols. (Florence, 1976), 2:59–60.

5. On Niccolò de' Tudeschi, see Knut Wolfgang Nörr, *Kirche und Konzil bei Nikolaus de Tudeschis (Panormitanus)* (Cologne: Böhlau, 1964).

6. See here also Appendix II.1.

7. The poem may well be, however, a literary fiction written by Marrasio himself.

ANGELINETUM

Marrasii Siciliensis ad Leonardum Arretinum
virum eloquentissimum in Angelinetum praefatio
incipit feliciter.

Hunc, Leonarde, tuo volui obsignare libellum
    Nomine, quo titulus luceat ipse magis.
Si quoi dandus honos Grai pariterque Latini
    Eloquii et quicquid laudis in orbe fuit,
5 Si quoi debetur fama immortalis avorum,
    Arretine, tibi gloria prima manet.
Effingis priscos nimia gravitate parentes
    Et superas veteres tu probitate viros.
Non solum dicant tibi se debere Latini,
10   Verum etiam Argolici teque tuosque colant.
Non minus in Graium conversus sermo Latinus
    Quam Graium per te lingua Latina tenet.
Eloquitur lepida ac ornata voce Latinus
    Factus Aristoteles: barbarus ante fuit.
15 Punica bella diu tot in annis mortua vivunt,
    Rex Cicero vivit non moriturque Plato.
Quid recitem libros te traduxisse Pelasgos
    Innumeros, totidem et composuisse novos?
Italiae lumen, per te venere Camenae
20   Ad Latium, per te dicta vetusta placent.
Indulgere velis nostro, Arretine, furori,
    Sive sit ille furor, sive sit ille dolor.
Iudicium facias nostro de carmine, sive
    Thura tegat, vel sint verbula digna legi.
25 Quae si iudicio fuerint laudata benigno,

The preface to the Angelinetum *of Marrasio Siculo
addressed to Leonardo Aretino, that most eloquent of men,
begins auspiciously.*

I desired to stamp this little book, Leonardo, with your name,
    So that its very title might shine the more.
If the glory of eloquence in Greek, and Latin too,
    Belongs to anyone, if there be any fame in the world,
If to anyone is owed the deathless renown of our ancestors,   5
    It is to you, Aretine, that the principal glory is due.
With your superabundant majesty you portray our forefathers
    And with your integrity you surpass the men of old.
Not only should the Latins say they are in debt to you,
    But the Greeks should also reverence you and yours.   10
Through you Latin speech has been transformed into Greek
    No less than the Latin tongue now possesses the Greek.
Though he was barbarian before, Aristotle, made a Latin,
    Speaks in an elegant and charming manner.
The Punic Wars, dead for so many years, are now alive,   15
    King Cicero lives, and Plato does not perish.
But why repeat that you have translated numberless Greek books
    When you have composed an equal number of your own?
Light of Italy, through you the Muses have come into Latium,
    Through you the sayings of the ancients delight once more.   20
May you indulge my madness, O man of Arezzo,
    Whether it be madness or suffering;
May you pass judgment on my poem — whether it should be
    Wrapping for incense, or whether my little words are worth
        reading.
If they should be praised by your gracious judgment,   25

Mordeat o quantum quisque poeta velit.
Nec pigeat nostris te respondere tabellis,
    Sive velis prosa, carmine sive velis.
Si mihi rescribes, Musas venisse putabo
30   Aonio ex fonte et numina sacra novem.
Indulgere velis nostro, Arretine, furori,
    Sive sit ille furor, sive sit ille dolor.
Quando novi vates ausi sunt tempore prisco
    Carmina, Phoebeos consuluere focos;
35 Nunc quaerenda meis non sunt oracla Sibyllae
    Versibus et Phoebus despiciendus erit:
Tu Cumaea mihi, tu Phoebeaeque sorores,
    Phoebus eris calamis Calliopeque meis.

Praefatio in Angelinetum *explicit.*

: II :

Marrasii Siciliensis Angelinetum *incipit feliciter
ad divam Angelinam.*

Angelina, meo si respondebis amori,
    Quanta fuit scribam Piccolomina domus.
Cantabo innumeros quos detulit illa triumphos,
    Quidve tuos primos nobilitavit avos.
5 Obducis frontem? rugabunt carmina nervi?
    Nec meus has segetes dente secabit equus?
Saepe boves validi diris lassantur aratris,
    Vexat et ingratus fortia corda labos?
Cunctos excruciat labor ingratissimus, acris
10 Et non grata necat solicitudo viros.

4

O let every poet criticize them however much he wants!
Please be unashamed to reply to my sketches,
    In prose if you want, or if you prefer, in poetry.
If you answer me, I shall believe that the nine sacred divinities,
    The Muses, have come from the Aeonian spring.   30
Do indulge my madness, O man of Arezzo,
    Whether it be madness or suffering.
When in ancient times new poets dared to make poems,
    They consulted the altars of Apollo;
Now my verses need not consult the oracles of the Sibyl   35
    And Apollo can be scorned.
You will be the Cumaean one for me, you the Phoebean sisters.
    You will be the Apollo and Calliope for my pen.

The preface to the Angelinetum *ends.*

: II :

The Angelinetum *of Marrasio Siculo to the divine*
Angelina begins auspiciously.

Angelina, if you will respond to my love,
    I will describe how great the house of Piccolomini has been,
I will sing of the numberless triumphs it has produced,
    And what ennobled your earliest ancestors.
You hide your face? Will my songs' vigor wrinkle your brow?   5
    Shall my horse not crop these fields with his teeth?
Are strong oxen often wearied by the dreaded plow,
    And does thankless toil trouble brave hearts?
Utterly thankless tasks torture everyone,
    Care that does not win thanks is the death of men.   10

Forsitan et titulos describi et gesta tuorum
    Contraxere aciem? Te prius ipse canam!
Et formam egregiam in primis flavosque capillos
    Et frontem atque manus a capite usque pedes,
15 Sideribus similes oculos, cristallina membra,
    Quae variat roseus dulcis odore rubor.
Mille tuas scribam praeclaro carmine laudes,
    Signa mihi primo si manifesta dabis.

∶ III ∶

Ad divam Angelinam
de laudibus suis complurimis.

Illaqueat risus dulcissimus Angelinai
    Marrasium; eius enim stillat ab ore favus,
Qui si Sardonias favus esset fusus in herbas
    Sardonii Siculis dulcia mella darent.
5 Me rapiunt oculi, qui sunt mihi sidera: apertis
    Lucent et tenebrae et Tartara opaca vident;
Per salebras ego tutus eo de nocte timendas,
    Clarus eo in latebras aspera perque iuga;
Non timor est mundo, Phoebo si lumina desunt
10   Aut si nocturna Cinthia luce caret.
Quando die nitidis mihi rides, Angela, ocellis,
    Non est splendidior sol neque luna prior.
Sideribus certant oculi, tua labra rubentes
    Corallos superant, alba ligustra genae.
15 Est gula lucenti tanto suffusa nitore,
    Ut timeam quando nigra Falerna bibis;

Has describing the honors and deeds of your family perhaps
     Made you withdraw your sight? Then I will sing of you first!
To begin, moving from head to foot, I will describe
     Your exceptional beauty and golden hair, your forehead and
          hands,
Eyes like stars, limbs gleaming like crystal,   15
     To which a rosy blush, sweet in its perfume, gives varied color.
I will write a thousand praises of you in a glorious poem,
     If you will first give me one clear sign.

∶　III　∶

To the divine Angelina:
Of her numerous praises.

Angela's utterly delicious laughter ensnares
     Marrasio; for honey drips from her lips.
Had this honey been poured out on the plants of Sardinia,
     The Sards would be giving sweet honey to the Sicilians.
Her eyes, which to me are stars, ravish me: when open,   5
     The darkness shines, and one can see in lightless Tartarus;
Through rough places fearful by night I pass safe,
     I go, brightly lit, into wild beasts' dens and over rough ridges;
The world has no fear, if Apollo's light should fail
     Or Cynthia lack her nocturnal splendor.   10
Whenever you laugh with your eyes gleaming, Angela,
     The sun is not more glorious nor the moon.
Your eyes vie with the stars, your lips excel
     The blushing coral, your cheeks the fair privet blossom.
Your throat is suffused with such a gleaming sheen,   15
     That I am fearful when you drink the black Falernian;

7

Sanguineos iugulos primo meditatus ad arma
    Issem, ni me tunc admonuisset amor.
Me macerat frons clara, velut quam numen adoro
20   Purior est speculo candidiorque nive.
Quom loqueris, rutilas fundunt tua labra favillas,
    Cinnama praeterea purpureasque rosas.
Pectora cristallus circumdat, longa hiacintus
    Lactea colla tenet, corpora tota nitor.
25 Haec mihi desiccant nimio fervore medullas
    Et mea dilaniat pectora longa sitis.
Arripiunt animam medio de corpore nostram
    Ista: voluptatis tu mihi prima quies.

: IV :

Ad divam ut eum cunctis amatoribus anteponat.

Si quis amandus erit vultu facieque serenus,
    Te Ganimedeus debet habere thorus;
Si placet armatus clipeo et fulgentibus armis,
    Belligerum Martem splendida forma petat;
5 Imperio aeternam si vis producere vitam,
    Iuppiter ardenti ferveat igne tuo;
Si moveat mentem tibi copia divitiarum,
    Mida petendus erit, ditior ante alios;
Si quis amore suo videatur dignus amari,
10   Marrasio nullus saucior esse potest.
Non quaerenda tibi est tantorum gloria regum:
    Hi periere duces hique obiere Ioves.

8

Thinking at first your throat to be bloodied, I might have
    resorted
  To arms, if love had not then admonished me.
Your bright brow, which I worship as a deity, torments me;
  It is clearer than a mirror, whiter than snow.   20
When you speak, your lips pour out glowing sparks
  Along with cinnamon and dark red roses.
Crystal clothes your breast, the hyacinth
  Your long milk-white neck, brilliance your whole person.
These things drain my vitals dry with intemperate ardor   25
  And enduring thirst ravages my breast.
These things snatch my soul from the midst of my body;
  You are the first repose of my delight.

: IV :

To his goddess, that she will rank him ahead of all her lovers.

If you must love anyone serene in face and form,
  Ganymede's couch should hold you;
If someone armed with shield and gleaming spear be your
    pleasure,
  Let your glowing loveliness seek out warlike Mars;
If you desire to bring forth a life immortal in power,   5
  Let Jupiter smolder with passion for you;
If abundance of wealth should stir your soul,
  You should seek out Midas, richer than all others;
But if anyone should seem worthy to be loved for his love,
  No one can be more smitten than Marrasio.   10
You should not seek the glory of such great rulers:
  Such leaders perish and such Joves die.

9

Restat ames qui primus amat, quem multa fatigant
    Tela, truci ex arcu missa sagitta tuo.
15 Et si forte ducum quos dixi pompa maneret,
    Ostendam ut cunctis antelocandus ero.
Vincit Amor faciem, prosternit tela Cupido,
    Vertit et imperium divitiasque premit.
Victus et Endimion fuit et subiectus Amori
20   Mars ferus et vidi cornua ferre Iovem.
Omnia quom superant et fortia et infima amores,
    Et meus est aliis fortior unus amor,
Et Venus et mores et te natura coercet,
    Inter amatores primus amator eam.
25 Sis veluti Italicis formosior una puellis,
    Angela, sic felix sisque benigna mihi.
Alternum quem iure peto mihi solvere amorem,
    Non mihi contracta tradere fronte velis.

: V :

Marrasii Siciliensis ad eloquentem et praeclarum virum
Iohannem Pratensem iurisconsultum responsio incipit.

Prate, meum numen, mea lux, mea gaudia, legi,
    Prate, tuos versus et placuere nimis.
Et te divinum possum appellare poetam:
    Namque elegos redoles Virgiliosque sapis.
5 Est gravior mihi poena, tuis quod privor ocellis
    Et quod te careo, quam tibi cura mei.
Si cupis alternis studiis nos iungere amores,
    Ast ego: vivamus tempora cuncta simul.

Just love him who loves you most of all, whom
    Many spears assail, arrows shot from a cruel bow.
And if by chance the pomp of those leaders I mentioned   15
    Should linger, I will show how I should outrank them all.
Love conquers appearances; he casts them down with his dart;
    He alters empire and subdues wealth.
Endymion was overcome, and wild Mars laid low
    By Love, and I have seen Jove wearing horns.   20
Since love conquers all things both strong and weak,
    And since my one love is stronger than the others;
And since Venus, custom, and nature constrain you,
    May I as a lover walk first among your lovers.
Just as you are the loveliest among the maidens of Italy,   25
    Angela, so may you be favorable and kindly to me.
Please pay me the love I rightly ask of you in return,
    And don't hand me payment with that grudging look.

: V :

An answer begins here from Marrasio Siculo to the
eloquent and famous jurist Giovanni da Prato.

Prato, my divinity, my guiding light, my joy, I have read
    Your verses, Prato, and they have pleased me much;
And now I can call *you* a divine poet:
    For you have the fragrance of elegy and Vergil's flavor.
That I miss you, that I am deprived of your dear eyes,   5
    Is for me a penalty heavier than your concern for me.
If you wish love poems to join us in mutual desire
    But I do too, we may live together always.

Nec fidei templum nec te, mea vita, fefelli:
10   Marrasius pereat si caret ipse fide.
Est mea salva fides: 'Veniam' dixisse fatebor;
        Quom dixi 'Veniam,' non sine lege fuit.
Pollicitus colere et villas et florea rura
        Fluminaque et rivos sole calente fui.
15   Praeteriere dies, iam iam cecinere cicadae
        Et folia arboribus iam cecidere suis.
Nunc deformis hiems me territat, angit et ipsum
        Me prope venturi principium studii.
Ergo nec advorsum me fundas, Prate, querelas;
20   Iratus quom sis, concutit ossa tremor.
Si veniam, non tecta tui, non alta subibo
        Atria, ut haec videam: te magis ipse petam.
Nec sine te villae, sine te nec rura placerent,
        Nec sine te fontes, nec mihi silva placet.
25   Quod petis a superis, ut me Angelina Sicanum
        Horreat, ut vultus horreat usque meos,
Istud idem faciam divis et thure Sabaeo,
        Ut fugiat vultus Francia bella tuos.
Sive velis nolisque etiam, deus annuat, ut, si
30   Illa meos oculos horreat, illa tuos.

: VI :

Ad divam Angelinam.

Quid furis, audaci nimium confisa iuventa?
        Praecipiti penna curva senecta venit.
Aspice: non semper vestita est terra virenti

I have neither tricked Fidelity's temple nor you, my dear;
    May Marrasio die if he is without fidelity.   10
Mine is intact. I shall confess that I said, "I shall come";
    When I said, "I shall come," it was a legitimate promise.
I promised to devote myself to country houses and flowery
        meadows
    And rivers and riverbanks under a warm sun.
Days have gone by, now; even now the cicadas have done singing,   15
    And now leaves have fallen from their trees.
Now ugly winter frightens me and torments me
    Just when I am going to begin my studies.
Therefore, Prato, don't pour out complaints against me,
    For when you are angry, trembling shakes my bones.   20
If I come, I shall not enter your dwelling nor its lofty courtyard
    That I might see them; it is you I shall be seeking.
Without you neither country houses nor country scenes delight,
    Without you neither streams nor woods please me either.
Because you beg the gods that Angelina should shrink   25
    From me, a Sicilian, that she should shrink from my face,
I will make the same request to the gods with Saban incense:
    That the lovely Francia may flee from your sight.
Whether you wish it or not, may God grant
    That if the one shuns my eyes, the other will shun yours.   30

: VI :

To the goddess Angelina.

Why do you rave, trusting overmuch in daring youth?
    Bent old age is coming with headlong wings.
Look: not always is the earth clothed with verdant grass,

Gramine, nec semper solibus usta riget,
5   Nec semper rutilos producit terra colores
Et niveas pariter purpureasque rosas,
Lilia saepe nitent placido redolentia odore,
Saepe gravant ramos dulcia poma suos,
Dulces saepe cibos dat nobis pampinus uvas;
10   Non semper fructus quaelibet arbor habet.
Sic te decipiet formosa et blanda iuventus,
Quae nunc est votis obsequiosa tuis.

: VII :

Ad divam Angelinam Marrasii eulogium.

Angelina, meos numquam miserata dolores,
Respice me: morior; respice me: morior.
Quid iuvat ut validis plangam mea pectora pugnis
Deque oculis lacrimae fluminis instar eant?
5   Me fugis, ut rapidos fugiunt armenta leones,
Ut timet horrendos parvula cerva lupos.
Non me lactavit Gaetula in valle leaena,
Non ursae aut tigres barbariaeque pecus.
Quem fugis? Obscuro non sum de sanguine natus:
10   Clara habuit genetrix nomina, clara pater.
Gloria magna tibi est perituro parcere amanti;
Cantabunt laudes carmina nostra tuas.
Si mihi nec lacrimae prosunt, nec carmina mille,
Nec centum laudes, nec rogitasse deos,
15   Praestat ut emoriar gladio traiectus acuto,
Finiat ut lacrimas mors furibunda meas.
Si dii iustitiae memores sunt atque nocentum,

14

Nor does it always stiffen, burned by the sun;
The earth does not always produce warm colors,   5
  Or white or dark red roses in equal measure.
Lilies often gleam, fragrant with mild perfume,
  Sweet fruit trees often load their branches,
Vine shoots often give us grapes, sweet as food.
  But every tree does not always bear fruit.   10
Fair and charming youth, for the moment obedient
  To your wishes, will in this way deceive you.

: VII :

Marrasio's eulogy to the divine Angelina.

Angelina, who has never taken pity on my sorrows,
  Look at me: I am dying; look at me: I am dying.
Why does it please you that I batter my breast with clenched fists
  And tears flow from my eyes like a river?
You flee from me as cattle flee from fierce lions,   5
  As the tender doe fears terrifying wolves.
No African lioness nursed me in a Gaetulian valley,
  No, nor she-bears nor tigers nor other savage beasts.
Whom do you flee? I am not sprung from obscure parentage:
  My mother had an illustrious name, as did my father.   10
You will win great glory by sparing a lover doomed to die;
  My poems will sing your praises.
If tears are no use to me, nor a thousand poems,
  Nor a hundred praises, nor pleading with the gods,
Then it is better to die pierced by a sharp sword,   15
  That furious death might put an end to my tears.
If the gods are mindful of justice and of those who do harm,

Nec meus effusus sanguis inultus erit.
Fata velint tales omni des tempore poenas:
20   Tu vehementer ames, impia, nullus amet.
Ascendam fontem medius qui praeminet urbi,
    Ut videas speculis funera nostra tuis.
Hinc me praecipitem postquam laniaverit ensis,
    Fons Gaius nostro sanguine plenus erit.
25 Eius marmoribus funebria carmina ponam,
    Saevitia ut cunctis sit manifesta tua:
'Marrasius moriens extremo murmure dixit:
    "Me genuit Nothum, me genuere Senae.
Mira quis haec credet, genitum bis tempore nostro
30   Marrasium Tusca tum Siculaque domo?
Informes primo Nothum mihi contulit artus
    Ossaque cum nervis, cum manibusque pedes.
Bis decies steteram corpus sine pectore: vitam,
    Ingenium atque animos Angela sola dedit.
35 Diruit haec eadem quae me construxerat una:
    Una meae vitae causa necisque fuit."'

Marrasii eulogium finit.

My blood will not have been spilled unavenged.
Let the Fates will it so that you pay such a penalty forever.
    May you burn with love, godless girl, and may no man love   20
        you.
I will go to the fountain that dominates the heart of the city,
    That you may see my death in your own mirror.
After the sword has ripped me apart, I will fall headlong,
    And the Fonte Gaia will be full of my blood.
On the fountain's marble I will set up my funerary verses,   25
    That your hardness of heart may be plain to all;
"The dying Marrasio said this with his last breath:
    'Noto bore me, Siena bore me.
Who would believe such marvels, that in our time Marrasio
    Was begotten twice—in his Sicilian home and then in   30
        Tuscany?
Noto first joined my shapeless limbs,
    My bones and sinews, hands and feet.
For twenty years I remained a body without a heart:
    Angela alone gave me life, talent, and feeling.
One and the same woman who built me up has now torn me   35
        down:
    She was the one reason for my life and one cause of my
        death.'"

Marrasio's eulogy is ended.

: VIII :

Ad praeclarum et ornatum virum
Thomasium Piccolominum epistola incipit.

Qua caret ex Erebo dicit, Thomasi, salutem
    Marrasius, foedat quoi mea membra cruor.
Squalida caesaries ubi turpi est sanguine tincta,
    Umbra mei ad Manes tabida movit iter.
5 Nudus ad infernas veni quom pallidus umbras,
    Nulla Charonte mihi remige cymba datur.
Illae, ubi me nudum placido caruisse sepulcro
    Conspexere, ruunt dilacerantque comas.
Tunc gemitu plenus fractas emictere voces
10   Incoepi et tremulo talia verba sono:
'Ex quo nec superis placuit mea vita nec atris
    Manibus umbra placet, respuat ossa lapis
Et lanient corpus rabidissima turba leonum,
    Ursa, lupi et tigres oraque cruda canum.
15 Crudius in terris monstrum si frendeat ullis
    Sive mari, veniat dilanietque caput
Et comedat, vomitet; si iterumque iterumque peredit,
    Irruat ut praeceps ad mea membra vorax.
O utinam haec videat quae nostrae mortis acerbae
20   Causa fuit! Nequeat funera flere volens!'
Audi quae patior Stigiis graviora repulsis:
    In caput inque pedes Corsica turba ruit.
Murmurat hic aliusque fabas cum cortice rodit,
    Caepas et porros ructat inepta cohors.
25 Bacchus in ore manet, nihil est nisi gloria vinum;

: VIII :

A letter to the famous and distinguished
Tommaso Piccolomini begins here.

From Erebus, Tommaso, Marrasio bids you good health –
    The one things he lacks, whose limbs gore defiles.
My hair is stained and matted with vile blood,
    My wasted shade makes its way toward the Underworld.
When I came naked and pale to the shades of the lower world.   5
    I am offered no boat-room by the oarsman Charon.
When the shades saw me naked and without a quiet tomb,
    They rush about and tear their hair.
Then, groaning, I began to utter feeble sounds,
    And with trembling voice such words as these: 10
"Since my life did not please the gods above, nor my shade
    The dark ones below, let my tomb spit out my bones
And let a rabid riot of lions, let the she-bear, let wolves
    And tigers, let the savage jaws of dogs mutilate my body.
If in any land or sea a starving monster gnashes its teeth,   15
    Let it come and tear off my head
And eat it and spew it out; once it has so eaten over and over,
    Let it rush headlong and insatiable upon my limbs.
O that she who was the cause of my cruel death might see it!
    Let her wish yet be unable to weep upon my corpse!   20
Hear what heavier things I suffer than rejection by the Styx:
    The Corsican crowd rushes to attack my head and feet.
One mutters and another gnaws beans and their shells,
    The useless crowd belches onions and leeks.
Bacchus stays in their mouth; wine is nothing but vainglory;   25

Ah madidos inter membra inhumata iacent!
Mallem terrificos morsus tolerare leonum,
    Corsica quam nostrum frangere verba caput!
Posthac quid puerique senes iuvenesque puellae,
30   Qui veniunt haustum pocula dulcis aquae,
Quom me conspiciunt tam dira tabe cruentum,
    Horrent et trepidant, nec capit ullus aquas?
Angela nec poterit de nocte aperire fenestras,
    Nec molles flatus ventus et aura dabit:
35 Irruet umbra ferox et se noctuque dieque
    Vexabit somnus, nec sibi gratus erit.
Quo circa, ut Stigiam possim transire paludem,
    Quod iacet ad fontem corpus humare velis.
Nulla puella velit me me sepelire iacentem;
40   Angela sola velit, si qua puella velit.
Angela si manibus claudat mea pectora busto,
    Thomasi, requies, tu mihi numen eris.
Dum vivis, quaecumque voles, quaecumque rogabis,
    Illa habeas laetus delitiasque Iovis.
45 Et quom maturos aetas compleverit annos,
    Coelicolae venient ad tua fata dei:
Marmoreum ad tumulum fundant et balsama, amomum,
    Et violae atque rosae molliter ossa premant.

Ah, my unburied limbs lie among drunkards!
I would rather endure the terrifying jaws of lions,
    Than have Corsican curses break my head!
Henceforth boys and old men or young girls,
    Who come to drink cups of sweet water,   30
When they see me all bloody with dreadful gore,
    Will they not shudder and tremble, and no one take a drop?
Angela will not be able to open her windows at night,
    Neither wind nor breeze will offer their soft breaths:
A fierce shade will rush in and her sleep will vex her   35
    Day and night, and will not refresh her.
Therefore, that I might be able to cross the Stygian swamp,
    You might wish to bury the body that lies at the spring.
No girl would like to bury me, poor me, lying there;
    Only Angela might want to, if any girl might.   40
If Angela with her hands should enclose my breast in the tomb,
    You, Tommaso, will be my rest, you my divinity.
While you live, whatever you shall want, whatever you shall ask,
    May you happily possess them and the pleasures of Jove.
And when time has rounded out ripe years for you   45
    The heaven-dwelling gods will come to your ending:
May they pour out balsam and amomum by your tomb
    And may violets and roses lie gently on your bones.

: IX :

Ad eloquentissimum et eruditissimum virum
Leonardum Arretinum.

Mos erat antiquis, sua quom trutinare volebant
    Ingenia, ad doctos saepe coire viros.
Marcum non puduit sapientem audire Catonem
    Multaque Aristotelem turba secuta fuit.
5 Te sequor: es toto vates celeberrimus orbe,
    Orator summus, rhetor in arte prior.
Arretine, fave, te tamquam numen adoro:
    Namque tibi placidam cessit Apollo liram.
Paeniteat nec te blando legisse libellum
10   Lumine, nec nugas inde dolare meas.
O utinam de te possem componere versus,
    Quales Virgilius Callimachusque tulit!
Si ad Maecenatem veteres scripsere poetae
    Carmina, Maecenas carmine dignus erat.
15 Si sunt grata animo quae scripsi verba, perennis
    Auspice te vivam tempora multa senex.

: IX :

To that most eloquent and learned of men
Leonardo Aretino.

It was a custom among the ancients that, when they wished
    To weigh their mental powers in the balance, they would often
        meet with learned men.
It was not shameful to listen to the wise Marcus Cato
    And a numerous crowd followed after Aristotle.
I am following you: you are a poet most famous throughout the   5
    world,
    A supreme orator, a rhetorician foremost in your art.
O Aretine, favor me, for I worship you as a god.
    Indeed, Apollo has granted you the peaceful lyre.
May you not be sorry to have read my little book with a fond eye,
    And to take the cudgel to these trifles of mine.   10
O, if only I could write lines about you
    Like those of Vergil and Callimachus!
If ancient poets wrote poems to Maecenas,
    Maecenas was worthy of the poem.
If the words I have written satisfy your judgment, I shall live   15
    For a long time, everlasting, an old man under your protection.

Ergo vale, et nugas, postquam limaveris, edam;
　　Si minus, in cista clausa papirus erit,
Quae cito si tinea non obtundetur iniqua,
20　　Vestiet ex chartis pharmacopola piper.

Marrasii Siculi Angelinetum
ad eloquentissimum virum Leonardum Arretinum
explicit feliciter.

Therefore, farewell, and after you have polished these trifles, I
    shall publish them;
  If not, then the papyrus will stay in a box,
And if it is not speedily eaten away by the spiteful bookworm,
  Some drug seller will wrap pepper in its paper.   20

The Angelinetum *of Marrasio Siculo,*
dedicated to Leonardo Aretino, most eloquent of men,
comes to an auspicious end.

CARMINA VARIA

MISCELLANEOUS POEMS

A

Antonii Panhormitae poetae epigramma
ad praeclarum ac divinum vatem
Marrasium Siculum incipit.

Angelinae oculis dedit aurea tela Cupido
    Donavitque genis, matre iubente, faces.
Os nectar, caput ambrosiam, flat pectus amomum
    Et, quod praetereo, balsama cunnus olet.
5 Haec eadem collo veros adnectit amores
    Deque sinu Veneris diva puella calet.
Hanc olim Siculus vates Marrasius ardet:
    Marrasius certe vult in amore mori.

B

Musa, age, sopitas in carmina concipe vires
    Ingeniumque tepens, pulcher Apollo, move.
Pauca canam nostro vati quem vulnera flentem
    Saeva pharetrato vidimus acta deo.
5 Ille est Marrasius, quem nostro Antonius aevo
    Clara Panhormigenae gloria gentis amat.
Vade, age, vade; suos solabere, Musa, dolores:
    Hoc primum nostri pignus amoris erit.
Fac etiam ut teneas nostri mandata Catonis,
10   Scilicet hunc salvum nomine adire suo.

A

An epigram of the poet Antonio Panormita
offered to the excellent and godlike bard,
Marrasio Siculo, begins here.

Cupid gave golden weapons to Angelina's eyes
  And, on his mother's orders, granted torches to her cheeks.
Her mouth breathes nectar, her head ambrosia, her breast
    amomum,
  And, what I don't say, her cunt is fragrant with balsam.   5
This same divine girl twines true loves about her neck
  And grows warmly amorous from the lap of Venus.
For ages the poet Marrasio Siculo has burned for her:
  In truth Marrasio wants to die in love.

B

The letter of Maffeo Vegio of Lodi
to Marrasio Siculo begins here.

Up, Muse, and summon my slumbering strength to song,
  And, lovely Apollo, rouse my tepid powers.
I will sing a few words to our poet whom we have seen
  Lamenting the cruel wounds inflicted by the quiver-bearing
    god.
He is that Marrasio whom Antonio loves: Antonio,   5
  Offspring of Palermo, the fame and glory of our age!
Come now, onward, Muse, comfort his sorrows:
  This will be the first pledge of my love.
See to it also that you heed the commands of our Cato,
  That is, to come to this man made safe by his name.   10

29

C

Maffei Vegii carmen ad Marrasium Siculum pro Angelina.

Quid quereris, quid te tanto maerore fatigas,
    Spes mea, blanditiae delitiaeque meae?
Quid gemis et totiens singultus pectora rumpunt?
    Quid lacrimis totiens lumina maesta madent?
5 Sume animos, lux nostra, animae pars altera nostrae,
    Qui vitae arbitrium mortis et unus habes.
Sume, age, sume animos, o vita dulcior, o mi
    Dulcis amor vita carior ipse mea,
Pone modum lacrimis, tantos compesce dolores;
10   Angelina rogat: quod rogat obsequere.
Heu miseram! Quot dura pii patiuntur amantes!
    Quantus in insano regnat amore dolor!
Quanta est credulitas tenero sub amore, quot ignes!
    Quam multi gemitus quantaque cura latet!
15 Quis mihi tunc animus, quom te crudelia vidi
    Facturum in Gaio funera fonte legens?
Nec mihi mens, nec vita fuit; labefacta pererrans
    Ossa tremor corpus debile pressit humo.
Pectus erat sine mente, caput sine voce, nec ullus,
20   Hei mihi, in exangui corpore sensus erat.
Utque animi rediere, dolor rediere pavorque;
    Percussit teneras utraque palma genas.
Vix tenui duro foderem quin pectora ferro
    Et fieret nostro sanguine turpis humus:
25 Fecissem aut tristi fregissem colla capistro,

C

Maffeo Vegio's poem to Marrasio Siculo on behalf of Angelina.

Why are you complaining, why do you weary yourself
    With such grief, my hope, my charm, my delight?
Why do you weep and why do sobs burst so often from your
      breast?
    Why are your sorrowful eyes so often wet with tears?
Pluck up your courage, my light, my soul's other half,   5
    Who alone have the power to decide my life and death.
Come, pluck up, pluck up your courage, O sweeter than life,
    O my sweet love, dearer than my very life to me,
Put an end to tears, suppress your sufferings;
    Angelina asks you: yield to what she asks.   10
Woe is me! How many hardships true lovers endure!
    How great the pain that governs love's insanity!
How much trustfulness tender love conceals, what burnings!
    How many sighs, what anxious cares lie hid there!
What was my state at that moment when, while reading,   15
    I saw you on the cruel point of death in Gaia's font?
Unconscious, lifeless was I; a trembling ran through
    My fainting frame and pressed my weak body to the earth.
My heart lost its will, my head its voice; nor was there
    Any feeling, alas! left in my bloodless body.   20
When my spirits returned, sorrow and fear returned as well;
    Both hands struck my tender cheeks,
I could scarce hold back from piercing my breast
    With hard iron and befouling the earth with my blood:
I would have done it or broken my neck with a grim noose   25

Ni tuus ardentem me tenuisset amor.
Ah! pudet et dicam: 'Quae tanta insania mentem
   Cepit, ut optares me sine velle mori?
Debuerat saltem, si te tua vita salusque
30   Non moveat, vitae tangere cura meae.
Dii melius fecere! Tuo si sanguine Gaius
   Forte cruentatas fons habuisset aquas,
Ipsa ego, nulla mora est, eadem per vulnera praeceps
   Foedassem limphas saucia ab ense suas.
35 Atque ut vos quondam fidi cecidistis amantes,
   Quorum purpureo mora cruore rubent,
Sic fuerat nobis aequali morte cadendum;
   Extinctos arbor texerat una duos,
Fons unusque duos traiectos ense tulisset
40   Et quae nunc vitrea est nunc aqua nigra foret.
Vos etiam ut semper memori vivetis in aevo,
   Sic nostrae mortis viveret altus honos.
Haec quoque marmoribus posuissem carmina nostris,
   Quae caneret molli quilibet ore legens:
45 "Marrasius propria periere atque Angela dextra;
   Consumpti cineres hic posuere suos."
Perge ergo ut valeas, vitae spes unica nostrae:
   Si valeas, nostrae causa salutis eris.
Nonne es tu ille meus quo non mihi carior ullus,
50   Marrasius Siculo vectus ab orbe meus?
Ille es qui tepidos movisti solus amores,
   Ille es flammatas qui geris ore faces,
Quem quotiens video, totiens incensa videndo
   Delitias videor laeta videre meas.
55 Ante tuos vultus posuit sua castra Cupido
   Deque tuis oculis spicula iacta volant.
Quae non arderet, saevis truculentior ursis

But that your love restrained me in my passion.
Ah, it shames me to say it: "What monstrous madness
  Seized you that you should wish to die without me?
Anxiety for *my* life ought at least to have touched you,
  Even if your own life and safety does not do so.   30
The gods did better! If perchance the Fonte Gaia
  Had its waters stained by your blood,
I myself, headlong and without hesitation, pierced by a sword,
  Would have defiled its clear water with like wounds.
And as once you fell, being faithful lovers,   35
  With whose crimson blood the mulberries grew red,
So we would have had to fall, by a similar death;
  As one tree had sheltered two dead lovers,
So one spring would have held two pierced by the sword
  And what is now clear water would be dark indeed.   40
Just as you two will live on always in long-remembering time,
  So the lofty glory of our deaths would live on.
I also might have placed on our tombs poems
  For someone to recite, reading with a gentle voice:
'Marrasio and Angela died by their own hands;   45
  Consumed by love, they placed here their own ashes.'
Therefore carry on, be strong, you, the one hope of our lives:
  If you are strong, you will be the source of our salvation.
Are you not mine own, more precious to me than any other,
  My Marrasio, who sailed from the region of Sicily?   50
You are he who alone stirred up my tepid desires,
  You are he who bears love's kindled torches in his face,
Whom, whenever I see you, inflamed by the sight of you,
  I joyfully seem to see my own delights.
Cupid has pitched his camp before your face   55
  And his darts fly from your eyes.
She who did not fall in love would be more ferocious

Esset et irato surdior illa freto.
Ferrea non ego sum neque sum de tigride nata,
60   At placidus sanguis nobile corpus alit;
Nec te crediderim rapidos genuisse leones,
    Nec rigidum fixo corde adamanta geris.
Te clari exornant mores, te vivida virtus,
    Te decor atque altae nobilitatis honos.
65 Et tibi frons laeta est et amica virentibus annis
    Ingenuusque tuo splendor in ore sedet.
Illa gerit silices et clauso in pectore ferrum,
    Quae talem imprudens nescit amare virum.
Cetera praetereo, sed me tua sancta poesis
70   Movit et ardentes misit in ore faces.
Illa animum miro tepidum succendit amore:
    Saeva pharetrati sentio tela dei.
Numen inest cunctis et mens divina poetis,
    Non laedit vates si movet ira Iovem;
75 Quicquid habent celebres a diis cepere poetae,
    Quicquid agant sanctis vatibus astra favent.
Quod cupiunt docti divorum munere vates
    Efficiunt; superos in sua vota trahunt.
Allicit ut reliquos, teneras sic Musa puellas;
80   Si nolint, summus Iuppiter ipse iubet.
Tutius est sanctos celebres et amare poetas:
    Cautius hi sapiunt quid sub amore latet.
Cetera turba ferat cupidas in proelia dextras,
    Vomere scindat humum vel mare navigiis.
85 Hoc proprium est vatum, propria est haec cura deorum,
    Quid sapit ardentes inscia turba focos?
At quia tu nostram potuisti inflectere mentem,
    Laetor in ingenio, clare poeta, tuo.

Than wild bears, and deafer than the angry sea.
I am not made of iron nor born of a tiger,
    But placid blood nourishes my noble body;   60
Nor would I believe that you were sired by fierce lions,
    Nor have you unbending adamant in an unmoving heart.
Fine manners, lively virtue, the glory and honor
    Of high nobility distinguish you.
Yours is a face joyful and friendly in its youthful years,   65
    And the glow of a freeborn man resides upon it.
She has flint and steel in her closed heart
    Who in her folly does not know to love such a man.
I will pass over the rest, for your divine poetry has stirred me
    And brought forth blazing love-torches upon my face.   70
It has set alight a tepid soul with wondrous love:
    I feel the fierce darts of the quiver-bearing god.
Godly power and a mind divine exist in all poets,
    Even if anger rouses Jove, he never injures bards;
The famous poets take from the gods whatever they possess;   75
    Whatever they do, the stars smile on the blessed bards.
Wise bards accomplish what they desire through gods' gift
    They draw the powers above to carry out their wishes.
Just as she does the rest, so the Muse entices tender maidens;
    Should they not wish it, high Jove himself commands.   80
It is safer to love holy and famous poets:
    Their knowledge is wiser of what lies hidden under love.
Let the rest of the mob bear eager hands to battle,
    Cleave the earth with a plow or the sea with ships.
Love belongs to poets, it is the proper concern of the gods.   85
    What does the thoughtless mob discern of its fiery altar?
Yes, and because you were able to change my mind,
    I rejoice, glorious poet, in your genius.

Ut quondam Gallo placuit sua blanda Licoris
90   Lesbiaque, ut fertur, grata, Catulle, tibi;
Ut fuit Ovidii cantata Corinna, Properti
      Cinthia et ut Nemesis pulchra, Tibulle, tua;
Sic ego Marrasii ferar Angelina Sicani,
      Aeternumque tuo carmine nomen erit.
95 Hoc unum superest, ut me miseratus amantem
      Excipias nostros in tua iura sinus.
Tu me ardere facis, tu me languere furentem:
      Causa meae vitae causaque mortis eris;
Tu nostrum sidus, tu gloria nostra perennis,
100   Omnia tu nostrae iura salutis habes;
Forsitan obducens mihi frontem et lumina fingo
      Interdum vultus nolle videre tuos.
Rectius id factum est meque ipsam cauta repressi,
      Ut lateant vulgus crimina nostra loquax.
105 Forma fuit teneris semper suspecta puellis,
      Blanda nocet sanctae forma pudicitiae.
Verum, si qua sapit, quod amat sapientius ardet;
      Saepe quod optaret docta puella negat.
Nunc ego per nostrum qui nos flammavit amorem
110   Te rogo perque alti regia celsa Iovis,
Hanc tueare animam quae in te conversa profundit
      Quotquot habet blandas, magne poeta, preces.'

Angelinae divae formosissimae epistola
ad Marrasium Siculum explicit.
Ex officina Maffei Veggii.

As once his charming Licoris pleased Gallus,
 And Lesbia, they say, pleased you, Catullus;   90
As Corinna was once sung by Ovid, Cynthia by Propertius,
 And your beautiful Nemesis by you, Tibullus:
So I, Angelina, will be exalted by Marrasio Siculo,
 And through your poems my name will be everlasting.
This one thing remains, that in pitying my love   95
 You should take my heart under your jurisdiction.
You make me burn, you make me swoon with passion;
 You will be the reason for my life and cause my death;
You are my star, you my eternal glory,
 You possess all rights over my welfare;   100
Meanwhile, covering my face and eyes, perhaps,
 I pretend to avoid your gaze.
This was well done, and prudently I held myself in check,
 That my crimes might be concealed from the chattering world.
Beauty in gentle maidens has always been held in suspicion,   105
 The attraction of beauty is harmful to holy modesty:
But if a girl has any wisdom, what she loves she burns for wisely;
 Often the well-taught girl says no to that which she desires.
Now I ask you, by that love which set us aflame
 And by the lofty kingdom of Jupiter on high,   110
That you watch over this soul who, being turned toward you,
 Pours forth, great poet, whatever sweet prayers she has."

*The letter of the most lovely goddess Angelina
to Marrasio Siculo comes to an end.
From the workshop of Maffeo Vegio.*

: I :

Marrasii Siculi responsio
ad Maffeum Veggium Laudensem incipit.

Maestus eram; veniunt ad me tua carmina, Veggi,
　　Excutiuntque meum dulcia verba metum.
Et decies postquam et totiens tua dicta relegi
　　Et quom terdecies, tunc placuere magis.
5　Namque lira et fidibus nostrum venere Camenae
　　Ad thalamum, cithara venit Apollo tua;
Et cecinit nivea vestitus pectora veste
　　Pexit et auricomum lucidus arte caput,
Quamvis incomptis solet errabunda capillis
10　　Tempora et incultas undique ferre comas;
Et cecinere tuum, Phoebo saltante, sorores
　　Carmen et alternis saltibus ille canit.
Splendida post sequitur coetum Angelina dearum
　　(Splendidior cunctis ipsa deabus erat)
15　Et gemitum et luctus et quem sufferre dolorem
　　Vix poteram excussit carmine sola tuo.
Tale tuum carmen, quo me solatus amantem es,
　　Quale fuit, dixit: 'Sicilis esse volo.'
Angela vera fuit, sed non persona locuta
20　　Ulla fuit, quamvis Angela ficta fuit.
Hos inter cantus subito moribunda resurgunt
　　Pectora, deinde abiit pallidus ore color;
Non minor et nostro datur his medicina labori
　　Quam data Romuleis quaeque Sabina fuit.
25　Praeterea ante oculos posuit tua Musa Catonem
　　Et te, quem pedibus sola elegia premit.
Antoni vatis divino carmine laeti

: I :

The answer of Marrasio Siculo
to Maffeo Vegio of Lodi begins.

I was all gloom; your verses come to me, Vegio,
    And their sweet words cast out my dread.
And straightway I reread your words ten times and ten again,
    And when read thirty times they delighted me even more,
For by your lyre and lute our own Muses came   5
    To my chamber, by your cithara Apollo came;
And he sang, his breast clothed with a snowy garment,
    And gleaming, skillfully combed his golden–haired head,
Although he usually carries his head waving back and forth
    With unkempt locks and leaves his hair utterly unadorned.   10
And then the sisters sang your song as Phoebus danced,
    And he alternated singing and dancing.
Brilliant Angelina followed after the company of goddesses
    (Herself more brilliant than all those goddesses);
She alone drove out, by your song, the groaning, grief   15
    And pain I was scarcely able to endure.
She spoke your song, such as it was, with which in my love
    You consoled me: "I want to be a Sicilian woman."
It was the true Angela, although it was a fictive Angela
    Yet no false character had spoken.   20
In the midst of these songs my dying spirits rose
    Straightway and the ashen color left my face;
No less a medicine is given to my suffering by these songs
    Than was each Sabine woman given to the sons of Romulus.
Moreover, before my eyes your Muse placed Cato   25
    And you too, whom elegy alone propels with its feet.
Future ages will honor the everlasting fame

Aeternam famam saecla futura colent:
Ovidii eloquium nec te, lascive Properti,
30   Horrescit, nec si vivus uterque foret.
Ante alios alium ponunt sua iura, Catonem,
    Quem Lex et Musae et sancta Poesis amant.
Magna tuis calamis referatur gratia, Veggi:
    Namque ego servatus carmine teque fui.
35 Dii te perpetuent, cuncta et per saecula laetum
    Reddant, sint vitae stamina longa tuae
Et, ne frigescant vires, mihi micte Thaliam
    Cum cithara et cantu carminibusque tuis.

D

Leonardi Arretini viri eloquentissimi
ad clarissimum adolescentem Marrasium Siculum
in Angelinetum *responsio*
incipit feliciter.

1   Leonardus Arretinus salutem dicit Marrasio Siculo.

Fons quidam, si fabulis picturisque credimus, esse perhibetur in
quo senes demersi iuventam recipiant: optandissimae profecto lim-
phae et quas operae pretium sit de Hibernia Taprobanam usque
peregrinando disquirere. Sed aliis quidem ubinam gentium reperi-
antur investigare sit cura; mihi vero tu nunc carminibus tuis mira-
bilissimi fontis huius latices, ut vere dixerim, superfudisti; iuvenes-
cere profecto me sensi statim atque illa perlegi graviorique deposita
2   aetate ad iuventam reduci. Natura hoc fieri dicemus an alia qua-

Of the poet Antonio, blessed with divine song:
He does not shrink from Ovid's diction nor from yours,
    wanton Propertius — not even should both return to life.   30
His own rules place before the others another man, Cato,
    Whom Law and the Muses and holy Poetry love.
Great gratitude will be repaid to your pen, Vegio;
    For I have been saved both by your poem and by you.
May the gods preserve you and may they keep you happy   35
    Through the ages, may the threads of your life be long,
And, lest your powers grow cold, send me Thalia
    Along with her lyre, her song, and your poetry.

D

*The answer of Leonardo Aretino, that most eloquent man,
to the brilliant youth Marrasio Siculo
about the* Angelinetum
begins auspiciously.

Leonardo Aretino greets Marrasio Siculo.   1
    If we can believe stories and pictures, there is reputed to be a certain spring in which old men, once having immersed themselves, received back their youth: undoubtedly waters very much to be desired and which it is worth one's while to investigate by traveling all the way from Spain to Sri Lanka. But let it be others' concern to search out among the peoples of the world where they may be found; in my case you have, in a very real sense, poured out in your poems the waters of that most marvelous spring; indeed I felt myself younger as soon as I read them, and laying aside the weight of age, returned to youth. Shall we say it happens by   2

piam ratione, ut in eorum affectuum quos attente inspicimus simi-
litudinem traducamur? Quod in risu et fletu licet intueri. Te igitur
amantem inspiciens ac toto affectu effuse loquentem, dispeream
nisi ipse quoque amare incoeperim!

3   Sed ante omnia illud discutiendum est quod de furore scripsisti
inquiens: 'Indulgere velis nostro, Arretine, furori' [I.21]. Id alius
forsan aliter, ego certe sic accipio, quasi laudis furor sit non vitupe-
rationis. Sunt enim furoris, ut a Platone traditur, species duae:
una ex humanis proveniens morbis, mala profecto res ac detes-
tanda, altera ex divina mentis alienatione; divini rursus furoris
partes quattuor: vaticinium, misterium, poesis et amor. His vero
deos totidem praeesse veteres putaverunt: nam vaticinium Apol-
lini, misterium Dionyso, poeticam Musis, amorem Veneri tribue-
4   bant. Et vaticinium quid tandem sit nemo fere qui modo quic-
quam legerit ignorat: est enim divinatio quaedam, sed non omnis
divinatio vaticinium est, sed illa tantummodo

          magnam quoi mentem animumque
     Delius inspirat vates aperitque futura,

ut Maro inquit. Nam haruspices et augures et coniectores ac cetera
huiusmodi turba nec vates quidem ipsi sunt nec eorum opus qui-
dem vaticinium est, sed sanorum hominum prudentia et ingeniosa
5   rerum futurarum coniectatio. Misteria vero circa religionem, ex-
piationes et propitiationes divini numinis versantur cum vehemen-
tiori quadam mentis concitatione, qualia in sacris libris permulta
ad placandam coelestem iram quibusdam suppliciis factitata legun-
6   tur. Poema quoque eandem fere determinationem recipit quam et

nature or by some other means that we acquire a likeness of the passions of those whom we study with close attention? This is something one may observe in the case of laughter and tears. Therefore, as I watch you loving and speaking so profusely with a full heart, hang me if I don't myself also begin to be in love!

But, first of all, I have to discuss what you've written about 3 madness, when you say, "Please indulge my madness, Aretinus" [I.21]. Another man may see the matter differently, but for my part, I certainly understand madness to be worthy of praise rather than censure. For there are, as we know from Plato, two kinds of madness: one springing from human infirmity, a thing undoubtedly evil and detestable, the other from a divine alienation of mind. Again, of the divine madness there are four species: prophecy, mystery, poetry, and love. Indeed the ancients thought that a like number of gods were in charge of these: they assigned prophecy to Apollo, the mystery rites to Dionysus, poetry to the Muses, and love to Venus. And practically no one who has read anything 4 at all does not know what prophecy is; for that is a particular kind of divination, though not all divination is prophecy, but only that whereby

> the Delian seer inspires a great mind
> And spirit and opens up the future,

as Vergil says. For it is not the diviners and augurs and soothsayers and the rest of that lot who are the real seers, nor is their activity real prophecy, but rather the wisdom of sane men and their clever inferences regarding future events. The mystery rites, by contrast, 5 have to do with religion, with prayers of expiation and propitiation of divine beings, accompanied by a certain more intense excitation of the mind, the sort of things we read about in sacred books, many of which are performed in order to appease the wrath of heaven by means of certain sacrifices. A poem also has virtually 6

de vaticinio supra dicebamus. Non enim omne opus poema est, ne si versibus quidem constet, sed illud praestans, illud hac honorata nuncupatione dignum quod afflatu quodam divino emittitur. Itaque quanto vaticinium coniectationi dignitate praestat, tanto poema, quod ex furore fit, sanorum hominum artificio est anteponendum; hinc illae sunt a bono poeta quasi vesani hominis emissae voces: 'unde iubetis ire, deae?'; et Virgilius:

> dicam horrida bella
> dicam acies actosque animis in proelia reges
> Tyrrhenamque manum totamque sub arma coactam
> Hesperiam. Maior rerum mihi nascitur ordo,
> maius opus moveo.

Quod totum vaticinantis more prolatum est a poeta.

7   Quid ergo vaticinium, quid misterium quidve poema hactenus mihi dictum sit; de amore autem postea dicemus. Nunc autem illud ostendendum est, has furoris species, de quibus supra diximus, non esse malas. Primum enim, ut a misteriis incipiam, quis alienationem istam ac furorem et quasi abstractionem raptumque hominis circa rem divinam dixerit esse malum? Quis vero non bonum atque laudabile? Amplo me in loco versari sentio: extant enim exempla paene innumerabilia divinorum hominum, si forte liberet hac in parte orationem extendere, sed prolixitatem in re conspicua reiciendam censeo. Circa misteria igitur furorem non esse malum
8   constat. Quid autem vaticinii? Furorem illum quoque non esse malum, vel ex eo patet quod bona permulta ab illo proveniunt. Sibyllae quippe et huiusmodi, furentes quidem dum essent, publice

the same definition as that which I was making above about prophecy. But not every literary production is a poem, not even if it is in verse, but that which is outstanding, that which is worthy of the honored name [of poetry], brought forth by a kind of divine inspiration. And so, by as much as prophecy surpasses guesswork in dignity, so much should a poem, because it comes into being by [divine] madness, be ranked before the contrivances of sober men; hence, the following words put forth by a good poet are the words, as it were, of an insane man: "Whence do you bid me go, goddesses?"; and Vergil:

> I will tell of dreadful wars
> I will tell of battle lines and of kings driven by anger into the
>   fray
> And of the Tyrrhenian band and all Italy compelled to arms.
> A greater pattern of affairs is coming to birth through me.
> I am mounting a greater work.

All of this was uttered by the poet in the manner of a seer.

Thus far I have said what prophecy is, what the mysteries are, and what poetry is; later I will speak about love. It must now be shown, however, that those kinds of madness about which I spoke earlier are not evils. To begin with the mysteries: who would say that such alienation and madness and, as it were, seizure and abstraction of a man in relation to divine matters is an evil? Who in fact would not say that it is good and praiseworthy? I feel that I am dealing with a huge topic, for there are well-nigh innumerable examples of men with supernatural power, especially if, on this subject, one was allowed to extend the discussion, but I recommend rejecting prolixity on such an obvious theme. Concerning the mysteries, therefore, it is a given that madness is not an evil. What about the madness of prophecy? That that form of madness also is not an evil is plain especially from the fact that very many good things issue from it. Indeed the Sibyls and suchlike, while

7

8

9 et privatim multis profuere, sanae vero exiguis aut nullis. Poetae quoque tunc demum boni existunt quom suo illo corripiuntur furore, qua de causa vates eos nuncupamus quasi furore quodam correptos. Qui vero absque furore Musarum poeticas ad fores, ut inquit Plato, accedit, sperans quasi arte quadam poetam se bonum evasurum, inanis est ipse atque eius poesis. Prae illa quae ex furore est, haec quae ex prudentia disperditur.

10 Poetarum ergo furor a Musis est; amantium vero a Venere. Oritur autem hic ex verae pulchritudinis contemplatione, cuius effigiem visu intuentes acerrimo ac violentissimo sensuum nostrorum, stupentes ac velut extra nos positi, totis affectibus in illum corripimur, ut non minus vere quam eleganter dictum sit amantis animam in alieno corpore vitam ducere. Haec igitur vehemens occupatio animi atque correptio amor vocatur: divina quaedam alienatio ac veluti sui ipsius oblivio et in id quoius pulchritudinem

11 admiramur transfusio. Quam si furorem ac vesaniam appellas, concedam etiam atque fatebor, dummodo intelligas neque poetam bonum esse ullum posse, nisi huiusmodi furore correptum, neque futura praevidere vaticinantes, nisi per huiusmodi furorem, neque perfecte neque eximie deum coli, nisi per huiusmodi mentis alienationem.

12 De furore igitur hactenus mihi dictum sit provocato verbis tuis. Equidem si talis est furor tuus qualem ipse modo descripsi, non modo indulgeo illi quod me flagitas, verum etiam ultro te ad illum cohortor. Qui enim amorem vituperat, quid tandem dici potest nisi dignum esse illum qui extremo in odio cunctorum versetur? Sed haec satis, in epistula praesertim, quae longitudinem renuit.

they were in a state of madness, were of benefit to many both publicly and privately, but while sane helped very few or none. Poets also only become good when they are seized by that mad- 9 ness, which is why we call those who are, as it were, seized by madness *vates*. He who, as Plato said, approaches the poetic threshold of the Muses without madness, hoping that he will come out a good poet, is foolish, as is his poetry. In comparison with the poetry which is produced by madness that which comes [merely] from practical wisdom is worthless.

Thus, while the poet's madness derives from the Muses, that of 10 lovers comes from Venus. It arises moreover from the beholding of true beauty; looking at its image with the most passionate and violent gaze, confounded and, as it were, placed outside ourselves, we are carried away with all the feelings of our senses fastened on it, so that it might be said no less truly than elegantly that the soul of the lover lives in another's body. Therefore this violent possession and seizure of the mind is called love: it is a certain divine alienation and, as it were, forgetfulness of self and a transformation into that thing whose beauty we marvel at. If you call this madness 11 and insanity, I shall even grant it and admit it as long as you understand that no poet can be good unless seized by such madness, nor can anyone who makes predictions foresee the future unless by madness of this sort, nor can god be worshipped perfectly and excellently unless by that same alienation of mind.

Therefore allow me—challenged by your words—to have spo- 12 ken thus far and no further about madness. For my part, if your madness is such as I have just described, I not only look kindly on it because you ask me to, but I also encourage you further toward it. What can be said of one who finds fault with love, except that he deserves to be the object of universal hatred? But these remarks are enough, especially in a letter, [a form] that declines elaborate treatments.

13   Carmina vero ipsa tua atque hanc scribendi amoenitatem usque
adeo probo, ut inter Nasones et Propertios et Tibullos te existi-
mem collocandum; hi enim emendatissime ornatissimeque om-
nium elegiam scripsisse putantur. Sed unum scias volo, me non
tam tibi eximiam hanc palmam esse tribuendam existimare quam
Amori. Ille est enim qui verba tibi dictat, qui sententias ostendit,
qui varietatem et copiam et elegantiam subministrat. Quod vero
me tantopere laudas carminibus tuis, fateor idem mihi quod The-
mistocli evenire; 'sed non ego credulus illis.' Nam conatum esse me
atque conari, ceterum longe abesse, te vero nequaquam adulatum
sed benivolentia mei deceptum intelligo.

14   Vale et quotidie scribere aliquid, ut facis, dignum Amore et
Musis ne cesses; gloria quippe agendo periclitandoque acquiritur,
nec spectantibus coronae sed certantibus parantur. Iterum vale.
    Nonis octobris Florentiae.

: II :

Marrasii Siculi responsio
ad eloquentissimum ac eruditissimum virum Leonardum
Arretinum de laudibus et numine Gaii fontis
feliciter incipit.

Non opus est Scithicum senibus disquirere fontem,
    Quo sub demersis prima iuventa redit.
Siccus apud Scithiam per saxa latentia repit,

48

But I commend your poems themselves and your charming way   13
of writing so much that I reckon that you should be ranked with
poets like Ovid and Propertius and Tibullus; for these are thought
to have written elegy the most faultlessly and elegantly of all. But
I want you to know one thing, that I think this choice honor
should be ascribed not so much to you as to Love. For it is he who
speaks the words to you, who shows you the thoughts, who fur-
nishes the variety, the abundance, the grace. But as to the fact that
you praise me so highly in your poems, I confess that it happens
for me as for Themistocles: "I just don't believe them." For I real-
ize, though I have tried and continue to try [for excellence], I am
still far off, whereas you have in no way flattered but have been
deceived by your goodwill toward me.

Farewell and do not cease to write something each day, as you   14
do, that is worthy of Love and the Muses. Glory, to be sure, is
won by doing and taking risks, and victory crowns are obtained
not by spectators, but by those taking part in the competition.
Again farewell.

October 7, in Florence.

⠒ II ⠒

*Marrasio Siculo's answer
to the most eloquent and learned Leonardo Aretino
concerning the glory and the divine spirit of the Fonte Gaia
begins auspiciously.*

It is not necessary for old men to seek out the Scythian spring,
   Beneath which their first youth returns to those immersed.
In thirsty Scythia it snakes through hidden rocks,

49

Funditat et limphas ante Senense forum.
5 Hic situs in media fons est argenteus urbe
     Et tumulus vivis ossibus ille meis.
  Phoebus ab Eoo roseas quom solvit habenas
     Mane, videt Gai lumine fontis aquas.
  Quaecumque hos latices haurit, quaecumque liquores,
10   Et calet in primis et iuvenescit anus.
  Vidi ego, Nestoreos qui iam transiverat annos,
     Summersum iuvenis membra referre senem.
  Sed si forte meis tete iuvenescere sentis
     Versibus, his limphis uda papyrus erat:
15 Non versus fecere mei, nec inepta poesis,
     Sed quibus aspersus saepe libellus aquis.
  Fons hic exornat iuvenes urbemque Senensem;
     Numen habet: laqueos, retia, mella, iocos,
  Sanguineos arcus, pharetram flammasque, sagittas
20   Deposuit Gaio candida fonte Venus.
  Hac satus ulterius nec vult volitare per auras:
     Exuit hic pennas deposuitque faces;
  Per turres tantum volitat nec moenia nostra
     Egreditur; fessus fonte Cupido sedet.
25 Algentes ardent et sunt in amore furentes,
     Quam primum biberint pocula dulcis aquae.
  Huc, Leonarde, veni, sacros hausture liquores:
     Sic iuvenis fies, sic in amore furens.
  Postquam marmoribus gelidoque in fonte resedi,
30   Plena fuere mihi corda furore gravi.
  Vellem divini raperent mea corda furores
     Ad quos me hortaris, dive poeta, tuos.
  Sed ne intemperiae dubito mea pectora vexent,
     ridiculum ut dicar qualibet urbe caput.
35 Si manifesta meam rapiet vesania mentem,

And pours out its waters in the Campo of Siena.
Placed here in the midst of the city is a silvery spring   5
    That shall be the tomb for my living bones.
When from the East Phoebus loosens the roseate reins in the
        morning,
    He sees by his light the Fonte Gaia's waters,
And whatever old woman drinks those refreshing waters
    Begins to grow warm and regains her youth.   10
I have seen one who already had passed the years of Nestor,
    Once immersed, recover a young man's limbs.
But if, by chance, you feel yourself rejuvenated
    By my verses, the paper was wet from those waters.
My verses have not made you so, not my clumsy poetry,   15
    But rather my little book, so often sprinkled with those waters.
This spring ennobles both the youth and the city of Siena;
    A divine spirit dwells there; there radiant Venus has left
Her snares, her nets, her honeyed drinks, her jests,
    Her bloody bow, her quiver, flames, and arrows.   20
Her offspring has no more wish to fly through the air:
    Here he has shed his wings and laid down his torches;
Cupid only flits about our towers and does not leave
    Our city walls; but when tired he sits by the spring.
The frigid burn and begin to rage in love   25
    As soon as they drink cups of that sweet water.
Come hither, Leonardo, to drink the sacred waters:
    Thus you will become young; thus you'll be madly in love.
After I sat again upon the marble by the chill fountain,
    My heart was filled with a heavy madness.   30
I wish that my heart would be seized by that divine madness
    Of yours, divine poet, to which you urge me in your writings,
But I fear that madness will so agitate my spirit
    That I shall be mocked in any city you like.
If open frenzy my mind shall seize, my first cure   35

Prima salus gelido mergere fonte comas.
Nam quem Gorgoneum primo appellare poetae,
    Hunc fontem Gaium tempora nostra vocant.
Cruda voluptatis si quid mea verba tulerunt,
40   Carminibus nostris si qua libido fuit,
Laus omnis Veneri detur, omnis gloria fonti:
    Quos cecini versus, hos mihi dictat aqua.
Quid tibi collibuit me inter numerare Tibullos?
    Credo meas nugas captus amore probes.
45 Si te ego descripsi priscos superare poetas,
    Me, licet immensus, anne fefellit amor?
Nec quia laudarit decepta est lingua, sed illa
    Nescivit laudes accumulare tuas.
Postremo, ne longa trahar per devia, sacros
50   Hic superat fontes numine, melle, ioco.
Huc, Leonarde, veni, suaves hausture liquores:
    Sic iuvenis fies, sic in amore furens.

E

Karoli Arretini viri eloquentissimi
in Homeri poetae clarissimi
Batrachomyomachiam,
idest Ranarum murumque pugnam,
ad Marrasium Siculum poetam clarum praefatio incipit.

1 Nuper, suavissime Marrasi, quom apud quosdam praestantissimos
iuvenes studiis humanitatis mirifice deditos Homerum summo-
pere laudassem dixissemque eum non solum in rebus magnis, quae
mediocri oratori vel poetae maximum orationis campum praestare

Would be to plunge my hair in the icy spring.
For this spring, which poets first named "the Gorgonian Spring,"
    Our own times calls "the Fonte Gaia."
If my rough words have brought you any pleasure,
    If by my songs you find delight,   40
Let all praise be given to Venus, all glory to the spring:
    The spring dictates to me the verses that I sing.
Why did it please you to account me another Tibullus?
    I think you approve my trifles because you're love's captive.
If I have written that you surpass the ancient poets,   45
    Has my love, though unbounded, really deceived me?
Not because it praised was my tongue deceitful, but rather
    Because it knew not how to heap praise high enough.
Finally, lest I be drawn far off the track, this spring surpasses
    All other holy springs in divinity, sweetness, and charm. 50
Come hither, Leonardo, to drink these waters:
    Thus you will become young, thus you will be madly in love.

E

A preamble by Carlo Aretino, the most eloquent of men,
to the Batrachomyomachia *or*
The Battle Between the Frogs and the Mice
of Homer, the most famous of poets,
addressed to Marrasio Siculo, a famous poet, begins.

Recently, most charming Marrasio, when, among a group of most   1
excellent young men wonderfully devoted to liberal studies, I had
praised Homer to the skies and had said that not only in great
matters, which customarily offer the widest field for expression to

solent, verum etiam in eo bello quod adolescens de ranis muribusque finxit quantum iam ingenio valeret ostendisse, et precibus et vi a me exegerunt ut id in Latinum converterem ac, si non valerem versu, saltem id, quoquo modo possem, soluta oratione transferrem. Itaque, cum eorum studiis nullo pacto obsistere quirem, liber omni pede id traducere aggressus sum; sed, cum perpaucos transtulissem versus, ita ea oratio incondita et incomposita mihi visa est, ut nihil suave, nihil elegans, nihil denique Homericum resonare videretur. Itaque mutato consilio, Musas invocavi, ut mihi aliquantulum aspirarent meaque labra si non Parnasi sacris undis, saltem lymphis illius Gaii fontis, de quo nuper quam plures suavissimos elegos edidisti, aspergerent. Ac si repente ex corvo (ut inquit ille) poeta prodirem, eis hecatombem pollicitus sum. Proxima deinde nocte in somnis mihi visum est Musarum gremio sublatum in Gaio fonte esse demersum, quamobrem paulo post experrectus, alacri animo ad scribendum accessi et hoc opusculum in nostram linguam transtuli. In quo si quid elegans visum fuerit, tum Homero, omnium poetarum praestantissimo, tum maxime illis undis, quibus tua carmina uda esse dicis, attribuito; sin autem aliquid ineptum offenderis, id a me editum esse credas.

2   Sed iam diu tecum iocor. Non tamen me latet videri Plutarcho haec Homero non esse tribuenda; putavit enim, ut arbitror, hanc clarissimi poetae summam fore laudem, si nihil illius nomine inscriberetur praeter illa duo egregia poemata, quorum altero bellum Troianum, altero Ulixis varios errores cecinit. Itaque et hoc et *Margitem* Homeri esse negavit; de *Hymnis* vero nullam fecit mentionem, sed non video cur sententia eorum qui haec Homero ascribunt vera esse non possit. Nam si noster Maro *Culicem, Co-*

middling orators and poets, but also in that war of the frogs and mice which he created as a young man, he even then possessed the power to show such great genius, by entreaty and by force they compelled me to translate it in whatever mode I could; if I weren't able to manage verse, then I should at least translate it in prose. And so, since there was no way for me to resist their eagerness, I set about translating it in meter; but when I had translated only a few lines, the text seemed to me so rough and awkward that it seemed to resonate with nothing charming, nothing tasteful, nothing in any way Homeric. And so I changed my plan and called upon the Muses to breathe on me a little bit and sprinkle my lips, if not with the holy waters of Parnassus, at least with those of the Fonte Gaia, about which you recently produced quite a few charming elegiac couplets. And if I suddenly was revealed as a poet (as that man says), having been a crow, I promised them a hecatomb. And the very next night I seemed in my sleep to be borne in the lap of the Muses and immersed in the Fonte Gaia; for this reason, I woke up a little later, turned to writing with an eager mind and translated this little book into our language. If anything seems graceful in it, attribute it first to Homer, the most excellent of all poets, then very much to those waters with which you say that your own poems are sprinkled; if you are put off by anything clumsy, you may trust that that portion was produced by me.

But I have been joking with you for some time. Still, I am not 2 unaware that Plutarch's view was that this work should not be attributed to Homer; he thought, I believe, that it would be the highest praise for the most famous of poets if no works carried his name apart from those two outstanding compositions, in one of which he sang of the Trojan War and in the other of the various wanderings of Ulysses. And so he denied that this and *Margites* were Homer's; he made no mention of the *Hymns*, but I do not see why the opinion of those who ascribe them to Homer cannot be right. For if our Vergil wrote *Culex*, *Copa*, and a number of other

pam nonnullaque alia exercendi ingenii gratia scripsit, ut tandem pastores, agros horrendaque bella caneret, quid mirum Homerum hoc opere bello Troiano praelusisse, praesertim quom verborum elegantia ab illo praeclaro opere minime dissentire videatur? Quamvis enim laudabile sit res magnas scribere, in parvis tamen aliquando se exercere haud absurdum est, et enim

> non sum animi dubius verbis ea dicere magnum
> quam sit et angustis hunc addere rebus honorem.

Nam, ut inquit praestantissimus poeta,

> in tenui labor; at tenuis non gloria.

3   Sed minime mirum nobis videri debet, si de hoc opere inter doctos aliquod certamen sit, quom de genere, de vita, de patria denique ipsius Homeri tam varias sententias esse videamus. Nam si ab Ephoro patriam quaeras, Cumaeum esse dicet; si a Pindaro omnium liricorum principe, tum Smyrnaeum tum Chium asseverabit; si ab Antimacho et Nicandro, Colophonium censebunt; sin autem ab Aristarcho et Dionysio Thracio, haud dubitabunt Atheniensem dicere; demum quom Simonides Chium, Aristoteles item fuisse scribat, non desunt qui eum ex Cypro, Salaminium aut Argivum esse concedant; qua item tempestate quibusve parentibus fuerit, tam variae sententiae sunt, ut satius sit de eo nihil affirmare quam tam diversas de eo opiniones proferre.

things just to exercise his talent, so that in due course he might sing of shepherds, fields, and dreadful wars, what wonder that Homer in this work composed a prelude to his Trojan war, especially since it seems to depart only very slightly from the verbal felicity of that famous work. For although it is praiseworthy to write of great matters, to exercise one's talent on small things is not at all inappropriate, for

> I am well aware how great a thing it is to speak of these
> matters
> With words and to confer this dignity on humble matters.

Indeed, as the most excellent of poets says,

> The work is modest in scope, but not the glory.

But it should not seem to us very remarkable if there should be 3 some debate among learned men about this work when we see that there are such varied opinions about the family, the life, and even the birthplace of Homer himself. For if you ask Ephorus about the birthplace, he will say Cumae; if you ask Pindar, the prince of lyric poets, he will say first that it is Smyrna, then Chios; but if you ask Antimachus and Nicander, they will judge it to be Colophon; however, if you ask Aristarchus and Dionysius of Thrace they will not hesitate to say Athens; lastly whereas Simonides writes that it was Chios, and Aristotle the same, there is no lack of those who allow that he was from Cyprus, Salamis, or Argos; as to when he was born or from what parentage he sprang there are such varied opinions that it is better to state nothing about him than to set forth such different views about him.

4   Nos autem, hanc omnem quaestionem relinquentes, ad te, Musarum decus, qui iam tantum carmine profecisti, ut inter Tibullos Propertios Gallos numerandus videaris, hoc opusculum tamquam Homeri mittimus, ut id emendes ac his diebus aliquo ridiculo animum relaxare possis. Vale.

: III :

Marrasii Siciliensis responsio quoi titulus est Hecatombe
*ad eloquentissimum virum Karolum Arretinum
incipit feliciter.*

Credebam Gaios latices coluisse Camenas,
    Solum quae canerent impare dicta sono;
Horrendas acies horrendaque proelia cerno,
    Karole, quae dictas his madefactus aquis.
5 Armatae veniunt, mirum est, e fonte sorores,
    Intrant et thalamum splendida turba meum.
Secum blanditias lascivaque verba ferebant
    Otiaque et plausus delitiasque prius:
Consuevere comas niveis ornare ligustris,
10   Cingebat frontem fulva corona suam;
Consuevere caput viridi connectere oliva,
    Stabat et auratis vestibus arte nitor;
Aurea per flavos serpebat spira capillos,
    Ornabat nitidas candida gemma manus.
15 Nunc clipeos hastasque ferunt parmamque sudemque
    Pilaque; sunt manibus tela verenda suis.
Carmen voce gravi me me offendere canentes,
    Ranarum et murum bella timenda Iovi.

Abandoning this whole question however, we send this little   4
work, as though it were by Homer, to you, glory of the Muses,
who have achieved so much in song that you seem to be numbered
among those like Tibullus, Propertius, and Gallus, in order that
that you may revise it and ease your mind during this time with
something amusing. Farewell.

: III :

Marrasio Siculo's answer, entitled Hecatomb,
*to that most eloquent of men, Carlo Aretino, begins
auspiciously.*

I once believed that the Muses dwelt in the Fonte Gaia,
    Muses who only sang songs to me with uneven sound;
I now see bristling battle lines and frightening battles,
    Which you, Carlo, compose, moistened by those same waters.
Amazing as it is, the sisters are coming armed from the fountain,   5
    And a glittering throng is entering my chamber.
Once they carried caresses and wanton words with them,
    Leisurely days and applause and pleasures:
They used to adorn their hair with snowy-white privet
    And a golden crown used to ring their foreheads;   10
They used to twine their heads with fresh olive branches,
    Their garments glittered, artfully embroidered with gold,
A golden coil wound through their fair hair,
    A shining jewel adorned their elegant hands.
Now they bear shields and spears, buckler and pike   15
    And javelins; fearsome weapons are in their hands.
They ran in to me, singing a song in weighty tones
    Of the wars of frogs and mice, which even Jove must fear.

Dum legerem timui Meridarpaga Borborophontem:
20   Ut timeam maior sollicitudo fuit.
Obstupui medius galeata per agmina murum:
    Territus hinc ranis, inde deabus eram.
Nec me interpellant nymphae tua dicta legentem;
    Talia perlectis una locuta fuit:
25 'Karolus udus aquis et nostro numine dignus
    Pollicitus centum est caedere rite boves.
Bos ubi centenus? Quando centena dabuntur
    Munera? Vota dei persoluenda volunt.
Ipse boves habeat centum totidemque capellas
30   Atque sua irroret iugera sola Tagus.
Nos volumus cantet titulos et numina nostra,
    Quom testudineam pulsat Apollo liram.
Centum elegos faciat, centena poemata nobis
    Poscat et accipiet grandia dona sinu.'
35 'Accipite hos, dixi, seque hoc absolvite voto:
    Centum elegos pro se composuisse libet.'
Illa refert: 'Sua sunt gratissima carmina nobis,
    Sunt et apollineis illa canenda sonis.
Lauro ornandus erit, nisi sit quod serta corymbis
40   Laurea nique hederas vincat honore comae.'
Inde abiere omnes et me sibi multa volentem
    Quaerere destituunt diffugiuntque thorum.
Centum elegos una petierunt voce puellae;
    Centum elegos placida scribere mente velis.
45 Karole, rivus aquae manat qui fonte Senensi
    Nec tibi nec cuiquam despiciendus eat.
Tarquini coniunx Gaios libasse liquores
    Fertur et ante alias facta puella proba est;
Hinc proba quaeque fuit primaeva aetate puella
50   Et Tanaquil primo Gaia vocata fuit.

While I read, I feared Meridarpaga Borborophontes:
    That I should be afraid was an even greater source of fear.   20
I marveled in the midst of the helmeted ranks of mice,
    I was terrified by the frogs on this side and the goddesses on
        that.
But the nymphs did not interrupt me as I read your words:
    When I had read them through, one spoke these words:
"Carlo, wet with our waters and worthy of our divinity,   25
    Has promised to sacrifice a hundred cows.
Where is that hecatomb? When will these hundred gifts
    Be given? Gods wish vows to be fulfilled.
Let the Tagus itself have the hundred cows
    And as many goats, and water only its own acres.   30
We want him to sing of our fame and our divinity,
    When Apollo strikes the tortoise-shell lyre.
Let him create a hundred elegiac verses; let him demand for us
    A hundred verses and let him receive great gifts in his lap."
"Receive these," I said, "absolve him from his promise: 35
    I would like to write a hundred elegiacs on his behalf."
She answered, "His songs are wondrously pleasing to us,
    And they must be sung to Apollonian strains.
He must be adorned with laurel, unless, to honor his locks,
    Something bests the laurel twined with berries or the ivy."   40
Then they all departed and ceased their asking, though I wanted
    To ask them many things, and they fled from my chamber.
With one voice a hundred maidens sought my elegiac verse:
    One wants a calm mind to write a hundred elegiac verses.
Carlo, the stream of water that flows from the Sienese fountain   45
    Should not flow scorned by you or anyone else.
Tarquin's wife is said to have drunk from the waters of Gaia
    And she as a maiden was made virtuous before others;
Hence every virtuous girl in her first youth was called Gaia
    And Tanaquil was the first to be called Gaia.   50

Hunc Gaium vocitant certe a probitate sororum
    Fontem, quem celebrant numina sacra novem.
Karole, crede mihi, non haec sententia nostra est:
    Quae cecini foliis verba Sibylla dedit.
55 Obsequere interea, quamvis tua carmina Homerum
    Spirant et quamvis numen Homerus habet.
Namque polita nimis nimis et limata fuere
    Carmina Phoebeo suscipienda sinu.
Certant Virgilio, sunt et certantia Homeri
60   Versibus et certant si qua Tibullus habet.
Sive Helicone tui fundantur saepe capilli,
    Sive caballina sparserit unda pedes,
Seu iuga Parnasi spatiere per ardua montis,
    Sive per Ascraeos iveris ipse lacus,
65 Sive habites villas aut florea rura pererres,
    Sive suburbanas legeris arte rosas,
Sive ubicumque velis requiescere, protinus illuc
    Adveniet celeri quaeque Thalia pede,
Ut timeam Gaio repetant te fonte relicto
70   Atque habitent pectus turba decora tuum.
Musas nec metuas, nam si te linquere vellent
    Et Phoebus fugeret, te Nicolaus amat:
Hic habet et Musas et mille poemata, mille
    Historias, priscos et bene noscit avos.
75 Eia agites, postquam cecinisti parva sub antro
    Maenalio, Antiphaten! Eia Ciclopa agites!
Non facile est clarum quicquam componere, siquis
    Neglexit primo scribere velle iocos.

And surely they call by the name "Gaia" the fountain which the
    nine divinities
    Celebrate because of the virtue of those sisters.
Carlo, believe me, this is not my opinion:
    I have sung words that the Sibyl gave to the leaves.
Yield meanwhile, though your poems breathe   55
    Of Homer, and Homer has divinity.
For your poems, worthy of being taken to Apollo's bosom,
    Have been exceedingly polished, exceedingly refined.
They vie with Vergil, and are in contention with the verses
    Of Homer and vie with anything of Tibullus.   60
Whether your hair is often washed in Helicon
    Or the nag's wave has sprinkled your feet,
Whether you walk along the lofty ridges of Mt. Parnassus,
    Or you in person have traversed the Ascraeon pools,
Whether you live in country houses or wander the flowery   65
    countryside.
    Or with your art you gather roses near the city,
Or whether you should wish to rest anywhere, straightway
    thither
    Each Thalia will come on swift feet,
So that I fear lest, after abandoning the Fonte Gaia,
    That lovely band will seek you and dwell in your breast.   70
May you not fear the Muses, for if they should wish to leave you
    And Phoebus were to flee away, yet Niccolò loves you still.
He possesses both the Muses and a thousand poems,
    A thousand histories, and he knows our ancient forefathers
    well.
Come then, you have sung of small things beneath the Maenalian 75
    cave;
    Come then, may you awake Antiphates, awake the Cyclops!
It is not easy to compose anything renowned if you have
    Neglected to desire at first to write playful things.

Non pelagi tumidos fluctus secuisset Iason,
80   Is nisi per tenues saepius isset aquas;
Qui postquam medium sulcavit nauta profundum,
     Auratae ad patriam vellera vexit ovis.
Cortice populeo ni sese armasset Achilles,
     Fixisset timidas ni prius ille feras,
85 Vulcani tam magna humeris numquam arma tulisset,
     Sanguine ab Hectoreo nec rubuisset humus.
Muribus et ranis nisi praelusisset Homerus
     Iliadi, magnum non cecinisset opus.
Et postquam eloquio cantasti parva rotundo,
90   Adgredere aeternam, te precor, *Iliadem.*
Ulterius proprias non vult errare per urbes
     Maeonides, Tuscas vult habitare domos.
Ilias, antiqui quam nescivere poetae
     Transferre et Latiis edere quippe novam,
95 Mavult in linguam per te migrare Latinam
     Quam velit Argolicas nunc habitare casas.
Te petit iste labor, tibi gloria summa relicta est
     Sitque humeris validis sarcina grata tuis.
Sed prius his nymphis placida parere decorum est
100   Mente: fac extollas nomen ad astra suum.
Centum elegos una petierunt voce puellae;
     Centum elegos placida scribere mente velis.

Marrasii Siciliensis Hecatombe
ad eloquentissimum virum Karolum Arretinum
explicit feliciter.

Jason would not have cut through the swollen waves of the sea
    If he had not often made his way through little streams;   80
After he had furrowed the ocean deeps as a sailor,
    He carried off the fleece of the golden sheep to his homeland.
If Achilles had not armed himself with poplar bark,
    If he had not first pierced the timid wild creatures,
He could never have borne Vulcan's huge armor on his shoulders,   85
    Nor reddened the earth with Hector's blood.
If Homer had not written about frogs and mice as a prelude
    To the *Iliad*, he would never have sung his great work.
And after you have sung of small matters with finished
      eloquence,
    You will move on, I beg you, to your immortal *Iliad*.   90
Homer does not want to wander any further
    Among his own cities, he wants to dwell in Tuscan homes.
The *Iliad*, which the poets of old did not know how to translate
    Or how to publish in a new form for the men of Latium,
Prefers to emigrate to the Latin tongue   95
    Than to continue dwelling in Greek houses.
This task seeks you, this highest of honors has been left for you,
    And may this burden be pleasing to your strong shoulders.
But first it is fitting to obey those nymphs with a calm
    Mind: see to it that you lift their name to the stars.   100
With one voice the maidens demanded a hundred elegiac verses;
    In an obliging mood please write a hundred elegiac verses.

        The Hecatomb *of Marrasio Siculo*
      to that most eloquent of men, Carlo Aretino,
          comes auspiciously to an end.

: IV :

*Ad Angelinam Cornelianam
ut Cornelio indulgeat ob pestem Senas fugienti.*

Cornelius, dirae pavidus formidine pestis,
   Se miserum! dixit: 'Terra beata vale!
Angelina vale tuque o formosa valeto
   Eva et convaleant gaudia nostra Senae!'
5 Cornelius mortem fugitat, non ut sibi vita
   Carior est oculis, Angela pulchra, tuis.
Se cruciat fugiens et te te hac lege relinquit:
   Quam primum salvas velle redire Senas.
Angela, candentes libeat mactare iuvencos
10 Atque boves aris multaque tura crema.
Cornelius salvus redeat vivatque saluber;
   Cornelio salvus sospite semper ero.
Ut tibi servetur, te, Corneliana, reliquit;
   Tuta manes: nullo tempore numen obit.
15 Vive, puella, annos ut Nestora vincere possis,
   Vincas Tithonum et Laomedontiaden.
Et postquam totidem tu, lux sua, vixeris annos.
   Non maculet roseam foeda senecta cutim
Et niveis semper sint candidiora ligustris
20 Pectora, sit semper Cornelianus amor.

Expliciunt.

: IV :

To Angelina Corneliana, that she might forgive Cornelio
for fleeing Siena because of the plague.

Cornelio (poor fellow!), trembling with fear
   Of the dreadful plague, said, "Farewell, blessed land!
Farewell, Angelina, and you, beautiful Eva,
   And farewell to all the joys of Siena!"
Let Cornelio flee death—not that life is   5
   Dearer to him than your eyes, lovely Angela.
Let the fugitive be tormented, having left you with this stricture:
   That he wants to return to a healthy Siena as soon as he can.
Angela, may it please you to sacrifice snow-white bullocks
   And cows at the altars and burn a deal of incense.   10
May Cornelio return safe and live in health:
   I shall always be safe if Cornelio is safe.
In order to be kept safe for you, Corneliana, he left you;
   You will remain safe, no divinity will ever destroy you.
Live, dear girl, that you may surpass Nestor in years,   15
   Surpass Tithonus and Priam.
And after you have lived as many years, light of his life,
   May foul old age not spoil your rosy skin.
And may your breasts be ever whiter than snowy privet blossoms,
   And may Cornelio's love be everlasting.   20

The end of the verses.

: V :

Ad Evam pro Sabino Siculo.

Eva, vale, quondam mea lux, mea vita, voluptas;
 Cornelius valeat, fidus ubique comes.
Servus eram laqueosque tuos et vincula solvo,
 Ut pedibus collum nulla puella premat.

: VI :

Ad Margaram ut Fabritium redamet
et Grifo Siculo in amore non respondeat.

Margara, siquis erit merito tibi dignus amari,
 Fabritius cunctis anteferendus erit.
Omnibus ex rebus sunt elicienda vetustis
 Quattuor, et praestant rebus honore novis.
5 Primum erit ex illis, quem flexo poplite adores,
 Qui laqueo illaqueat colla fugacis, Amor.
Consule Fabritium et tu nosces cetera, namque
 Dimidiam nostri detinet ille animam.
Pone novum et veterem repetas dulcedine amorem:
10 Cantabunt laudes carmina nostra tuas.

: V :

To Eva on behalf of Sabino Siculo.

Eva, farewell, once my light, my life, my pleasure;
  Bid Cornelio farewell, ever a loyal comrade.
I was a slave, but I am loosing your snares and chains,
  So that no girl may put her feet on my neck.

: VI :

To Margara that she may return Fabrizio's love and not respond lovingly to Grifo Siculo.

Margara, if anyone shall be worthy of being loved by you,
  Fabrizio must be ranked above all others.
Of all the old concerns four should be evoked,
  And they are greater in worth than any new ones.
The first of these will be Love, whom you adore on bended   5
  Knee, who catches in his noose the neck of the one who flees.
Ask Fabrizio and you will know the rest,
  For he keeps back half my soul.
Put aside your new love and sweetly seek once more the old:
  Our poems will sing your praises.   10

: VII :

Ad Evam pro Sabino suo.

Esset apud Latias formosior Eva puellas,
    Pectora ni glacie frigidiora forent.
Algentem video sese noctuque dieque
    Et friget quotiens itque reditque via.
5 Ignibus Aetnaeis maiores pectore flammas
    Ardentesque faces corde Sabinus habet.
Frigida, quid dubitas manibus disrumpere pectus?
    Carior est facies, quam sibi vita, tua.

: VIII :

Ad Evam puellam pro Sabino suo.

'Postquam limato iecisti spicula ferro,
    Audes "quis moritur?" dicere cruda mihi.
Quis moritur? Pulchrae moritur dilector Evai.
    Te miseram! mortem Siciliensis obit.
5 Mortuus hoc tumulo tam dira morte Sabinus
    Claudetur; lacrimis funera flebo meis.'
'Si lacrimis te flere iuvat, me claudier isto
    Marmore, ut aeternum nox premat una duos.
Aut ego cum lacrimis animam revocabo Sabini,
10   Postquam coniungam nostra labella suis,
Aut superincumbens moriar consumpta dolore
    Et quem non vivens mortua habebo virum.'

: VII :

To Eva on behalf of his friend Sabino.

Among the maidens of Latium Eva would be lovelier
  If her bosom were not colder than ice.
Night and day I see her, freezing cold,
  And whenever she comes and goes she's colder than ice.
Sabino's breast holds flames greater than Etna's fires   5
  And his heart holds blazing torches.
Ice-cold woman, why don't you just rip open his breast with your
    hands?
  To him, your beauty is more precious than his life.

: VIII :

To the maiden Eva on behalf of his friend Sabino.

"After you have hurled a spear of sharpened iron,
  Cruel woman, you dare to say to me, 'Who is dying?'
Who is dying? It's Eva's lover who is dying,
  You wretch! The Sicilian is going to meet his death.
The dead Sabino will be enclosed in this tomb   5
  By so dire a death; I shall weep over his dead body."
"If it helps you to bewail with tears that I am enclosed
  In that marble, may one night forever crush two souls.
Either I with my tears will call back Sabino's soul
  After I have joined my lips to his,   10
Or I'll die lying down upon him, eaten away by grief
  And the man I did not hold while living I will hold in death."

: IX :

Ad clarum virum Petrum Victorinum
pro Fabritio suae animae dimidio.

Si maiore opera celebres clarosque poetas
    Aut elegos coleres, doctior ipse fores.
Vellem te Musis dulces adhibere labores;
    Cures ingenium nobilitare tuum.
5 Aeterni vates, aeterno carmine laeti,
    Aeternam famam saecula cuncta tenent.
Sed si alio te ducit amor et pectora torquet,
    Si illaqueat mentem pulchra puella tuam,
Ut facilem reddas versu nugeris amantem
10   Et dominam flectes calliditate metri.
Omnis carminibus donata est, Petre, potestas:
    Mitescunt duri saxea corda viri.
Si tamen aeternos velles conscribere versus,
    Virgilium ante oculos nocte dieque tene;
15 Si tu lascivas velles vocitare Camenas,
    Nasonis primo sit tibi nota domus.

: X :

Ad Barnabam studia humanitatis deserere volentem.

Qua monitus fueras mihi dulcis epistola ad aures
    Venit, ab ornatis verba legenda viris.
Scriptum erat in primis: 'Barnabeu, trado salutem

: IX :

*To the famous man Piero Vittorino
on behalf of Fabrizio, half his soul.*

If you were devoting yourself to famous and illustrious poets
    And to elegy with greater effort, you would be more learned.
I would like you to devote sweet labors to the Muses;
    May you take care to win fame for your talent.
Immortal poets, happy in their immortal poetry,   5
    Keep their immortal renown through all the ages.
But if love leads you elsewhere and torments your heart,
    If a lovely girl should ensnare your mind,
Then trifle at playing the lover in verse to make her pliable,
    And bend your mistress with your metrical cunning.   10
Every power has been given, Piero, to poems;
    They soften the stony heart of a hard man.
If you still would like to compose immortal verse,
    Hold Vergil before your eyes night and day;
If you would like to summon wanton Muses   15
    Let Ovid' house become familiar to you first.

: X :

To Barnaba who wants to desert humanistic studies.

The charming letter in which you had been admonished has come
    To my ears, words that ought to be read by distinguished men.
At the beginning was written: "Barnaba, gracious friend,

Ad te ego Petrucius, comis amice, meam.'
5   Non dubito is faciet limato te atque vetusto
     Eloquio ad priscam protinus ire viam.
    Flecteret immitem quo quondam capta noverca est
     Hippolytum Phaedra et mortua nulla foret.
    Si Phalaris quemquam vellet comburere tauro,
10   Voce sua accensum extingueret ante focum.
    Proposito affixos poterit deflectere divos
     Deque tuis humeris solvere, Phoebe, liram.
    Sed risu dignam volui prius ipse fabellam
     Scribere, et attendes carmina mixta ioco.
15   Cur sereret nullas segetes quaesivit egenum
     Dives; respondit: 'Semina quisque serit.
    Tempestate alia pauci sulcare solebant
     Horrebamque famem, frigora longa, sitim.
    Tunc ego fortis humo mandabam semina, laetus
20   Excepi fructum ac aurea poma simul;
    Nunc potero ad tantas aliorum vivere terras,
     Dulcia vina bibam, dulcia mala legam.'
    Dives ad haec: 'Propriis implebunt horrea granis
     Agricolae et frugis quisquis avarus erit.
25   Adventante hieme et longaevo frigore noctis,
     Tu sine pane bibes pocula tristis aquae.'
    Despexit ditem cautum sententia egeni
     Atque urgente fame mortuus ille fuit.
    Non aliam poteris causam praebere roganti
30   Quam de fruge habuit dives ab agricola.
    Audes humanis studiis indicere bellum?
     Indignum facinus tempora nostra vident!
    Monstra quis haec credat? Medias sitibundus ad undas
     Non bibit, ille vorax despuit ore cibos.

I, Petrucci, impart my greetings to you."
I don't doubt that he will make you return to your old path.   5
    By his polished and classical eloquence.
He might have influenced the cruel Hippolytus, with whom
    His stepmother Phaedra once was smitten, and no woman
        would be dead.
If Phalaris wished to burn anyone in his bull, his voice
    Might have extinguished the kindled hearth first.   10
He could thwart the fixed intentions of the gods;
    He could loosen the lyre from your shoulders, Phoebus.
But I first wanted to write a story that deserves a laugh;
    You'll listen to poetry varied with jokes.
A rich man asked a poor man why he sowed no crops,   15
    And he answered, "Every man is sowing seeds.
In another time few were wont to plow the fields
    And I shuddered at hunger, long cold, and thirst.
Then I bravely sowed seed in the ground, and happily
    I harvested a crop and golden fruit at the same time.   20
Now I will be able to live on the wide lands of others,
    I shall drink sweet wines and pluck sweet apples."
The rich man replied, "Farmers will fill their barns with their
    Own grain, and each man will be miserly with his own crops.
With winter coming and nights of long-lasting cold   25
    You will, without bread, drink bitter cups of water."
The needy man took thought, despised the rich man's caution,
    And when winter came, hunger crushed him to death.
When someone asks, you won't be able to give a different reason
    Than the rich man gave about the farmer's crops.   30
Do you dare declare war on the studies of humanity?
    That our age should see such a shameful crime!
Who would believe these horrors? The parched man does not
        drink
    Amid the waters, the hungry man spits food from his mouth!

35 Temporibus primis tu solus in urbe colebas
  Rhetores, et quamvis nullus in urbe foret,
Pauperie tunc dives eras, nunc copia egenum
  Te facit: affluxus rhetoris ipse nocet.
Non opus est monitu, quom te Andreotius ardens
40 Admonuit: placidos edidit ille sales.
Si a se discedis, tu te discedis ab ipso
  Deque viro armato factus inermis eris.
Si studia atque artes fugies tu pectore nostras,
  Ex Erebo infernas ipse vocabo deas,
45 Non nisi Tisiphonen et Tisiphonesque sorores
  Aut si quid Stygio gurgite peius erit.
Irruet ante oculos Furiarum turba; timebis
  Flagra dei inferni et milia, crede, faces.
At si non fugies, sacras vocitabo Camenas,
50 Aut si quid coelo dignius esse potest;
At si non fugies, suaves opobalsama odores
  Spirent et violae, spargat et aura crocos.
Aut repetas Musas aut tot pellemus ab urbe
  Rhetores, et primas ique redique vias.

: XI :

Ad Mauritium Lutium
ut suae nuptae primos flores decerpat.

Tonia formosa est et sanguine clara parentum
  Et veterum fama est nobilitata patrum.
Quando puella uterum matris delinquit et aura
  Vescitur, adventant Iuno, Diana, Venus.
5 Iuno thorum speciemque Venus, sed Luna pudorem

76

In your youth you alone in the city would devote yourself   35
   To rhetoricians, and, although there wasn't one in the city,
Then you were rich amid poverty; now, plenty makes you poor;
   The very abundance of rhetoric harms you.
You should not need to be warned, since zealous Andreozzo
   Admonished you; he uttered gentle raillery.   40
If you part company with him, you part company with yourself,
   And, once a man-at-arms, you'll become a man defenseless.
If in your heart you flee from our studies and our arts,
   I myself will summon the infernal goddesses from Erebus,
Not excepting Tisiphon and Tisiphon's sisters,   45
   Or whatever will be worse from the Stygian abyss.
A crowd of Furies will rush in before your eyes; believe me,
   You'll fear the whips and fires of the god of Hell.
But if you do not flee, I shall summon the holy Muses
   Or whatever can be worthier from heaven above.   50
But if you do not flee, may violets and balsam
   Breathe sweet odors, and may breezes sprinkle saffron.
Either seek again the Muses, and come and go in your early ways,
   Or we will drive from our city the arts of eloquence.

∶ XI ∶

To Maurizio Luti
that he pluck the first flowers of his bride.

Tonia is beautiful and renowned for her parents' ancestry,
   And the fame of her forefathers is well known.
When she left her mother's womb and began to feed
   On air, Juno, Diana, and Venus appeared.
Juno brought the marriage bed, Venus beauty, but Luna   5

Affert: quaeque suo munere donat eam.
Luna verecundo depinxit in ore ruborem
    Et posuit capiti sidera bina suo.
Haec ubi facta, Venus nitidis arrisit ocellis
10   Et dixit: 'Rutilas spargo per ora rosas.'
Et triplici dono donata est virgo pudica:
    Connubio stabili est tradita Mauritio;
Et manibus divum facta est Antonia sacris
    Splendidior speculo candidiorque nive.
15 Felix ante alias tanto exornata marito,
    Quae thalamum intrabit splendida nympha tuum!
Festina hibernas secum consumere noctes
    Et matutinas collige prime rosas!

: XII :

Ad Aeneam Silvium responsio incipit.

Non hilarem accipiat meme Trinacria tellus,
    Ni dedero Aeneae carmina mille prius.
Verbula quae niveo tu vis mea marmore pingi
    Sunt tectura piper, cinnama, thura, crocum.
5 Versibus ornasti tantis Marrasia Tempe,
    Ut me immortalem longa papyrus agat.
Nugas non agito, nisi sint mea plena furore
    Pectora: tunc scribo quom venit ille furor.
Silvius Aeneas cantabitur atque decora
10   Picula et alteruter carmina nostra leget.

Brought modesty; each endowed her with her own gift.
Luna painted a rosy color on her modest mouth
    And placed a pair of stars upon her head.
When she had done this, Venus with shining eyes smiled
    And said, "I sprinkle red roses all over her face."   10
And so the chaste virgin was given a threefold gift.
    She was given to Maurizio in steadfast wedlock,
And by the goddesses' holy hands Antonia was made
    More brilliant than a mirror and whiter than the snow.
Happy before all others, to be adorned for such a husband;   15
    What a dazzling nymph will enter your marriage chamber!
Hurry to devour these long winter nights with her
    And gather to the fullest the roses of dawn.

⁝ XII ⁝

An answer to Eneo Silvio begins here.

The land of Sicily would receive me in an unhappy state
    If I don't first give Eneo a thousand poems beforehand.
My little words that you would have carven on white marble
    Will end up wrapping pepper, cinnamon, incense, and saffron.
You've adorned the Tempe of Marrasio with such long verses   5
    That just the length of the paper will make me immortal.
I do not work on composing my trifles, unless my heart is full
    Of a divine madness: when the madness comes, I write.
Eneo Silvio will be celebrated in my poems, and so will lovely
    Picula, and both of them will read my songs.   10

Ipse vale et laudes si mille optaveris, ora
   Ut cito diripiat pectora nostra furor.

Marrasii Siculi ad Aeneam Silvium explicit.

: XIII :

Marrasii Siculi poetae praeclari ad deas aquarum.

Nymphae, carus amor fugit hinc: vos currere ad ortus
   Incipite et Venetam correvocate meam.

Et te cymba, precor, nostrum quae ducis amorem,
   Quam modo puppis aquam, nunc tua prora secet.
5 Cymba, redi subito; nam te rediisse iuvabit:
   Lignea quae modo sis, aurea puppis eris.
Fluminaque ad proram veluti nunc saxa rigete,
   Ut redeat lasso remige cymba suo.
Nymphae, carus amor fugit hinc: vos currere ad ortus
10   Incipite et Venetam correvocate meam.

Dicite Hamadryades et rustica numina clament:
   'Clausum iter ad Venetos, clausum iter ad Venetos.'
Semper Hamadryadum coluit qui templa puerque
   Navit qui latices saepius ipse fui.
15 Exclament omnes et concava saxa vocabunt:

Be well yourself, and if you should want a thousand praises,
  Pray that a divine madness swiftly tear asunder my breast.

Marrasio Siculo's answer to Eneo Silvio ends here.

: XIII :

From Marrasio Siculo to the goddesses of the waters.

Nymphs, my dear love is fleeing hence; go hurry to the East
  And together summon back my Venetian girl to me.

And you, little boat, I pray, who carry my love, may your prow
  Now cleave the water which a while ago your stern was
    cleaving.
Little boat, come back quickly; for you will be happy you came   5
    back:
  Though you be only wood, you shall be a ship of gold.
And waves, grow hard as rocks now at the prow,
  So that, its oarsmen exhausted, the little boat may come back.
Nymphs, my dear love is fleeing hence; go hurry to the East
  And together summon back my Venetian girl to me.   10

Tell the Hamadryads and rustic divinities to shout:
  "The way is closed to Venetians, the way is closed to
    Venetians."
I have been one who always worshipped at the temples
  Of the Hamadryads and as a boy swam so often in these
    waters.
Let them all cry out and the hollow rocks will shout: 15

'Clausum iter ad Venetos, clausum iter ad Venetos.'
Nymphae, carus amor fugit hinc: vos currere ad ortus
    Incipite et Venetam correvocate meam.

Tu, Neptune, velis extollere ad astra procellas.
20   Territus ut fugiat nauta pericla maris,
Aut tenui astrictum mare sit glacieque geluque,
    Ut neque sit remo nec via tuta pede.
Tunc tibi, Neptuno, niveum mactabo iuvencum:
    Gnosia, si libeat, Gnosia vacca cadet.
25 Nymphae, carus amor fugit hinc: vos currere ad ortus
    Incipite et Venetam correvocate meam.

Te, Venus, humanos superant si fata dolores
    Adversa, in saxum si mea membra rigent,
Oro, animam e nostris fugientem siste medullis,
30   Neve anima primum corpus inerme ruat.
Sed praesens facilisque meo succurre dolori;
    Corruet ante tuos candida vacca focos.
Nymphae, carus amor fugit hinc: vos currere ad ortus
    Incipite et Venetam correvocate meam.

"The way is closed to Venetians, the way is closed to
    Venetians."
Nymphs, my dear love is fleeing hence; go hurry to the East
    And together summon back my Venetian girl to me.

And you, Neptune, please raise storms to the stars.
    May the frightened sailor shun the dangers of the sea,   20
Or may the sea be bound with clear ice and frost
    So that the way is not safe by oar or foot.
Then, Neptune, I will slaughter for you a snowy bullock;
    A Cretan cow if you like — yes, a Cretan cow — shall fall.
Nymphs, my dear love is fleeing hence; go hurry to the East   25
    And together summon back my Venetian girl to me.

And you, Venus, if adverse fates shall have the upper hand
    Over human suffering, if my limbs should stiffen into stone,
Stop, soul, stop! I'll pray, as it flees my inward marrow,
    Don't let my defenseless body collapse before my soul!   30
But be here and ready to help me in my grief;
    And a white cow will fall before your altars.
Nymphs, my dear love is fleeing hence; go hurry to the East
    And together summon back my Venetian girl to me.

: XIV :

Marrasii Siculi ad Franciscum Tallonum,
qualem puellam cantari dignam eligere debeat Ferrariae,
ubi puellae amantis mores describuntur,
feliciter incipit.

Pestis ab Etrusca postquam me depulit ora,
    Ingenio et Musis et sine amore fui,
Et raucae nostrum ranae excussere cerebrum,
    Quae Patavi fines et loca spurca natant.
5   Tris inter medicos vigilavi squalidus annos,
    Hippocraten legi non sine rege Arabo.
Expertus varias herbas variosque liquores,
    Aegrotis didici ferre libenter opem.
Interea nullo caluerunt pectora amore,
10   Saeva nec iniecit spicula acerbus Amor.
Nunc ego limosas timeo algentesque paludes
    Inviaque et steriles undique stagna lacus,
Ut dubitem in saxum subito mea corpora vertant,
    Neu rigeant veluti frigida corda nives.
15   Cum, Francisce, tibi divum non defuit umquam
    Ingenium versus atque decoris item,
Cum relegis nostros atque oblectaris eisdem
    Versibus, et nugae cum placuere meae,
Ut redeant primae citharae Musaeque priores,
20   Nunc tibi arundinea est quaeque petenda palus;
Fluminaque et rivi, fontes et stagna petantur
    Et quoscumque locos splendida nympha colit.
Saepe inter salices nymphas errare videmus,
    Saepe inter calamos, saepius inter aquas.

: XIV :

*A poem of Marrasio Siculo to Francesco Tallone,
asking that he choose the sort of girl from Ferrara that
is worthy of song, wherein the ways of a loving girl
are described, begins auspiciously.*

After the plague drove me from Tuscan parts,
    I was without inspiration or Muses or love.
And the noisy frogs that swim in the area of the Po
    And its filthy places rattled my brain.
For three miserable years I studied hard among the doctors,   5
    I read Hippocrates, not without the kingly Arab.
Having tried various herbs and various potions
    I willingly learned to bring help to the sick.
Meanwhile no love warmed my heart,
    And cruel Love threw no savage darts at me.   10
Now I am afraid of the cold and slimy swamps,
    The pathless fens and the lifeless lakes.
So that I wonder if my body might suddenly turn to stone,
    Or my heart grow stiff and cold as snow.
Since your godlike talent for verses and beauty as well   15
    Has never failed you, Francesco,
And since you read and reread mine and are amused by them,
    And since my trifles have pleased you
So that our youthful Muses and earlier lyrics return,
    Now you must seek out every reedy swamp;   20
You must seek out rivers and streams, springs and pools,
    And whatever places the shining nymphs inhabit.
I see nymphs wandering often among the willows,
    Often among the reeds, and very often in the waters.

25 Excerpenda tibi nunc est ex vallibus istis
   Nympha decora meis saepe canenda sonis.
   Hos habeat mores: mentemque animumque modestum,
   Nec modo sit facilis, nec modo cruda nimis;
   Gaudeat interdum me praetereunte, revolvat
30   Interdum faciem dissimuletque suam;
   Nec me discruciet quotiens me viderit illa,
   Laeta nec ex abitu saepe sit illa meo;
   Illa mihi facie nitida vultuque sereno
   Rideat, ut nostrum bulliat igne iecur;
35 Illa Medusaeo nec me respexerit ore:
   Sim velut Aglauros, frigidus unde lapis;
   Me flentem si quando etiam tristemque videret,
   Se mitem atque hilarem praebeat illa mihi.
   Hanc mihi si dederis divam, Francisce, puellam,
40   Mille elegos fingam conficiamque sibi.
   Hoc mihi natura est: nisi sim devinctus amore,
   Nulla fluunt nostro carmina docta sinu.
   Nec tibi deficient ex nostro carmine laudes
   Atque mihi aeterno tempore amicus eris.

Valeas qui legeris.
Ferrariae Idibus Aprilis.

Now you must choose for me a comely nymph   25
    From these vales for me to sing of often in my songs.
Let her have these ways: a modest mind and spirit,
    Neither too compliant, nor yet too unresponsive;
Sometimes let her be happy when I pass by,
    Other times let her turn away and hide her face.   30
Let her not torture me as often as she sees me,
    Nor let her often be happy at my departure.
With a shining glace and a calm countenance
    Let her smile at me so that my liver boils with fire.
Let her not look on me with the face of Medusa: 35
    I would then be like Aglauros, who was changed to stone.
If at some moment she should see me weeping and sad,
    She should present herself to me as kind and cheerful.
If you give me this divine girl, Francesco, for her
    I will invent and polish a thousand elegiac verses.   40
My nature is this: unless I am overcome by love,
    No learned poems flow from my bosom.
My poems will not lack praises for you
    And you will be my friend for time everlasting.

May you who read this be well.
Ferrara, April 13.

: XV :

Marrasii Siculi poema
de transmutatione ac laboriosa amatorum vita
ad Medusam divam puellam feliciter incipit.

Quam timui, ante meos oculos obiecta Medusa es
    Et mea tu laqueo colla superba ligas.
Scis, renui faciemque tuam mihi saepe minantem
    Extimui et mores insidiasque tuas.
5 Quid, si te fugio, me firmius ipsa catena
    Stringis? Si redeo, me quid iniqua fugis?
Tu quotiens nostros mutasti carmine vultus?
    Tu quotiens oculis pectora tota tuis?
Saepe ego vipereos sumo cervice capillos
10   Oraque terna humeris stant rabiosa canis;
Saepe fui mitis, tenero mansuetior agno
    Et mea caesaries aurea saepe fuit.
Ah, quotiens stabulis foenum paleamque momordi!
    Excubui quotiens more timentis apri!
15 Me celerem quotiens texit furnaria vestis,
    Nec mihi pistori ianua aperta fuit!
In me praecipites veniunt qui moenia lustrant,
    Pervigiles cursant in mea crura canes;
Teque iubente canis mea sumpsit imago figuram:
20   Quem lanient hostem non habuere canes.
Efficior tener atque macer, pinguissimus; adde
    Uno eodemque die vir, puer atque senex.
Quid referam? Convertor amans in mille figuras
    Quaque die et totidem nocte silente novas.
25 Brachia tu quamvis mutasti et corpora nostra,

፥ XV ፥

Marrasio Siculo's poem to that divine girl Medusa
about the transmutation and toilsome life of lovers
begins auspiciously.

You whom I feared, Medusa, are cast before my eyes,
    And are binding my proud neck with your noose.
You know I have rejected your face that often threatens me
    And have dreaded your ways and your treacherous traps.
Why, if I flee you, do you bind me more firmly with your chains?   5
    And why, if I come back, wicked one, do you flee me?
How often have you changed my looks through song?
    How often have you changed my whole heart with your eyes?
Often I feel your snaky hair on my neck
    And the triple rabid faces of the dog stand on my shoulders.   10
Often I was kind, milder than a tender lamb
    And often my flowing hair was golden.
Ah! How often did I nibble hay and straw in the stables!
    How often did I sleep outdoors like the fearful boar!
How often did a baker's garment cover me in my swift flight!   15
    And no door was open to me, baker as I was!
Those who patrol the city walls come lunging for me,
    Their watchdogs are rushing for my legs;
At your command my appearance took the shape of a dog:
    The dogs did not have an enemy they could rip apart.   20
Once very plump, I am become frail and thin; in addition
    In one and the same day, a man, a boy and a codger.
Why go on? As a lover I am changed into a thousand new shapes
    Each day, and the same number each silent night.
Although you have transformed my arms and my body,   25

Non animum poteris, blanda Medusa, meum.
Contribuere mihi nascenti sidera legem
    Et connexa pari fila fuere manu,
Ut numquam sine amore velint mea corda manere,
30   Seu Paris ipse mihi, seu mihi Nestor ero.
Ergo si quis erit qui me prohibebit amare,
    Ixionis poterit sistere nempe rotam,
Tantaleamve sitim poterit sedare famemque
    Vulturis; impleta vasa ferentur aqua.
35 Brachia tu quamvis mutasti et corpora nostra,
    Non animum poteris, blanda Medusa, meum.
Te propter quotiens faciem percusserat imber
    Dempserat et capiti tegmina nostra furens!
Saepe per ardentes movi vestigia soles
40   Et redii hiberna quam madefactus aqua;
Saepe mihi placuit ventis committere navem,
    Saepe suam ventis commaculare fidem.
Mobilior quamquam tu sis quam ventus et unda,
    Cur tamen in te una stat mea fixa fides?
45 Herculeos sibi quisque animos assumat amator,
    Damnaque sub domina deteriora feret.
Ipse ego pro nihilo facio, mihi crede, labores
    Herculis: ingredior Tartara mille vices,
Tartareusque canis, superas extractus ad auras,
50   Venit et extimuit meque meamque manum;
Et Furiae infernae me cognovere furentem
    Et mirata meum dira Chimaera caput.
Ad me confugiat Stygiam transnare paludem
    Qui cupit, inferni si bene nescit iter:
55 Notum iter et sedes et quae sub nocte volantes
    Perpetiuntur aves et vada, cymba, Charon.
Vix poteram prius ipse leves sufferre labores,

Captivating Medusa, you will not be able to alter my soul.
The stars laid down their law for me at my birth
    And my life threads were spun with an even hand,
So that my heart may never wish to remain without love,
    Whether I be like Paris himself or like Nestor.   30
Therefore, if there is anyone who will forbid me to love,
    Doubtless he could also bring Ixion's wheel to a stop,
Could slake the thirst of Tantalus, and the hunger
    Of the vulture; and the urns of water would be forever full.
Although you have transformed my arms and my body,   35
    You will never, charming Medusa, be able to change my soul.
How often on your account had a raging storm struck
    My face and torn the covering from my head!
Often I have walked under burning suns
    And come home drenched by a winter downpour;   40
Often I delighted to expose my ship to the winds,
    Often I decided to sully her trust in the winds.
Although you are more inconstant than wind and wave,
    Why is it that in you alone my faith is fixed?
Let each lover take for himself the courage of Hercules,   45
    And under his mistress he will suffer worse losses.
Believe me, I myself reckon the labors of Hercules at naught,
    I have walked into Hell a thousand times,
And the hound of Hell, dragged into the upper air,
    Came, and dreaded me and my fist;   50
And the Furies of Hell have known me in my madness
    And the dread Chimera was awestruck at my head.
Let whoever wishes to cross the Stygian swamp come
    Straight to me if he is ignorant of the best way to Hell:
I know the way and its abodes, and what the birds suffer   55
    Who fly in darkness; I know the passage, the boat, Charon
        himself.
Before this, I was scarcely able to endure the lightest labors,

Nunc graviora libens et leviora puto.
Nulla subest illi potior medicina labori,
60   Quam veniat, domina, sub dicione tua.
Ah, quotiens volui committere lumina somno!
     Fugerat at somnus lumina clausa meus.
Ante tuos postes noctem vigilavimus omnem;
     Praeterii ante illos lumine mille vices.
65 Si qua datur somno requies, si lassa quiescunt
     Membra thoro, in mentem, blanda Medusa, venis.
Aestivus quotiens dum sol exureret agros,
     Intrarunt guttur pocula nulla meum!
Multotiens sine pane diem consumpsimus omnem,
70   Vexabat quamvis viscera nostra fames.
Consueram lacrimas nullas perfundere, sive
     Mortua mater erat, vel meus ipse pater;
Unde sit admiror mihi nunc data copia flendi:
     Non nisi sunt lacrimis lumina plena meis.
75 Iuppiter, ut fama est, periuria ridet amantum,
     Sic lacrimas ridet nocte dieque meas.
Totque fui postquam poenas ego passus amaras,
     Tu nostri luctus es miserata graves
Et mihi dixisti: 'Relegas quid epistola dictat
80   Nostra brevis, quam nunc aurea fila ligant.'
Tunc ego: 'Complures oculos quam pastor habebat
     Argus, quam coelo sidera nocte micant.'
Et subito, nivea vestitus pectora veste,
     Nocte sub obscura prata secanda peto.
85 Luciferi ante ortum felicia gramina legi,
     Quae fuerant atro sanguine tincta lupi;
Et mihi per gelidos campos quaesita cicuta est
     Et quae cantantes adiuvat herba manus.
Quin etiam ad tumulos media sub nocte resedi
90   Et traxi digitis virginis ossa meis.

Now I gladly undergo the heaviest and think them light.
No remedy is powerful enough for the suffering
    That comes under your domination, my lady.   60
Ah, how often have I wanted to entrust my eyes to sleep!
    But sleep has fled from my closed eyes.
Before your doorposts I have watched the night through;
    With my eyes I have passed before them a thousand times.
If any rest is offered by sleep, if my exhausted limbs   65
    Lie quiet on my bed, you come to mind, captivating Medusa.
How often, while the summer sun is burning the fields,
    No draft of liquid touches my throat!
How many times have I passed the whole day without food,
    Although hunger gnawed my vitals.   70
I used not to weep many tears, whether my mother
    Was dead, or even my father himself;
Now I am amazed that such a store of tears is given me:
    My eyes are full of nothing but tears.
Jupiter, so the story goes, laughs at the false oaths of lovers,   75
    He laughs night and day at my tears.
After I had suffered so many bitter punishments,
    You took pity on my burden of grief
And said to me: "Read over what my short letter
    Says, the one tied with a golden thread."   80
Then I said: "As many eyes as the shepherd Argus had,
    As many as the stars that shine in the night sky."
And at once, clothing my breast in a snowy robe,
    I seek a meadow to be mown by the dark of night.
Before the rising of the Daystar I plucked the fortunate grasses   85
    Which had been stained by the black blood of a wolf.
And amid the cool fields I sought a reed pipe,
    And the plant that aids the hands of singers.
Yes, and in the middle of the night I even sat among the tombs
    And drew out the bones of a virgin with my fingers.   90

Per similes artus facta est tibi cerea imago
    Et cordi infixa est ferrea fortis acus.
Suppositum Veneri Martem cum vidimus omnes,
    Collecta artifici profuit herba suo.
95 Tunc incude faber ferii et fornace metallum
    Excoxi et factus anulus inde fuit.
Quantum in amore valet tu scis, mea diva puella,
    Aureus hic nostra circulus arte cavus.
Namque obscura die facta est nox clarior omni,
100 Qua concessisti gaudia cuncta thori.
Tecum si possem tales consumere noctes!
    Nox aeterna, veni; lux reditura, fuge.

Explicit transmutatio ac
laboriosa amatorum vita ad Medusam.

: XVI :

Marrasii Siculi congratulatio de pace
ad illustrissimum principem Leonellum Estensem
feliciter incipit.

Non nisi de sancta volui, clarissime princeps,
    Pace loqui nostris versibus atque iocis.
Pax tranquilla tuos populos sine fine tenebit:
    Tu pius et verus pacis amator ades.
5 Fortis es et iustus non iusto tempore princeps,
    Quem tibi subiecti numinis instar habent;
Tu iuvenis natu, sed prudentissimus heros,
    Tu regis imperiis regna paterna tuis;

I made for you a waxen image with limbs like yours
    And a strong needle was imbedded in its heart.
Although we all have seen Mars subjugated to Venus,
    The plant gathered was of use to her artisan husband.
Then with anvil and furnace like a blacksmith   95
    I struck and heated metal and made from it a little ring.
You know, my goddess girl, how this golden band,
    Hollowed out by my skill, is so powerful in love,
For the dark night on which you granted all the delights
    Of your bed became brighter than any day.   100
If only I could spend such nights with you!
    Come, eternal night; returning light, be gone.

The transmutation and toilsome life of lovers
addressed to Medusa is ended.

∶ XVI ∶

Marrasio Siculo's words of congratulation for the peace
to that most illustrious prince Leonello d'Este
begins auspiciously.

I wanted, most brilliant prince, to speak of nothing
    In my verses and playful poems except holy peace.
Peace, endless, serene, will hold sway over your peoples:
    You, the true and dutiful lover of peace, are at hand.
Your are a brave and just prince in an unjust age,   5
    Whom your subjects hold equal to a divinity;
You are young in years, but the most sagacious of heroes,
    You rule your father's kingdom by your own authority;

Atque ita tu populos, cives gentemque gubernas,
10   Ut videare tuis anteferendus avis;
Atque ita tu cunctis dignos largiris honores,
    Ut te divinum quilibet esse putet.
Est opulenta viris urbs haec Ferraria multis:
    Hospitium pacis te duce semper erit.
15 Non minus et patris semper fuit aucta triumphis
    Tellus finitimis invidiosa locis.
Hesperia de gente truces mortale duellum
    Expleturi hostes hic habuere locum.
Indixere diem pro se sibi quisque tyrannus:
20   Armati veniunt ad fera bella viri;
Dumque animus dubio, dum mors vicina videtur,
    Divisit sapiens proelia voce parens:
Quos neque magna ducum nec magna potentia regum,
    Hos potuit genitor conciliare tuus.
25 Adde quod et Latiis erat exitiale periclum
    Urbibus et multis bella futura malis,
Et populi atque duces accingebantur ad arma
    Atque erat Italicis una ruina deis
Ni pater illustris tecum posuisset opimam
30   Pacem inter Venetos anguigerumque Ducem.
Conticeo proavos quibus exornaris ab aevo,
    Unde Estense genus, quis, Leonelle, parens.
Magnum opus et magnas res scribere non sine magno
    Ingenio et nostrum quam puerile vides.
35 Sed si forte meum nunc fortunatius esset
    Ingenium, canerem teque tuamque domum.
Gaudeo quod studiis, rarum est hoc tempore, princeps
    Deditus humanis clarus et eloquio es.

And you so govern its peoples, citizens and nations
    That you seem to rank ahead of your forefathers.   10
And you bestow such worthy honors on all
    That anyone would think you godlike.
The city of Ferrara is rich in its multitude of men:
    While you are ruler it will always be the dwelling of peace.
Your territory, a land that is the envy of its neighbors,   15
    Was no less augmented by your father's victories.
Fierce enemies from a Western race, about to engage
    In a deadly duel, made this city their dueling ground:
Each tyrant had declared a day for the combat;
    Armed men were coming for a barbarous war.   20
While courage was in doubt, while death seemed imminent,
    Your wise father separated the combatants with a word:
Men whom neither powerful warlords nor mighty kings
    Could bring together, your father was able to reconcile.
There was, besides, the ruinous danger to the Latian cities   25
    And risk of future wars with their many evils.
The people and their leaders were preparing themselves for war
    And a single ruin seemed destined for Italy's gods,
If you and your illustrious father had not imposed
    Fruitful peace between the Venetians and the snake-bearing   30
        duke.
I say nothing about your ancestors whose timeless honor you
        enhance,
    Nor the origins of the Este, Leonello, nor your father.
One cannot write a great work about great matters
    Without great talent, and you see how immature mine is.
But if somehow my talent were now to become more prosperous,   35
    I would sing of you and your house.
I rejoice because you are—something rare in this age—a prince
    Devoted to humane studies and famous for eloquence.

Maecenas obiit, simul oppetiere poetae;
40   Sed tibi nascetur, dive, poeta tuus.
Est opulenta viris urbs haec Ferraria multis:
      Hospitium pacis te duce semper erit.
Est Baccho Cererique etiam gratissima; Phoebus
      Hanc amat hancque colit hancque tuetur Amor.
45 Tantis culta deis visa est mihi dulcis; amavi
      Hanc urbem, placuit mosque genusque suum,
Ut nulla sub parte poli perpessus iniquas
      Tot fuerim poenas totque timenda mala.
Res mira, et nostris non est audita nec ullis
50   Temporibus, volui quot fera bella pati.
Audi et vera leges quot sunt discrimina amantum
      Quotque viae et quantis subdita vita malis:
Pro nihilo faciunt et mille pericula, mille
      Mortes atque volunt mille perire modis.
55 Haec mihi nota via est per quam vestigia movi
      Saepius et vidi quam sit amara via.
Si tantis adiecta malis est vita, voluptas
      Una subest illi, quae mihi pluris erat;
Haec erat ut facerem placidam facilemque puellam,
60   Ut veniat domina sub dicione mea.
Post multos luctus, lites saevosque labores
      Pax tranquilla fuit non habitura modum.
Et iuvenes pacem retinent pacemque puellae:
      Si quid agunt, pacis omnia plena vides.
65 Pax tranquilla tuos populos sine fine tenebit:
      Tu pius et verus pacis amator ades.

Explicit.

Maecenas died, and poets at once met their deaths,
    But a poet of your own will be born for you, divine one.   40
This city of Ferrara is rich in its multitude of men,
    While you are its ruler it will always be the home of peace.
It is also most pleasing to Bacchus and Ceres; Phoebus loves
    This city and dwells here, and Love watches over it.
Cared for by such great gods, it has seemed sweet to me;   45
    I've loved this city, enjoyed its ways and its people.
So that under no other sky might I have endured to the end
    So many unfair punishments or so many fearful evils.
It is a wondrous thing, unheard of in our time or any other,
    How many savage combats I have wished to suffer.   50
Listen and you will read how many true disputes lovers have,
    How many are their paths, how many evils their lives endure;
Even a thousand dangers, a thousand deaths, they count as
       naught,
    And they desire to perish in a thousand different ways.
I have known this path and too often have I followed it   55
    And I have seen how bitter a path it is.
If life has hurled so many evils at me, it has offered
    One pleasure, more to me than all the pain:
This was that I should make a girl kindly and indulgent,
    So that, as my mistress, she would come beneath my sway.   60
After many griefs, disputes, and cruel sufferings
    There was tranquil peace that would not have had an end.
Young men keep peace and young women, too;
    If they do anything, you see all things full of peace.
Peace, endless, serene, will hold sway over your peoples;   65
    You, the true and dutiful lover of peace, are at hand.

The poem ends here.

⸫ XVII ⸫

*Marrasii Siculi poema de ortu, obitu et vita larvarum
pro Sucino Bentio suo ad illustrissimum principem
Nicolaum Marchionem Estensem feliciter incipit.*

Larvati dicunt, princeps animose, salutem,
    Marchio, quos genuit desidiosa Venus.
Nos uno partu, nulli coniuncta marito,
    Parturiit caeca lucida nocte parens,
5 Et nobis geminas facies oculosque quaternos
    Confinxit celeri composuitque manu.
Hinc Lachesis timuit cuicumque revolvere fila
    Per geminos fusos per geminasque colos.
Fata deam flentem sunt et miserata timentem
10   Et statuere uno funera nostra die.
Tandem nostra parens divos et fata rogavit,
    Nec potuit lacrimis fata movere suis,
Sed sibi deflenti nos concessere renasci
    Postque mori, annalis conficiendo iocos.
15 'Vita brevis sit, laeta tamen, sat mensibus unis,
    Dixere, ut Lachesis stamina pauca neat.
Larva oculis oculos comedat digitosque nitentes
    Cum digitis, crescat semper edendo fames.
Protea Vertumnumque patrem Dryopemque sequantur,
20   Censores habeant undique mille senes
Et dicant quaecumque velint impune loquentes,
    Sive iocosa velint, sive pudenda velint.
Bacchus avus: celebrent sua dulcia templa nepotes
    Larvati, epotent munera lauta patris.'
25 Cum spatium vitae breve sit, Venus ipsa medetur

: XVII :

Marrasio Siculo's poem about the birth, death, and life of masques on behalf of Sozzino Benzi to that most illustrious prince, Niccolò, Marquis of Este, begins auspiciously.

The maskers speak their greeting, brave prince and marquis,
    Maskers whom in her idleness Venus brought to birth.
Our shining parent, not joined to any husband, brought us forth
    In a single birth in the blindness of night.
With a swift hand she shaped us and fastened on us   5
    Twin faces and four eyes each.
Hence Lachesis was afraid to twist the threads of each
    Through the two spindles and the two distaffs.
The Fates pitied the goddess, weeping and fearful,
    And they put off our funeral for one day.   10
Then our mother entreated the gods and the Fates;
    She could not move the Fates with her tears,
But they granted to her tears that, by establishing annual shows,
    We should be reborn and afterward die each year.
"Let your life be brief, yet happy," they said. "Let single months   15
    Be enough for Lachesis to spin out a few threads.
Let the mask consume eyes with its eyes, and shining fingers
    With its fingers, and may its hunger always grow by eating.
Let them follow Proteus and father Vertumnus, and Dryops,
    Let them have a thousand old men on all sides as censors,   20
And let them say whatever they want and speak with impunity,
    Whether they want to say jesting things or scandalous ones.
Bacchus is their grandfather; let his masker-grandsons throng
    His sweet temples and drink their father's splendid gifts."
Since our space of life is short, Venus herself cures   25

Huic morbo cantu, saltibus atque lyra;
Et nos edocuit citharam sua verba sequentem
    Artificesque pedes organa docta sequi,
Et iussit nos tela pati quaecumque Cupido
30   Coniceret: nobis dux fuit ipse datus.
Nos monet hoc versu noctuque dieque canendo
    (Aspera non illi vox neque rauca manet):
'Si vixit paucos, multos si vixerat annos,
    Saxeus ille fuit, qui sine amore fuit.
35 Nil Iove maius erat, nil et Iove maius habetur:
    Coepit amare puer, nec sine amore senex.'
Sed quoniam nobis est vita brevissima, ludos
    Ipse velis, festos et celebrare dies.
Marchio concelebra, heroum clarissime princeps,
40   Qui laeta efficient funera nostra iocos.
Formosae pulchraeque petant tua tecta puellae,
    Est quibus aurata et candida vestis honos,
Et cunctae Veneres, tua quas Ferraria nutrit,
    Et si qua auratis vestibus una decor,
45 Ut digitos digitis possint coniungere nostris,
    Ad citharam ut possit quaeque movere pedes.
Haec si praecipias, ex Gaio fonte Camenas
    Traducam ad clari brachia longa Padi.
Maiorum laudes, titulos et gesta tuorum
50   Illustremque domum et te, Leonelle, canam.
Dii tibi dent quaecumque velis, quaecumque rogabis:
    Asper qui fuerat sit tibi mitis Amor.
Dii te perpetuent, cuncta et per saecula laetum
    Reddant, nec subeat vita beata necem.
55 Unum oro: nostros iocundo lumine versus
    Perlege; Sicanios incipe amare viros.

Explicit. Valeas qui legeris.

This ailment with song, dance, and the lyre;
She taught us the lyre that accompanies her words
   And the organ that has been taught to follow skillful feet.
And she ordered us to endure whatever weapons
   Cupid hurled; he himself was given us as leader.   30
She admonished us by singing this verse night and day,
   (Her voice is neither rough nor grating):
"Whether he lived a few years, or whether he lived many,
   He who lived without love was like a stone.
Nothing was greater than Jove and Jove holds nothing greater: 35
   He began to love as a boy, and as an old man loves still."
But since our life is so very short, may it please you,
   Celebrate games and festival days.
Celebrate, marquis, most glorious prince of heroes,
   The festivities that will bring to pass our happy deaths.   40
Let lovely and fair young women seek your palace,
   Women decked in gold and gleaming garments,
All the Venuses whom your Ferrara fosters,
   Any pretty one with golden garments,
So that they can join their fingers to ours   45
   And each can move her feet to our lyre.
If you so command, I shall lead the Muses from the Fonte Gaia
   To the long reaches of the glorious Po.
I shall sing the praises of your ancestors, their honors and deeds,
   Your illustrious house and you, Leonello.   50
May the gods give you whatever you want, whatever you ask:
   May love, who has been harsh, be gentle to you.
May the gods make you everlasting, and give you joy
   Through the ages, and may your blessed life be deathless.
One thing I ask: read through my verses with a jocund eye;   55
   Begin to love the men of Sicily.

The poem is ended. May the reader be well.

F

Illustrissimus princeps Nicolaus Marchio Estensis
ad doctissimos viros Succinum Bentium et Marrasium Siculum
feliciter incipit.

Vos laetis oculis, laetis complector et ulnis,
    Laetitiae nati laetitiaeque patres.
Vos pax dulcis alit placidusque per otia risus,
    Vos iocus et ludus, vos comitatur amor.
5 Talis nostra deos Ferraria fertilis optat,
    Cum lascivus ager urbsque canora salit.
Non ego vos claros obscura nocte creatos
    Crediderim: melior iactat origo suos.
Nam vates celeber, tragici decus ordinis, olim
10   Aeschylus in scaenam multa notanda tulit,
Inter quae larvam mimis pulchrosque cothurnos:
    Sic locupletat eam versibus atque habitu.
Hinc personatae primum sonuere Camenae;
    Nutriit ast larvas insidiosa Venus.
15 Palpat amans, loquitur tractatque licentius artem,
    Dum larva, ut clipeo, retia operta iacit.
Nec minus antiquus larvam tibicen habebat,
    Quom festos coluit maxima Roma dies.
Larva oritur ceu myrrha, croci, rosa, lilia, odorae
20   Ceu violae: cessant tempore quaeque suo.
Pectoribus tacitis generosi vivit amantis,
    Pascitur haec venis, cordibus ipsa viget.
Ergo patres nacti tales, his moribus alti:
    Ad nos non pudeat ferre gradum propius.
25 In primis magno veniens Ugone parente,

F

*A letter from the most illustrious Niccolò, Marquis of Este,
to those very learned men, Sozzino Benzi and Marrasio
Siculo, begins auspiciously.*

I embrace you with happy eyes and happy arms,
    Sons of joy, fathers of joy.
Sweet peace and gentle laughter nourish you in leisure hours,
    Jest, Play, and Love are your companions.
While the wanton fields and melodious city dance,   5
    Our fertile Ferrara longs for such gods.
I would not have believed that noted figures like yourselves
    Were born in the dark of night: a better origin boasts its birth.
For the famous poet Aeschylus, the glory of the tragic band,
    In time past brought many innovations to the stage,   10
Including the mask and handsome buskins:
    Thus enriching the stage with his verses and with costume.
That was when the Muses of the masque first spoke out;
    But deceitful Venus nurtured the masques.
Lovingly she strokes and addresses and wantonly fondles the art,   15
    As she casts hidden nets from the mask as from behind a
        shield.
When greatest Rome celebrated festival days,
    The flute player of old also wore a mask.
The masque arises like myrrh, roses, lilies, and saffron,
    Like scented violets: each ceases in its own time.   20
It lives in the silent hearts of the noble lover,
    Feeds on his veins, flourishes in his heart.
Thus met with such fathers, nurtured in these ways:
    May they not be ashamed to approach nearer to us.
Especially you who come from your great father, Ugo,   25

Quem Phoebus lustrat quemque Minerva colit,
Insignis Succine veni, comitante poeta
    Marrasio; Musis regia nostra sonet.
Ocius hic adsint ornatae faxo puellae,
30   Narcissi plures cumque Helenis Parides.
Cantibus et cithara saltus agitate decoros,
    Ut satyri cunctos exhilarate choros,
Virgo senex vir nupta, ioco invitante procaci.
    Huius laetitiae quo meminisse queant,
35 Intentus cunctos citat, ecce, Cupidinis arcus:
    Si fugiant, laesus vulnera acerba dabit.
Is namque imperium terris exercet et undis
    Inque deos omnes: sola Minerva vacat.
Huius signa subit quisquis victricia miles,
40   Membra senex fiet, ast animo iuvenis.
Dum sinit ipsa dies, dum vestra decentius aetas,
    Carpite iocundo gaudia plena sinu.
Aspicite ut celeres serpant ad tempora cani,
    Quis modo caesaries flava nimis fuerat.
45 Aspera mox veniet dapibus regina severis,
    Quae luxum frangat, corpora tota domet,
Urgeat edicto sensus frenare petulcos,
    Ferre sitim et duram viscera nostra famem,
Post cantus lacrimis sanctos audire prophetas
50   Et nudo ad templa saepius ire pede
Atque oculis castis alienam cernere nuptam,
    Stringere labra simul nullaque vana loqui.
Dum datur ergo animis manifesta licentia vestris,
    Lascivum moveant ora, pedes, oculi.
55 Dulcior interea gnatus pia cura parentis
    Sit Leonellus ovans saltibus atque ioco,

Whom Phoebus illumines and Minerva fosters.
Come, distinguished Sozzino, with the poet Marrasio
    As your companion; let my palace resound with the Muses.
I shall cause pretty maidens to come quickly hither,
    Many a Paris with many Helens of Troy,   30
Set afoot dances decorous with songs and the lyre,
    Like satyrs, gladden every dancing band,
Maiden, old man, husband, bride, enticing them with saucy jests.
    And in order that they may remember this joy,
Let Cupid's drawn bow, look! stir everyone up.   35
    Should they flee, the offended boy will give them sharp
        wounds.
For he exercises empire over earth and sea
    And over all the gods; only Minerva is spared.
Whatever soldier submits to this god's flag of victory
    Will become old in his limbs, but young in spirit.   40
While time permits, while your age decently allows,
    Seize delights to the full with a joyful breast.
Look how quickly white hair creeps onto your temples,
    Where your locks had once been ever so golden.
Soon the harsh queen will come with her grim food,   45
    To shatter indulgence and master entire bodies,
Urging us by her edict to restrain our wanton senses,
    To endure thirst and hard hunger in our guts;
And, after singing, to listen with tears to the holy prophets
    And to go often to the temples with naked foot,   50
And to look with chaste eyes at someone else's bride,
    To compress one's lips and say nothing foolish.
Therefore, while manifest license is permitted to your spirits,
    Let it be mouth, feet, and eyes that move wantonly.
Meanwhile, may my son Leonello, his father's dutiful care,   55
    Rejoice more fondly in dances and jests,

Promptior ut Musas ac Pallada deinde revisat:
Intermissus enim fit labor ipse levis.

*Explicit. Ex officina Guarini Veronensis
pro illustrissimo principe Nicolao Marchione.*

: XVIII :

*Incipit Marrasii Siculi responsio
ad Guarinum Veronensem virum litteratissimum.*

Postquam tu nostris respondes, dive, tabellis,
    Postquam complacuit nostra Camena tibi,
Gloria Marrasio dabitur non parva Sicano
    Atque futurus honos non mihi parcus erit.
5 Omnia quae veteres nostri scripsere Latini
    Carmine, prosa etiam, cuncta, Guarine, sapis;
Nec minus et Graias inter doctissimus artes,
    Sive velis prosa, carmine sive velis.
Adde quod historias scripsit quas, doctior Argis,
10 Plutarchus transfers et meliora doces.
Non ego descripsi quam prima theatra colebant
    Larvam, sed quam nunc regia quaeque tenet.
Si primos ortus primaeva ab origine vellem
    Scribere, principium tunc mihi Tespis erat.
15 Post Tespim palla cum mimis atque cothurnis
    Aeschilus ad nostri tecta secundus eat.
Tunc me oblectarent dicentem haec omnia, sed nunc
    Faece nihil calamos ora peruncta iuvant.
Idcirco mimos, scaenam grandemque cothurnum

So that he may then be readier to see the Muses and Pallas again:
  And may his toil be put aside for a time and may it be light.

The poem is ended. From the study of Guarino of Verona
on behalf of the most illustrious prince Niccolò the Marquis.

ː XVIII ː

Here begins Marrasio the Sicilian's answer
to that most literary of men, Guarino of Verona.

Now that you answer my letter, godlike one,
  Now that my Muse has won your approval,
No small praise will be given to Marrasio the Sicilian
  And in the future I shall have no small renown.
Everything our ancient Latin authors wrote in verse   5
  And in prose too, Guarino — you know it all;
And you are no less learned in Greek studies,
  Whether they be works in prose or in poetry.
Moreover, you translate the histories that Plutarch wrote,
  Being wiser than the Greeks, and your teaching is better.   10
I have not written about the masque which the first theaters
  Practiced, but that which every court now has.
If I had wanted to write about its primitive origins in antiquity,
  Then I would have made Thespis the starting point;
After Thespis, Aeschylus, with his mantle, mimes, and buskins   15
  Of tragedy would come second to my dwelling.
In that case, I would have loved to have spoken about all that,
  But as it is, faces smeared with dregs are of no use to my
    pipes.
That's why I've omitted actors, the stage, and high tragedy,

20   Praeterii: non hos fabula nostra colit.
    A me tibicen, populus spectator et omnis
        Tibia praeterita est praeteritaeque tubae;
    Sed ne cui dubio foret haec mea larva legenti,
        Personae alterius tempora et arma canis,
25   Quae, veluti flores quando cecidere, moritur.
        Larvatus moritur, quom sua larva cadit.
    Nil moritur; cessare suo si tempore dicam
        Nonque mori: cessat ceu rosa quisquis homo.
    Quam mihi misisti larvam, sine matre novercam
30   Ipsa habet et plures est sibi nacta patres;
    Quam tibi, nullus inest genitor, sed candida mater
        Mitior atque illi nulla noverca fuit.
    Ipse meam tuque ipse tuam iungamus utrasque
        Coniugioque adsint Bacchus et ipsa Venus.
35   Ex his ambabus nascetur filius unus,
        Monstrum, quod vultus continet ante retro.
    Haec iocor, haec habui festis aptanda diebus,
        Officii ingratus ne ferar ipse tui.
    Maxima carminibus referatur gratia, namque
40   Perpetuo vivent carmina nostra tuis.

Marrasii Siculi poema
de ortu, obitu et vita larvarum
feliciter explicit.

My play does not deal with them.   20
The flute player, the watching populace, every flute
    And every trumpet I have all omitted.
But lest anyone reading this should be in doubt about my
        masque,
    You are singing of times and gear from another sort of mask.
One that is dead, like flowers that have fallen.   25
    When his mask falls, the masker dies;
He doesn't die entirely; I should say: he ceases in his own time
    But doesn't die: every man, like the rose, ceases to be.
The mask you sent me has a stepmother without a mother,
    And it has acquired a great many fathers for itself, too;   30
The one I sent you has no father, but a splendid mother
    And a kinder one, and had no stepmother at all.
Let us unite mine and yours, and let Bacchus
    And Venus herself be there for their wedding.
From these two a single son will be born   35
    A monster, facing both forward and back.
These are jokes; I've adapted them to the days of festival,
    Lest I shall be held ungrateful for your kind service.
Let the greatest possible thanks be given to your poems,
    For my poetry will live forever because of yours.   40

*Marrasio Siculo's poem
about the birth, death, and life of masques
is finished auspiciously.*

: XIX :

Ad Kyriacum Anconitanum
rerum vetustarum indagatorem diligentissimum.

Si qua fuere virum divina epigrammata saxis
    Insculpta obscuro nomine, clara facis.
Tanta libido animo veterum monumenta videndi
    Fixa tuo, ut mundus area parva fuit.
5 Hinc tibi praeclaro Musae arrisere Latinae
    Hincque tibi Argivae mille dedere iocos.
Comis es et frugi vel sancto dignus honore,
    Kyriace; hinc larvas accipe, amice, novas.
Illis si quid inest crudum aut non auribus aequum,
10   Si qua iuventa illis nunc videatur iners,
Id reseca, sive ipse tua fac arte senescat,
    Iocundo ut possint lumine verba legi.
Kyriace, hoc pacto capias munuscula nostra,
    Ut mihi larvato tu comes esse velis.

Expliciunt.

: XIX :

To Cyriac of Ancona
that most assiduous investigator of antiquity.

If men have carved any divine inscriptions on rocks
    Whose names are dark, you make them clear.
So great was the desire of seeing the ancients' monuments fixed
    In your soul that the universe was but a small space.
From one side the Latin Muses smiled on you, famous man,   5
    From the other the Greek ones gave you a thousand shafts of
        wit.
You are gracious and sober, and worthy of sacred love,
    Cyriac; hence, my friend, receive these new masques.
If there is in them anything coarse and not right to the ear,
    If any clumsy youthfulness appears in them now,   10
Cut it out, or by your skill make it fully mature,
    So that the work can be read with a jocund eye.
On this understanding, Cyriacus, take my little gifts,
    And please be my companion in the masque.

The end.

: XX :

Marrasii Siculi ad serenissimum ac invictissimum principem
Sigismundum Ungariae et Boemiae regem
nec non Romanorum Caesarem semper Augustum
congratulatio de assumpta laurea
et exhortatio ad totius orbis aeternam pacem
feliciter incipit.

Temporibus diris laetor tibi, maxime Caesar,
    Postquam serta tuum circumiere caput
Et fasces meriti vetus et diadema priorum,
    Frontem etiam cinxit fulva corona tuam.
5 Hoc facinus clarum, quod non potuere Latini,
    Complesti, Romam quom tetigere pedes.
Italiam confectam odiis et ad arma furentem
    Venisti atque etiam ad bella cruenta ducum,
Auspiciisque tuis tranquilla pace relinquis
10   Tu Latios populos, oppida, rura, focos.
Maecenas studiis cum sis et Iulius armis,
    Augustus pace totius orbis eris.
Si claro voluit Maecenas vivere versu,
    Aeternus versu maluit esse deus,
15 Quam sua membra forent in duro sculpta metallo,
    Aurea sive forent aenea sive forent.
Sciverat aeternos homines non posse metallum
    Efficere, historicus sive poeta facit.
Extinctus merito maiori est laude canendus
20   Maecenas, vivus quam fuit ullus Otho,

: XX :

From Marrasio Siculo to the most serene and invincible prince
Sigismund, King of Hungary and Bohemia,
as well as August Emperor of the Romans,
a poem of congratulation for his assumption of the laurel
and a prayer for the everlasting peace of the whole world
begins auspiciously.

In these dire times, greatest Caesar, I rejoice for you,
    Now that the garland has encircled your head
And the well-deserved fasces and the ancient diadem of our
        ancestors,
    And the golden crown, as well, has bound your forehead.
You accomplished this brilliant thing, which the Latins   5
    Could not, as soon as your feet touched Rome.
You came to an Italy consumed by hatreds and mad for arms
    And even for the bloody wars of her leaders,
You leave the Italian peoples, its towns, its countryside,
    Its homes, in tranquil peace under your authority.   10
Although you may be a Maecenas in studies and a Julius in arms,
    You will be the Augustus of peace for the whole world.
If Maecenas wanted to live through noble verse,
    He preferred to be an everlasting god by means of verse,
Rather than have his limbs be sculpted from hard metal   15
    Whether it were gold or it were bronze.
He knew that metal cannot make men everlasting;
    A poet or an historian does that.
Maecenas dead must be hymned with greater praise,
    And rightly so, than any Otho was while still alive.   20

Illius extincti nomen delere senectus
　　Non poterit, vivus mortuus hicque fuit.
Humanis studiis quom sis ornatus et armis,
　　Arma tenes: defit qui tua gesta canat.
25　Numquam animo heroes, numquam ardua facta deorum
　　Scribere, non umquam fortia bella fuit.
Horridus in primis strepitus, concursus equorum
　　Audax, dirus erat sanguinolentus eques.
Ipse ego te postquam vidi, invictissime Caesar,
30　　Mutavi mentem propositumque meum,
Unde elegos, lusus et mollia carmina linquam
　　Cantaboque pari regia bella pede.
Nulla dies nostro fuit hac iocundior aevo,
　　Qua tibi nunc dico: 'Maxime Caesar, ave.
35　Maecenas studiis cum sis et Iulius armis,
　　Augustus pace totius orbis eris.
Restat ut hunc mundum discordi lite cadentem
　　Concilies: nam te sidera et astra vocant.
Parendum est superis, quorum terrena potestas
40　　Numine et augurio consilioque datur.
Humani generis fatum pendere videtur,
　　Imminet et cunctis summa ruina deis.
Ergo, age, discordes animi iungantur in unum,
　　Ne in priscum redeant tempora nostra chaos.
45　Dissidia et lites et tot discrimina postquam
　　Dempseris ipse tua, maxime Caesar, ope,
Tum genus et proavos et felicissima patrum
　　Nomina teque prius et tua gesta canam.'

Expliciunt.

Age could not wipe out the name of the former man
    After death; even dead he is living and here.
Although you are eminent in liberal studies and in arms,
    You stick with arms: a man to sing your deeds is wanting.
It was never my intention to write of heroes,   25
    The lofty deeds of the gods, the courageous battles.
Dreadful was the clamor in the front ranks, the bold clashes
    Between horses, grim was the bloodstained horseman.
After I saw you myself, invincible Caesar,
    I changed my mind and my theme.   30
Now I will abandon elegiacs, pleasantries, and tender poetry
    And will sing of royal wars in matching verse.
There has been no happier day in my life than this,
    On which I now say to you: "Hail, greatest Caesar.
Although you be a Maecenas in studies and a Julius in arms,   35
    You shall be an Augustus of peace for all the world.
All that remains is for you to unite this world, perishing
    From discordant strife: for the starry heavens call you.
One must obey the gods above, whose earthly power
    Is granted by divinity and prophecy and by reason.   40
The fate of humankind seems to hang in the balance,
    And total ruin threatens all the gods.
Therefore, come, let discordant minds be joined in unity,
    And let not our age return to primeval chaos.
After you have removed by your help these many   45
    Disagreements, disputes, and differences, greatest Caesar,
Then shall I sing of your ancestry and the blessed names
    Of your forefathers, and of you and your deeds before the
        rest."

The end.

: XXI :

Marrasius ad Panhormitam divum poetam,
ut solvat duo problemata quae ei Venus ante oculos adiecit:
unde est ⟨ut⟩ unus gallus centum gallinarum sufficiens fututor
sit, centum homines non unius feminae; alterum ut
pulcherrima puella uni paediconi superabundans sit,
milia vero epheborum vix sufficiunt.

Si quis erit Latio, qui possit solvere nodos,
    Quos mihi subridens attulit alma Venus,
Ipsus eris, sacrum calamum cui cessit Apollo
    et citharam suavem et, sancte poeta, lyram.
5 Centum gallinas cum gallus pressitet unus,
    Gallus sufficiens omnibus unus erit;
Non satura est centum mulier nec lassa priapis;
    Comperta est dicens femina nulla: 'sat est.'
Una supervacua est etsi pulcherrima virgo
10   Robusto iuveni, si foret illa Venus;
Si teneros centum quis paedicaret ephebos,
    Milia si veniant, non erit ille satur.
Unde est orta animis tantum diversa voluptas?
    Si sapis, ornabunt myrtea serta caput.
15 Haec Cytherea mihi solvenda aenigmata mandat:
    Ni faciam, ex coetu me fugat illa suo.
Antoni vates, aeterno carmine laetus,
    Aeternam famam saecula cuncta tenes.
Enuclees mihi verba deae commixta tenebris;

: XXI :

Marrasio to the divine poet Panormita,
that he solve two questions that Venus has set before his eyes:
whence is it that one cock is sufficient as a fucker of a hundred
hens, but a hundred men are not sufficient for one woman;
and second, that the most beautiful girl is too much for
one sodomite, but a thousand boys on the verge of
manhood are scarcely enough.

If there were anyone in Italy who could untie the knots
    That kindly Venus, all smiles, has tied me in,
You are the one, to whom Apollo has yielded his sacred pipe,
    His sweet cithara and his lyre, blessed poet.
When one cock hammers a hundred hens,   5
    One cock will be sufficient for all;
But a woman isn't sated or worn out by a hundred cocks;
    You can't find a woman who says, "Enough!"
While one maiden — though utterly beautiful — is more than
      enough
    For a lusty young man, if she be his Venus,   10
If someone should bugger a hundred tender lads,
    — Nay, thousands — he won't be satisfied.
How did pleasure come to vary in the mind so much?
    If you know, garlands of myrtle will ring your head.
Cytherea orders me to resolve this enigma: 15
    If I don't, she will cast me out of her band.
Antonio, my seer, happy in your eternal song,
    You keep your eternal fame for all the ages.
Expound for me the goddess' confusing words;

20   Est mea vita tuas inter, amice, manus.
      Implicitum his curis tu me, divine poeta,
        Extricare velis, dive poeta, velis?

                Senis XIII Kalendas Decembres.

                    ⁝ XXII ⁝

          Marrasius Antonino suo salutem.

    Antonine, tuos quotiens numerabis amicos,
      Fac meus in prima parte legatur amor.
    Me tulit Alvriacus non longe a litore collis,
      Me dudum Tusci detinuere Lares.
5   Hinc me diva suis revocatum cepit ocellis
      Angela, nunc lauro me tegit ipsa sua.

                    ⁝ XXIII ⁝

    Marrasii epigramma sculptum in fonte Gaio Senis.

    Marrasius moriens vitamque animamque reliquit
      Fonte sub hoc; retegit frigidus ossa lapis.

My life, dear friend, is in your hands.   20
Won't you, won't you, divine poet, disentangle me
    Who am tied up, godlike poet, in these perplexities?

Siena, November 19.

: XXII :

Marrasio greets his Antonino.

My dear Antonino, whenever you count up your friends
    Put my love down at the head of the list.
The hill of Alveria, not far from the shore, bore me,
    I remained for long amid the household gods of Tuscany.
From here the divine Angela called me back with her cute eyes,   5
    And captured me; now it is she who covers me with laurel.

: XXIII :

Marrasio's epigram carved upon the Fonte Gaia in Siena.

The dying Marrasio left his life and soul at the foot
    Of this fountain; the cold stone makes known his bones.

: XXIV :

Marrasii Siculi ad sanctissimum dominum nostrum
Nicolaum Papam quintum
in alios elegos praefatio. Lege feliciter.

Quam tibi cui melius poteram committere versus
    Quos castigandos sciverit esse meos?
Illis si quid inest crudum aut non auribus aequum,
    Aut lima aut dolabra tu resecare potes.
5 Humani interitus si quid male concino, quis te
    Philosophos inter clarior unus adest?
Arbitrii nostri si quid male colligo, nemo
    Divinum poterit te superare virum.
Sidereos motus, errantia sidera septem
10   Atque retrocessus quis trutinare potest
Et melius praebere vias lunaeque labores
    Dicere et aequatos connumerare dies?
Saturni atque Iovis si ex triplicitate volarunt
    Sidera et amborum linea centra scidit,
15 Quicquid agit natura potens et viribus instat,
    Omne aenigma potes solvere, sancte pater.
Philosophi centum non suffecere Latini
    Nec tibi, si quid habet, lingua Latina decus.
Omnia rimatus veterum commenta, novorum
20   Si quid honoris habent visa fuere satis.
Ingenii vis magna tui contenta Latino
    Non fuit eloquio; Graeca videre libet.
Argolicas artes, divina volumina ab Argis
    Edita, quae a claris scripta fuere viris

: XXIV :

A preface of Marrasio Siculo to his other elegiac verses addressed to our most holy lord, Pope Nicholas V. Happy reading!

To whom could I better entrust my verses than to you,
   Verses which, needing correction, anyone would know were
      mine?
If there is in them anything rough or jarring to the ear
   You can cut it away with a file or a pick.
If I sing badly of human mortality, what individual is at hand   5
   More distinguished than you among philosophers?
If my own powers of judgment misunderstand some point,
   No one can surpass you, divine man.
Who can balance the forward and retrograde motions   10
   Of the constellations, the seven planets,
Or better lay out the paths of the moon and describe
   Her eclipses or reckon up the solstices and equinoxes?
If the planets Saturn and Jupiter travel with three movements,
   And if their line cuts the center points of both.
Whatever potent nature does or threatens with its powers,   15
   You can solve every mystery, holy father.
A hundred Latin philosophers were not enough for you,
   Nor did the beauty of the Latin tongue, if any, suffice for you.
Having searched all the arguments of the ancients, you looked
   Among the moderns to see if there were any worthy of honor.   20
The great power of your mind was not content with Latin
   Eloquence; you wished to examine the Greek.
Having consumed the Greek manuals, and the divine books
   Published by Greeks, which had been written by famous men,

25 Et quaesita diu tandemque inventa, Latine
   Nunc translata vides et bene lecta sapis.
  Argolicis opulenta viris est reddita, quamvis
   Dives erat doctis lingua Latina suis.
  Philosophi plures temptant quadrare rotundum:
30   Palma Syracusio iam data palma fuit.
  Amplior atque minor reperitur circulus, ergo
   Quadrato aequalis: talia Brisso refert.
  Antiphon in trigonis trigona accumulare laborat,
   Ut tandem in curvam linea recta cadat.
35 Hi suadere queunt quod demonstrare volebant:
   Nulla sagitta ferit proxima signa virum.
  Musa Syracusium voluit cantare Maronis
   Theocritum extinctum saecula trina senem;
  Sed Iacobus, Graium genuit quem Mantua civem,
40   Transtulit in linguam Dorica scripta meam.
  Sicelides Musae tibi se debere fatentur,
   Mantua, quas nulla laude perire sinis.
  Pontifici summo peragatur gratia primo,
   Qui transferre facis mortua dicta viri.
45 Mortua millenos ac incinerata per annos
   Spera Syracusii sive cylindrus erat.
  Incipit a spira quum vult quadrare rotundum,
   Sed trigonum et spirae quadra rotunda probant.
  Quadratura fuit per saecula nulla nec aevum
50   Scita: Syracusio cognita prima fuit.
  Theophrasti veteres plantas facit ecce novellas
   Theodorus, Graecus natus, in Urbe probus.
  Conticeo innumeros quae sunt memoranda per annos,
   Quae traducta facis: solus Homerus abest.
55 Ulterius proprias non vult errare per urbes
   Maeonides; Latias vult habitare domos.

Long sought and finally found, you now oversee their translation   25
    Into Latin, and you understand well what you have read.
Although the Latin tongue was rich in its own scholars,
    It has been made opulent by the Greeks.
Many philosophers try to square the circle:
    The palm has already been given to the man from Syracuse.   30
A circle larger and smaller than the square is found,
    Therefore [some circle must be] equal to it: so Bryson states.
Antiphon labors to pile triangle on triangle.
    So that at length a straight line might become a curve.
But they were able to persuade us of what they wished to prove: 35
    No arrow, being a proximate point, strikes a man.
The Muse of Vergil wished to sing of Theocritus of Syracuse,
    An old man dead for three hundred years;
But Jacopo, a Greek citizen whom Mantua produced,
    Translated Doric writing into my language.   40
The Sicilian Muses confess that they are in debt to you,
    The Muses whom you, Mantua, allow to die without praise.
Let thanks be offered first to the exalted Pope,
    You who caused to be translated a dead man's words.
The sphere or cylinder of the Syracusan
    Was dead and reduced to ashes for thousands of years.   45
When someone wants to square a circle he begins with a spiral,
    But a triangle and spirals demonstrate round squares.
The squaring of the circle was unknown for ages
    And ages: it was first understood by the Syracusan.   50
See how Theodorus, born a Greek, a worthy man in Rome,
    Made the old plants of Theophrastus young again.
I pass over in silence the works you cause to be translated,
    Which will be remembered forever; only Homer is missing.
He does not wish to wander farther among his own   55
    Maeonian cities; he wants to dwell in Latin homes.

Si barathro ex imo revocabis ad aethera nostrum,
    Incola Romanus factus Homerus erit.
Ilias, antiqui quam nescivere Latini
60   Transferre et Latiis edere quippe novam,
    Mavult in linguam per te migrare Latinam
    Quam velit Argivas nunc habitare casas.
    Roma viros claros — quot sint mirabile dictu —
    Pascit pane tuo, ditat et aere tuo.
65 Nam quota pars orbis melior subiecta Tonanti
    Te petit atque tuos est venerata pedes.
    Magnificos sumptus abs te pro Caesare factos
    Praetereo: illud agam posteriore die.
    Est opus ingenio; veniunt in carmina divi;
70 Non timeo: versus censor amicus eris.
    A te principium, nostri quoque carminis auctor;
    Quicquid agam, semper tu mihi numen eris.

Explicit praefatio ad sanctissimum dominum nostrum
papam Nicolaum V.
Romae V. Kalendas maias 1452.

: XXV :

Marrasius Siculus domino nostro papae Nicolao V
Romae III. Nonas aprilis 1452.

Quis quis es, insignis, triplicis cui machina mundi
    Obsequitur nutu clausa et aperta tuo?
Infera regna timent, coelestia gaudia sumunt;
    Sunt homines medii, qui inter utrumque natant.

If you will only call him up from the depth of the abyss
    To our upper air, Homer will become a resident of Rome.
The *Iliad*, which the ancient Latins knew not how
    To translate and produce new for themselves,   60
Prefers to emigrate through your agency into the Latin tongue
    Rather than dwell anymore in Greek houses.
Rome feeds with your bread famous men and enriches them
    With your coin; how many there are is amazing to say.
For how much of the better part of the world subject   65
    To Jupiter seeks you and worships at your feet.
I pass over the splendid expenditures made by you
    On Caesar's behalf. I will deal with that at a later day.
Poetic talent is essential; divine beings come to us in poetry;
    I am not afraid: you will be a kindly censor of my verse.   70
You are the source, the wellspring of my song;
    Whatever I do, you will always be a divinity for me.

Here ends the preface to our most holy lord,
Pope Nicholas V.
At Rome, April 26, 1452.

: XXV :

Marrasio Siculo to our lord Pope Nicholas V
at Rome, April 2, 1452.

Who, who are you, remarkable man, for whom the fabric of
    The threefold world submits to open and close at your nod?
The lower kingdoms fear you, the heavenly ones derive their joy;
    Human beings are in the middle, swimming between both.

ː XXVI ː

Sanctissimi domini nostri Nicolai papae V responsio.

Sarsana quem genuit, Thomas sum, nunc Nicolaus
    Papa vocor quintus nomine velle Dei,
Cui Pater omnipotens coelum terramque patentem,
    Cui sub posse meo Tartara nigra dedit.

ː XXVII ː

Marrasii vaticinium ante XX annos ultra de sanctissimo
domino nostro Nicolao Papa V actum Bononiae.

Quum vidi te velle omnes superare legendo
    Et rebus sacris velle praeesse deis,
Praetereundo pares nec non aequando priores,
    Doctrinam cunctis posse docere tuam
5 (Nec conferre pares, nec te superare priores,
    Nec tacitum poterant reddere voce sua,
Sed tua sublimis cunctas superabat, ut omnes
    Argumenta queant discere acuta tua),
Praesagire animum fecisti haec omina nostrum
10   Et te praedixi vincere posse deos.
Non me Tiresias docuit nec Apollinis aedes,
    Sed divum ingenium cum probitate tuum.

: XXVI :

The response of our most holy lord, Pope Nicholas V.

I am Thomas, to whom Sarzana gave birth, now called
    Nicholas the Fifth, Pope by the will of God,
To whom the Almighty Father has given the heavens
    And the spreading earth, and put dark Hell under my power.

: XXVII :

The prophecy of Marrasio Siculo made twenty years ago in Bologna concerning his Holiness our lord Pope Nicholas V.

When I saw that you wanted to best everyone in reading
    And wished to excel the gods in sacred matters,
Surpassing your peers and equaling your ancestors,
    And that you could teach your doctrine to everyone
(Your peers could not be compared to you, nor your superiors   5
    Surpass you, nor could they silence you with their voice,
But your lofty voice conquered them all, so that they all
    Could learn to recognize your acute arguments),
You made my spirit feel a presentiment of these things
    And I foretold that you could defeat the gods.   10
Neither Tiresias' nor Apollo's shrine taught me this,
    But your divine talent along with your virtue.

: XXVIII :

Marrasii Siculi congratulatio dignitatis supremae ultimaeque laudes de rebus gestis, in ea unionis scilicet propulso scismate, Magnae Veniae, pacis Italie, aedis praesidii novae aedificationis ac reparationis melioris ad sanctissimum dominum nostrum Nicolaum papam V. Lege feliciter.

Proh Deus in terris, cui tanta potentia regum
    Atque ducum paret, Caesaris alta subest,
Et quicquid magno et salso est a gurgite cinctum,
    Sis felix, felix: te duce scisma ruit.
5 Nullum maius inest monstrum et letale venenum
    Ecclesiae, humanum corruit unde genus.
Scisma cadens inter cives populosque ferendum est,
    Firma suo regi si datur una fides.
Si caput arripuit grave et insanabile vulnus,
10   Ni fuerit cervix secta bipenne mala,
Dissidia et plebis rixas et iurgia princeps
    Castigat, si non conciliare potest.
Diviso templo geminum caput esse necesse est:
    Utrumque istorum iusta fovere putat.
15 Si facile est multos cives coniungere in unum
    Discordesque animos inde tenere manu,
Vix synodus poterit pastores iungere binos,
    Alter ut alterius det sua colla iugo.
Evertunt hereses populos et vota potentum;
20   Scisma sequestrat eos a meliore sinu.
Ambigitur quis peior homo: qui mittit ad ignem

: XXVIII :

Marrasio Siculo's words of congratulation and utmost praise
for his deeds of highest worthiness, namely, the expulsion of
schism within the Union, the Great Pardon, the peace of Italy,
the rebuilding and repair of defenses, addressed to his Holiness
our lord Pope Nicholas V. Happy reading!

Ah! God on earth, whom the great might of kings and warlords
    Obeys, to whom the high power of Caesar submits,
And whatever is girt by the great salty deep,
    Be blessed, be blessed! Under your leadership schism collapses.
There is no greater monstrosity or to the Church no greater   5
    poison,
    Whence the human race is brought to ruin.
Schism falling among the citizens and peoples must be borne
    If a single, steadfast faith is given to their king.
The prince punishes the dissensions and quarrels and disputes
    Of the people, if he is unable to reconcile them.   10
But if a serious and incurable wound has seized the head,
    Unless the evil neck is cut with a twin-edged ax,
Inevitably, with the church divided, there will be twin heads:
    Each of the two thinks it is pursuing just aims.
If it is easy to unite many citizens as one   15
    And thereby restrain their conflicting spirits,
A synod will scarcely be able to unite two shepherds,
    So that one would bow its neck to the other's yoke.
Heresies overturn peoples and the prayers of the powerful:
    Schism separates them from their better refuge.   20
It is hard to decide which is the worse man: he who sends

Tot populos aut qui pellit ab aede bonos.
Gloria magna tibi, quam non habuere priores:
Unio namque tuo tempore facta fuit
25 Immensamque tuis veniam feliciter annis
Addidit omnipotens, vota suprema, Deus.
Unio cum venia duo sunt clarissima mundo,
Quas supra optari res bona nulla potest:
Una ministrat opes, pacem vitamque quietam,
30 Altera laeta Deum, sidera et astra videt.
Unam forte alii, geminas tu solus adeptus;
Famam hanc extingui tempora nulla queunt.
Venit ab extremis hominum pars maxima Romam,
Ploeripedes celeres ulterioris humi;
35 Eoi venere, austri gelidique triones
Et zephyri, quartas quas tuus orbis habet,
Atque inter medios homines misere canentes
Tellus quaeque suos et plaga quaeque suos.
Nocte sub ingenti parvo et sub sole morantes
40 Iurant astra suum deposuisse situm.
Est conata tuam faciem vultumque videre
Parrhasis et nequiit pondere pressa suo.
Laudibus addo tuis: orator principe ab Indo
Missus iter vetitum transiit atque novum.
45 Res mira audita est nullo neque tempore visa,
Postremis Indis has patuisse vias.
Abbatem fluctus Siculas divertit ad oras:
Acceptus patria non sine honore fuit.
Lauta fuere suo placido condita sapore

Many peoples to Hell or the one who drives good ones from
    church.
A great glory is yours, one your predecessors did not have:
    For in your time unity has been achieved
And Almighty God has happily added the Great Pardon,   25
    The utmost of our prayers, during your pontificate.
Unity and pardon are the two most glorious things in the world;
    No good thing can be desired that is above these:
One offers wealth, peace, and a quiet life,
    The other looks joyfully to God, the stars, and the heavens.   30
Some by chance have achieved the one, you alone have secured
        both;
    No passage of time can extinguish this achievement.
The greatest part of mankind come to Rome on numberless feet,
    Swiftly they come from the furthest parts of the earth;
From the East they come, the South, and the chill Northern   35
        lands.
    And from those of the West wind, from all quarters of your
        world,
Each land, each region has sent its own inhabitants,
    Each chanting *Miserere* in the midst of mankind.
Those dwelling under a vast night and brief sun
    Swear that the stars have left their abode.   40
Callisto tried to glimpse your face and countenance
    And could not, burdened by her own weight.
I will add this to your praises: an envoy sent from an Indian
        prince
    Made the new and forbidden journey.
Never was such a marvelous thing seen or heard of,   45
    That this route had opened up from farthest India.
The currents diverted the abbot to the shores of Sicily,
    He was received in my homeland with the highest respect.
Splendid courses were seasoned with their own subtle flavor

50   Fercula, diversae complacuere dapes.
    Fine epulis posito et quae praebet mensa secunda
        Expletis, cecinit quae iubet alma fides.
    Convenere viri nostri, statuere coronam
        Et cupidi quae fert India mira rogant.
55 Hic sermone suo, mediante interprete, fatur
        Armatos barrum ad proelia ferre viros;
    Maioresque canes nec non genus omne luporum,
        Denique erat nostris grandius omne pecus.
    Sincipitis medio affixis cornibus unis
60   Est fera, quae volucres unica vincit aves.
    Maxima quaeque refert animalia vivere terra
        Et quae pontus habet grandia monstra natant
    Diversa in specie nostris — hic nescius audet
        Dicere quam maius non variatque minus —
65 Thus et ebur sileant illaque opobalsama quis non
        Est lac concretum vel sua gutta natat,
    Plurima praeterea redolentia aromata, gemmae
        Et lapidum species grata colore suo.
    De Phoenice parum, de Nilo multa recludit
70   Codicibus nostris consona verba nimis;
    Enarrat fontes magna virtute feraces.
        Vix Siculi credunt, qui uberiora tenent.
    Unius scatebras describam, limpida cuius
        Ab radice Aetnae frigida bullit aqua.
75 Intense nigrum capiet tela alba colorem
        Mersa sub hac: vidi haec experimenta probans.
    Extat Agrigenti species salis: igne repostus
        Liquitur at refugit vel crepitabit aqua.
    Tandem ego: 'Fare, precor, vestro de principe verum
80   An fictum quicquid fama perennis alit?
    Relligiosus homo fertur vitaeque sacerdos
        Caelibis, uxoris pondera nulla gerens.

And various dishes took his fancy.   50
When the banquet was over and dessert was finished,
    He sang what gentle trust dictated.
Our people gathered together, they made a circle
    And eagerly they asked what marvels India contained.
In his speech, with the help of an interpreter, he told of   55
    Armed men bringing an elephant into battle;
Of huge dogs and every kind of wolf
    And even all kinds of domestic animals, all larger than ours;
A wild beast with a single horn in the middle of its head
    Which alone can defeat winged birds.   60
He described the largest animals living on earth,
    And the great sea monsters, different in appearance from ours,
Swimming there—the man ignorantly dares to say
    How greater and smaller things do not much differ—
Not to mention incense and ivory and the balm of Gilead   65
    Whose sap is not solid and whose drops flow,
And a great many fragrant perfumes as well, and gems
    And a type of stone pleasing in its color.
About the Phoenix he says little; but about the Nile he reveals
    Many things, very much in accordance with our sources.   70
He tells of springs productive of great power; but
    The Sicilians, who have richer things, scarce believe him.
I shall describe one bubbling spring whose icy clear water
    Bursts from the very foot of Mt. Aetna.
A white cloth will take on a deep black color when immersed   75
    In this spring: I have seen and can certify the experiment.
A type of salt is found in Agrigento: when placed in fire
    It liquefies, but it recoils from water or crackles.
At last I said: "Tell us, please, about your ruler;
    Are the old stories about him true or false?   80
He is said to be a religious man and a priest
    Of celibate life, without the burden of a wife.

Reges atque duces magni sua sceptra verentes
    Subiecti et solus pace gubernat eos.'

85 Dixit: 'Habet natos et pignora cara probamque
    Uxorem, generos ingenuasque nurus.

Esse sacerdotem, cui nulla potentia compar,
    Verum est, et reges sub iuga colla tenent.

Indus ab his Indis venio; sub principe tanto
90   Dego; mei reditus sit comes ipse Deus.

Antoni sancti gracilem mea dextra bacillum,
    Laeva crucemque gerit, pondera grata mihi.'

Post haec plura refert quae non sunt digna relatu,
    Pace viri, surdis auribus illa meis.

95 Quando redire meus poterit pes lapsus ad Indos,
    Qui tot per leucas distat ab Urbe tua?

Mercurio similis, talis qui nexuit alas,
    Necte tibi pennas, pes meus, atque vola.

Non opus est aura, remo pedibusque volantis
100   Fulmineo cursu dona petentis equi.

Ausoniam petito, felicia templa Deumque
    Quem colis et supplex ad sua tecta redi.

En redii montes et flumina et aequora mensus;
    Tam celeri penna nulla rediret avis.

105 Protinus Italicas cum sis regressus ad oras,
    Incipe ab Ausonia dicere, si quid habes.

Italiam confectam odiis et ad arma furentem
    Vidisti et regum et proelia longa ducum.

Auspicioque tuo cessarunt bella minaeque;
110   Reges atque duces pax tenet atque fides.

Pax tranquilla placet nec sanguinolenta ministrant
    Arma; tibi excudit fulmina nemo faber;

Scorpio, funda, arcus, tormentum, blida, sagittae,
    Hasta, aries, iaculum, pila, macera vacant,

115 Atque horum generum quibus est sua vita futura

Kings and great leaders fearing his power are subject
　　To him and he alone rules them in peace."
He answered: "He has wellborn, legitimate sons　　　　　　　85
　　And a virtuous wife, and noble daughters-in-law.
It is true that he is a priest, to whom no power is equal.
　　And kings hold their necks under his yoke.
I come as an Indian from these Indies; I dwell subject
　　To this great prince; may God Himself accompany my return.　　90
My right hand carries the slender staff of St. Anthony,
　　My left a cross, both welcome burdens."
After this he said much more which, to my deaf ears,
　　Was not worth the telling, with all due respect to the man.
When shall my foot, wandering in the Indies, be able to return,　　95
　　My foot, which is so many leagues away from your City?
O my foot, bind on wings for yourself like Mercury's,
　　He who bound on wings of this kind, and fly.
I do not have need of wind, nor of oar nor of the feet
　　Of a horse flying with lightening speed as it seeks gifts.　　100
Seek out Italy, its blessed churches, and the God
　　Whom you worship, and return as a suppliant under His roof.
See, I have returned, having traversed mountains, rivers, and seas.
　　No bird would return with so swift a wing.
When you return forthwith to the shores of Italy,　　　　　　105
　　Begin to speak about Italy, if you have anything to say.
You have seen an Italy destroyed by hatred and raging for war,
　　And the protracted battles of kings and warlords.
Under your leadership wars and threats of wars have ceased;
　　Peace and trust binds kings and warlords.　　　　　　　110
Tranquil peace pleases them and they do not supply
　　Bloody weapons; no smith forges thunderbolts for you.
Artillery, sling, bow, catapult, fiery darts, arrows,
　　Spear, battering ram, javelin, pike, siege engine are gone.
And weapons of this kind, harmful to men, lie buried,　　　　115

Perniciosa viris arma sepulta iacent.
Quae, si quando Dei bellis vexilla praeibunt,
    Resplendere suo lumine acuta voles.
Reiecta galea tutum te reddit amictus
120   Et quae circumdat magna tiara caput.
Non lorica tuos thorax nec protegit artus,
    Alba sed ardentis stamine texta Dei.
Tu baculo templum, populos tu pace gubernas,
    Romam, alias ‹urbes›, oppida, rura, focos.
125 Uberius laudes cumula, cape laudis acervos
    Et laudum cumulis ditior unus eris.
Nil melius, nil maius erit, nil sanctius orbe
    Quam Christum pedibus menteque corde sequi.
Eius sectaris vitam et vestigia, mores,
130   Pacem quam cunctis iusserat ipse dari.
Nonne reservatas tibi per tot saecula laudes
    Aspicis? Et merito: contulit ista Deus.
Unio quem tollit propulso scismate? Magna
    Quem venia? Ausonia est pacificata cui?
135 India, quae reges multos alit ampla potentes
    Atque suus princeps, quos adivere pedes?
Expediam paucis ad quem confluxit ab omni
    Parte orbis melius quod plaga quaeque tenet?
Et casura quibus manibus vitare ruinam
140   Templa datum primis et meliora dari?
Maxima quae aedificas sacrata palatia Romae
    Ceu troni superant tecta superba tua.
Te Pater aeternus multo ad maiora reservat,
    Ut sanctos inter connumereris avos.
145 Annua festa tibi celebrabunt templa per orbem,
    Interiment laudes saecula nulla tuas.

Weapons that will have a future life
If ever the standards of God lead the way to war,
    You will wish them, sharpened, to glitter with their own light.
The helmet spurned, your vestments and the great tiara
    That surrounds your head keep you safe.   120
Neither corselet nor cuirass protects your limbs,
    But only the white-woven cloth of our radiant God.
With your staff you govern in peace the church, the populace,
    Rome, other cities, towns, the countryside, and homes.
Heap up praise more abundantly, take great stacks of praise,   125
    And you alone will be the richer for those heaps of praise.
Nothing will be better, nothing greater, nothing holier in the
        world
    Than to follow Christ's footsteps in mind and in heart.
You constantly follow his life, his footsteps, his ways,
    His peace that He commanded be given to all.   130
Surely you see the praises reserved for you through so many
    Centuries? And rightly so: for God has bestowed them.
Whom does Unity exalt now, with schism driven out?
    Whom does the Jubilee exalt? Who pacified Italy?
Wide India, which fosters many powerful kings   135
    And its ruler — whose feet did they approach?
Shall I sum up to whom there flowed from every part
    Of the globe the best that each region holds?
To what hands was it first granted that tottering churches
    Avoid ruin and that better churches be founded?   140
The great sacred buildings that you are raising in Rome
    Like thrones rise above your magnificent dwelling.
The eternal Father is keeping you for much greater things;
    That you might be numbered among the saints of old.
Churches throughout the world will celebrate your feast day,   145
    And no future ages will put an end to your praise.

: XXIX :

Marrasii Siculi exhortatio ad movendum bellum iustum
contra Syros, qui Terram Sanctam occuparunt,
ad sanctissimm dominum nostrum Nicolaum papam V.

Si quis forte roget qua sit ratione gerendum
    Imperium, Augusti nomen habere putet.
Quid fundare novas aut amplificare pusillas
    Aut urbes proprio iure tenere iubet?
5 Moenia sancta suo sunt expugnanda labore,
    Quae possessa diu perfidus hostis habet
Aut quae iam nostra sub relligione manebant,
    Aut si qua infidis pergama rapta videt.
Barbara gens pereat, pereant qui bella retardant,
10   Quae poteris contra iusta movere Syros.
Nulla prior sacris accessit gloria rebus,
    Quam poteris titulis accumulare tuis.
Eia age, frange moras; nam nec violenta movebis
    Proelia, natura non fugiente necem.
15 Sponte sua venient; venient non forte vocati
    Quos aluit reges unica nostra fides;
Et transalpini venient sine munere reges
    Atque duces quibus est oppida parva focus.
Pauperis est animo fixum sua pignora Parthis
20   Vendere et uxorem, si qua pudica manet.
Cum caput in terris, tua cum sit prima voluntas,
    Ipse quid expectas? Erige signa crucis!
Quanta mala eriperes! Et quanta strage careret
    Nostra fides! Quanto stercore munda foret!

: XXIX :

An exhortation by Marrasio Siculo to our most holy lord,
Pope Nicholas V, to make just war against the Syrians
who have occupied the Holy Land.

If by chance anyone will ask why he must exercise imperial
    Power, let him consider that he bears the name Augustus.
Why else does he order new cities to be founded, small ones
    Enlarged or others to be sovereign and independent?
Holy walls must be besieged by his effort,   5
    Walls which the faithless enemy holds and has long held
Or which once remained subject to our religion,
    Or if he sees any citadel captured by infidels.
May the barbarous race perish, may they perish who impede the
        wars
    Which you will be able justly to declare against the Syrians!   10
No glory was added earlier to sacred matters
    That you could add to your distinctions.
Come now, break through delays; for you will not be
    launching violent battles nor the slaughter that nature shuns.
They will come of their own accord; kings will come,   15
    Whom our united faith has nourished, called not by chance;
Without gifts kings from across the Alps will come
    And warlords whose home is but a small town.
It is fixed in the mind of the poor man to sell his children
    To the Parthians, and his wife too, if any remain chaste.   20
Since you are the earthly head, since your will is first,
    What are you waiting for? Lift the sign of the cross!
How much evil you would remove! And how much bloodshed
    Would our faith avoid! Of how much filth would it be
        cleansed!

25 Nam quae cruda solent immittere bella fideles,
Ultrices vertes ad tua signa manus.
Pax tranquilla tuos fidos sine fine tenebit,
Unde tibi aeternum nomen adesse potest.
Tunc tibi, dive pater, divina poemata nectam
30 Cantaboque pari proelia iusta pede
Et simul heroes et regia bella ducesque,
Si fuerit mores turma secuta tuos.
Fama perennis erit cunctis tua castra secutis;
Numine namque tuo splendida semper erit.

: XXX :

Marrasii Siculi aegroti ad Deum omnium rerum opificem
summum, ut ab aegritudine ipsum liberet et tempus
paenitentiae concedat. Lege feliciter.

Summe opifex, aeterne Deus mundique creator,
Incommutabili qui ordine cuncta regis
Praeter vota hominum, quibus est sua tota voluntas
Libera, quae nullo vimine nexa manet,
5 Arbitrii libertatem veram puto causam
Totius esse mali, totius esse boni.
Hinc video horrendas poenas tolerare nocentes,
Hinc bona quaeque suum concomitantur opus.
Si sic, peccandi quibus est ablata potestas?
10 Humano arbitrio subdita semper erit.
Deliqui, fateor, nec me peccasse negabo;
Indulgere tuum est, sed cecidisse meum.
Ipse meas tuque ipse tuas agitemus utrasque

For against the savage wars which they would let loose upon   25
    The faithful, at your signal you would turn avenging bands.
Calm, endless peace will possess your faithful people,
    And thus an everlasting fame will cling to you.
Then for you, divine father, I shall weave a divine poem
    And I shall sing in epic meter of your just wars   30
As well as the heroes and warlords and royal battles,
    If the troops have followed your example.
There will be everlasting fame for all who have followed your
       camps.
    It will always gleam brilliantly with your divine spirit.

: XXX :

A poem of Marrasio Siculo in his illness to God,
highest artificer of all things, that He might free him from
sickness and grant him time to repent. Happy reading!

Most lofty maker, eternal God, and creator of the world,
    Who rules everything by unchangeable design,
Beyond the prayers of humans, who have a completely
    Free will that remains unbound by any tie,
I think that the true cause of the totality of what is bad   5
    And of what is good lies in that freedom of choice.
Hence I see the guilty endure terrible punishments,
    Hence the rewards that accompany good work.
If this is so, from whom has the ability to sin been removed?
    It will always be subject to human inclination.   10
I have fallen short, I confess, nor will I deny that I have sinned;
    Yours it is to show kindness, mine to have fallen.
Let us each play our parts, I mine and you yours;

Partes: tu clemens, ipse beatus ero.
15 Esse Deum decuit, docuit clementia patrem
    Esse, inclementem non decet esse Deum.
    Philosophi primam causam dixere moventem
    Omnia posse nisi falsaque vera simul;
    Nil mixti, nil compositi, nil materialis,
20   Sed sine mensura cuncta tenere bona;
    Vivere praeterea, qua nec praestantior ulla
    Vita nec posset quis meliore frui.
    Assentire placet, fidei non ista repugnant;
    Assensi postquam, non ea sola iuvant.
25 Adde quod, humana fracta compagine, quidam
    Compositum totum morte perire tenent;
    Quidam animam, quidam corpus consurgere, utrumque
    Quidam, alii neutrum sed velut una mori.
    Haec fugienda mihi praeter consurgere utrumque,
30   Pugnant cum nostra verba sonora fide.
    Multa canunt vates sancta et cecinere prophetae:
    Extant naturae dicta superba nimis.
    Ite procul, vates, procul hinc vos ite, prophetae;
    Tartara nam vinctos vos tenuere diu.
35 Peccarunt primi qui nos genuere parentes,
    Tam subito manibus membra creata tuis.
    Adde quod humana melior natura superbi
    Luciferi e coelo decidit ima petens.
    Errarunt sancti patres, cecidere eremitae
40   Immaculati annos per quadraginta prius;
    Quamquam diva canant, iam deliquere prophetae.
    Occidere homines unus et alter item:
    Clamque viro uxorem rapuit, iubet inde maritum
    Ire aciem ad primam perniciemque suam;
45 Alter quem necuit sicca sepelivit arena,
    Fugit et atrocem, dira ferendo, necem.

If you will be merciful, I shall be blessed.
It is fitting that God exists, Mercy has taught that He   15
    Is a father; it is not fitting that God lack mercy.
Philosophers have said that the prime mover can cause
    All things, except false to be true at the same time,
That it is unmixed, incomposite, and immaterial,
    But contains all good things without measure.   20
Moreover its life is one than which no life can be
    More excellent, nor can anyone enjoy a better one.
I resolve to agree, as such things are not contrary to faith;
    But having assented, those things by themselves do not help.
Moreover, some people hold, once the human frame is broken,   25
    That the whole composite perishes in death;
Some say the soul rises again, some the body, some both,
    Others neither one, but that both perish together.
Excepting the one that both shall arise, I must flee these views,
    Since fine-sounding words conflict with our faith.   30
Seers and prophets sing and have sung many holy things:
    They offer overproud utterances on nature.
Go hence, seers, go far from here, prophets;
    For Tartarus has held you in chains for ages.
Our first parents, who sired us, sinned,   35
    Our parents, created so suddenly by your hands.
Plus the nature of proud Lucifer, better than human,
    Fell from the heavens and sought the depths.
Our sainted forefathers erred, eremites fell,
    Who had lived unstained for forty years;   40
Though they sung of holy things, the prophets still fell short.
    One after the other they killed their fellow men.
Secretly one stole a man's wife, then bade the husband
    To go to the front of the battle to his death;
Another buried in dry sand a man whom he killed,   45
    And, enduring dire things, fled his frightful death.

A cuius facie ille fugit? Mandata refutat
    Cuius? Et ad Tarsos quo prohibente fugit?
Hic freta conscendit, putat hic evadere frustra;
50   Carpit iter: velo et remige tutus erit?
Nam salis intumuere undae fluctuque procella
    Et nimbo atque imbri pellitur ipsa rates.
Naufragium timuere omnes dum causa latebat;
    Viva freto iacitur sarcina iniqua rati;
55 Torrentem superare suis qui viribus audet
    Mergitur, a multa saepe repulsus aqua.
In mare proiectum sorbes, balena, ciboque
    Laeta manes; vivas non coquis ipsa dapes,
Speque cibi fueras cum tu fraudata, putabas
60   Pasci et eras pastus vivaque cymba seni.
Tresque dies mirum gravida quod vixit in alvo,
    Sed magis hunc stomachum posse nutrire cibum.
Tertia cum rutilans ad nos aurora redibit,
    Ad litus venies tunc vomitura virum.
65 Evomitus Ninivem venit, intrat, moenia lustrat;
    Praedicat hos cita morte perire viros,
Clamitat atque: 'Dei ira est subversura nocentes,
    Urbem, delicias et pecus omne simul,
Ni vos paeniteat scelerum; ieiunia servent
70   Usque ad oves, carnem pallia dura tegant.'
Egrediturque urbem ne, si subvertitur, illum
    Ipsum hiet; ast hederae tutior umbra sibi.
Meque coquente aestu tenuit? sat tectus ab illa?
    Non concessa basis nec mihi cuspis erat!
75 Debuerat cuicumque aegro, et si non morituro,
    Se praebere hilarem se facilemque mihi.

And that man, whose face does he flee? Whose commands is he
    Refusing? And against whose orders does he flee to Tarshish?
This man goes to sea, in vain he thinks to escape;
    He seizes the way: will he be safe by sail and oar?   50
The sea waves swelled up and a storm was driven
    By the surge, and the boat itself by cloud and rain.
Everyone feared shipwreck, while the cause lay hidden;
    The burden, too great for the ship, is cast alive on the deep;
That one, daring by his own strength to stay above the torrent   55
    Is submerged, pushed down by the whelming waters.
You swallow, O whale, the man thrown into the sea,
    Happy for the food; but you do not digest the living meal,
And though cheated in your hope of food, thinking to feed,
    You provide food and a living boat for the old man.   60
How wondrous that he lives in your swollen belly for three days,
    But more wondrous that this stomach could nourish its own
        food.
When the third glowing dawn shall return to our lands,
    You will come to the seashore to vomit up the man.
The vomited one comes to Nineveh, enters it, surveys its walls;   65
    He predicts that these men will die a swift death,
And cries out: "The wrath of God will overthrow the wicked,
    The city and its luxuries, and its livestock all at once,
Unless you repent of your wickedness; let the people fast
    Including the sheep; let sackcloth cover your flesh."   70
He leaves the city lest, if it be overthrown, it swallow him too;
    But the shade of God's spreading ivy is safer for him.
Did it keep me too from the burning heat? Did it cover me
        enough?
    Neither the base nor a branch of it was granted to me!
It should have offered itself to any sick man, dying or not,   75
    And been offered to me cheerfully and made easy for me.

Fastidit: vomerem citius quam sorbere vellem;
   Fastidit: stomacho nausea facta meo.
Non mirum si illum vomuit testudo, sed illum
80   Quod potuit ternos ventre tenere dies.
Ipse tibi invideo; poenas pro crimine mallem
   Saepe dedisse tuas quam tolerasse meas.
Integer atque propheta aliis praedicere casus
   Missus es; in nostros pellimur ire rogos.
85 Si medias iactus tumidas proclivis in undas
   Decidis, in primis labor et inde cremor.
Tris te ventre dies servat testudo sepultum;
   Ipse annos totidem febribus ustus humor.
Solibus aestivis hederae protectus ab umbra es,
90   Quae mihi non solum, sed prohibentur aquae.
Iamque vale, ingredior nunc portas quam fugis urbis
   Inveniamque umbram et qui mihi tecta dabit.
Non poterit Ninivita meos spectare dolores
   Nec poterit fletus ipse tenere suos.
95 Tu siccis oculis, tu cruda mente videbas,
   Nec lacrimis siccae commaduere genae.
Est gravior mihi poena meis ex carnibus esse
   Et saccum et cinerem et graviora pati;
Est rugata cutis saccis et durior illis
100   Quos Ninivita humeros induit atque latus;
Nec mihi deficiunt cineres: cum scalpere pellem
   Incipio, multus decidit ungue cinis.
Est consumpta dies longisque ambagibus acta;
   Pauperis ex hedera regia tecta peto.
105 Quam cito mutata est lacrimis superbia regis!
   Ira remollita est, quae prius acris erat.
Scivi equidem et menti nulla est oblivio, cui iam est
   Posse datum vita per tria lustra frui.
Quisquis es, o nimium plorasti ultroque dedisti

148

It scorns me: I would vomit sooner than swallow;
　　It scorns me: nausea has gripped my stomach.
It is no wonder that the monster spit him out, but rather
　　That it could hold him three days in his belly.　　　　80
I envy you; I would prefer to have paid your penalty
　　For my crime many times than to have borne my own.
You were sent as a blameless prophet to foretell disaster
　　To others; I am compelled to go to my own funeral pyre.
If you are tossed overboard and sink down amid the　　85
　　Swollen seas, I slip first and then I am burned.
The monster kept you three days buried in its belly;
　　My moisture was burned by fever for as many years.
You were protected from summer suns by an ivy's shade,
　　Not only shade, but water is forbidden me.　　　　90
So farewell, I enter now the gates of a city you flee,
　　And I shall find shade and someone to give me shelter.
Nineveh will be unable to gaze upon my sufferings
　　Nor able to hold back in its own tears.
You saw with dry eyes, you saw with unfeeling mind,　　95
　　And your dry cheeks did not moisten with tears.
My punishment is the heavier as it weighs on my flesh
　　And I endure sackcloth and ashes and heavier pains;
My wrinkled skin is harsher than that sackcloth
　　With which Nineveh clothed its shoulders and sides;　　100
I am not without ashes, either: when I start to scrape
　　My skin, a great many flakes fall from my nails.
The day has been used up, consumed in long digressions;
　　Instead of a poor man's ivy, I seek a royal dwelling.
How quickly has a king's disdain been turned to tears!　　105
　　His anger, so sharp at first, has been softened.
Indeed I know and remember well, I to whom it was given
　　To enjoy life for three times five years.
O you, whoever you are, who have wept much and given

149

110   Mitem animum, unde Dei lenior ira venit,
      Non me animo miti superas nec fletibus ullis,
        Sed regno atque opibus divitiisque tuis.
      Consueram lacrimas nullas perfundere, sive
        Mortua mater erat, vel meus ipse pater;
115 Unde sit admiror mihi nunc data copia flendi:
        Non nisi sunt lacrimis lumina plena meis.
      Depost enixas pecudes tu sceptra tenebis,
        Speluncam fugies quae tibi vita fuit.
      Persequitur si te validum regemque futurum
120   Rex ferus, hospitia ac atria tutus habes.
      Rure, foco, patria, templis et flumine, villis
        Aeger et extorris pellor et exul agor.
      Exilium patria ampla foret: nam figere sedem
        Concessum, necubi spes datur ulla mihi.
125 Psallentis cithara vox exaudita; reflentis
        Plorantisque mei bucina surda gemit.
      Quid referam cunctos primaeva ab origine, cum sint
        Ausi omnes vitam commaculare suam?
      Ipse ad me redeo peregrinaque crimina curae
130   Sint aliis; nostrum discutiatur onus.
      Si scelera admisi me damnatura nocentem,
        Si struxere meam Tartara nigra domum,
      Audi quae patior Stygias superantia poenas
        Tormenta: et tauri est aerea poena levis.
135 Ipse bis undenos steteram sanissimus annos;
        Nescio nostra salus cui invidiosa fuit.
      Non potuit plus mula meos quam rumpere renes,
        Turbidus argilla dum fluit amnis aqua.
      Haud sibi consueto saltu vada prosilit uno,
140   Quae volucer pedibus nullus adiret equus,
      Unde fui e tota sublatus circiter ulnam
        Sede; repercussae condoluere nates.

Willingly a gentle spirit, whence God's anger is softer,   110
You best me not by a gentle spirit nor by any tears,
    But by your kingship, your power, and your riches.
I had become accustomed to shed no tears, either
    When my mother died nor even my father;
So I marvel at myself now, at such a flood of weeping: 115
    My eyes are full of nothing if not tears.
From behind your zealous flock you will hold the scepter,
    You will flee from the cave that was your life.
If a barbarian king hunts you, a strong man, a future king,
    You are safe, and have shelter and fine homes.   120
Sick and banished, I am driven from fields, hearth, and home,
    From farms, churches, and the river, and wander an exile.
A spacious homeland would be exile; for no hope of settling
    My abode anywhere has been given me.
The voice of the lute player is heard; the trumpet moans,   125
    Deaf to my weeping and my laments.
Why should I mention every man from the dawn of time,
    When they all dared to defile their own lives?
I must return to myself and let the misdeeds of others
    Be their concern; I must shake off my own burden.   130
If I have admitted crimes that will damn me as guilty,
    If black Tartarus has built a home for me,
Hear the torments I suffer, surpassing Stygian penalties:
    Even the bull of bronze is a light penalty.
I had lived the healthiest of lives for twice eleven years;   135
    I know not who it was who envied my health.
The mule did its worst and ruptured my kidneys,
    While the stream flowed by, muddied by potter's clay.
In one leap (for it unusual), the mule leaped over the water,
    Something no fleet-footed horse would dare do.   140
Thus was I lifted whole about a foot from my seat.
    My buttocks were in severe pain from the shock.

Nox media aestivis dum solibus alta teneret
 Frigidus excussit percita membra tremor
145 Successitque calor febrilis, sanguinis uber
 Mictus; magnus erat pectinis inde dolor.
Hic calor accensus crescit, desiccat et urit;
 Extenuat carnes et coquit ardor epar;
Dimminuit vires per venas fusus in omne
150 Corpus et assidue me cruciare solet.
Nec requies datur ulla mihi, nec somnus amicus;
 Lis est cum somno magna labore meo.
Ipse animo lassus quotiens mea membra quieti
 Commendo, requies ac si inimica fugit.
155 Est mihi cum somno bellum; pax nulla futura;
 Si innocuus fugit et si nociturus adest.
Claudo vigil quotiens oculos, phantasmata terrent
 Pallida et atra caput, squalida et hirta comas,
Per varios conficta modos variasque figuras,
160 Manibus ut Furias velle nocere putes.
Tragelaphos centum, hircocervos atque Chimaeras
 Harum, quae apparent, una figura gerit.
Adde quod in Cancro sol ferventissimus extat,
 Miscuit et vires fervidus ipse Canis;
165 Praeteriitque gradus omnes et corda Leonis
 Cernebatque suus Virginis ora rubor;
Et lances geminas aequali pondere Librae
 Intravit, quamvis non sua tecta forent.
Sol, focus et ventus, febris, phantasmata vexant;
170 Cuncta simul nobis agglomerata nocent.
Unus Sole satus si orbem combussit et astra,
 Huic tot coniunctis ustio maior erat.
Circumsaepta domus longo certamine ab igne
 Et flammis validis extitit ustus ager.

Though midnight stood high in the summer heavens,
    A chill shiver shook my agitated limbs,
And feverish heat followed; I urinated copious amounts   145
    Of bloody fluid; then great pain filled my groin.
The heat, once kindled, grew, dried me out and burned me;
    The burning thinned out my flesh and roasted my liver,
Spread throughout my veins into my whole body;
    It reduced my strength and tortured me without pause.   150
It gave me no rest, no sleep was my friend;
    A great struggle arose between sleep and suffering.
As often as I, in exhaustion, commended my limbs to rest,
    Thus often did rest flee like an enemy.
Sleep made war against me; there could be no peace;   155
    Whatever was harmless fled, what was harmful present.
Whenever I closed my eyes while awake, ghosts terrified me,
    Pale ghosts with dark heads, filthy and shaggy-haired,
Devised in various ways and shapes, so you'd think
    That the Furies wanted to harm the Spirits of the Dead.   160
Of the shapes that appeared, one bore the features of
    A hundred horse-stags and goat-deer and Chimeras.
On top of that, the sun at its hottest was in Cancer
    And the blazing Dog Star added its virulence too.
It went past all degrees and the heart of Leo   165
    And its red glow saw the face of Virgo.
It entered also Libra's twin scales with their equal weight
    Although these would not be its seat.
Sun, fire and wind, fever, ghosts, all harried me;
    The whole mass of them together did me great harm.   170
If the one seed of the Sun had burned down the world and its
        stars,
    My burning was greater than all those linked to him.
My house was girt by fire in a long-lasting contest
    And my fields were burned by the powerful flames.

175 Pro zephyro molli regnabat turbidus auster,
        Ut gelidae extiterit percalefactor aquae;
    Unde inspiratus tam primum expellitur aer,
        Quam primum calidi limina cordis adit.
    Non sunt de numero quae torquent accipientem,
180   Pharmaca amara nimis linguaque fissa siti
    Ah, volui quotiens ardentem extinguere febrem!
        Ustio poscit aquam, lingua crepata fugit.
    Interea exurit, depasta est pessima corpus
        Febris; parvum olei nostra lucerna tenet.
185 Arida facta cutis; sunt haec exausta medullis
        Ossa; caro fluxit; spiritus unus inest
    Artubus exustis; mirum est ex corpore toto
        Unde fluit sudor nabilis instar aquae.
    Indefessa meum torquent haec omnia corpus;
190   Maius supplitium est tot mala ferre simul.
    Non possem graviora pati si Tartara adirem;
        Si natura hominis limite clausa suo est,
    Ad flagrum mihi cuncta manent, haec aspera vitam
        Prosternunt, sanctis vix toleranda viris.
195 Tartarus a multis et subterraneus orbis
        In centro terrae creditur esse locus;
    Credo super terram, patior cum vulnere poenam,
        †Aut sine cur subter Tartara opaca fore.†
    Sorte mea si forte ratum vel fixa voluntas
200   Te mihi supremam constituisse piram,
    Ante obitum concede, precor, tam poplite flexo
        Quam capite obstipo, numen adire meum.
    Me ad steriles artes et barbara regna tenentem
        Atque rebellem hominem forsitan esse putas?
205 Hic virtute puer, cum pubertate virebat,

The violent south wind ruled in place of the gentle west one,   175
    And the south wind heated up the cold water;
Thus air, once breathed in, was exhaled as soon
    As it approached the threshold of my overheated heart.
Numberless were the things that tormented the recipient,
    Very bitter drugs and a tongue cracked by thirst.   180
Oh! how often I longed to quench the burning fever!
    My fire demanded water, my parched tongue fled from it.
Meanwhile the worst of fevers was burning up my body;
    It consumed it; my lamp held very little oil.
My skin dried up; my bones were worn down to the marrow;   185
    My flesh melted away; a single breath lived
In my parched limbs; the sweat from my whole body,
    Amazingly, flowed like a stream you could swim in.
All these things tortured my body relentlessly;
    To bear so many evils at once made the suffering greater.   190
I could not have suffered more if I had gone to Tartarus;
    If man's nature is bounded by a limit,
All these sufferings kept flogging me, pressing the life
    From me, things scarcely to be borne by the saints.
Many believe Tartarus and the subterranean world   195
    To be a place at the center of the earth:
When I suffer the penalty for my wound, I believe it above
      ground,
    [Or allow why Tartarus will be dark beneath.]
If my fate is decided and your purpose immoveable,
    And you have prepared my funeral pyre,   200
Before I die, grant me, I pray on bended knee
    And with bowed head, to approach your divinity in prayer.
Do you perhaps think that I am holding on to useless arts
    And barbarous kingdoms, that I am a rebellious person?
This boy possessed virtue when he was green with youth   205

Virque, senex fidus nunc tibi semper erit.
Hunc ego, tu nosti melius, qui totius orbis
   Imperium mavis quod regat omne tuum.
Romam habitat, quem tota cohors regumque ducumque
210   Caesareumque colit supplice voce caput.
Multa loquenda tacens et plura tacenda locutus
   Si fuerim, quae scis praetereunda loquor.
Quid memoro poenam, qua non violentior ulla
   Scitur posse dari nec truculenta magis?
215 Si e medio tollar non viso numine nostro,
   Nil mihi sub terra saevius esse potest.
Visa mihi totiens sunt infera regna deique
   Tartarei et quid agant: est mihi tota cohors.
Pro nihilo facio quod sub tellure timetur;
220   Assueto flagris sunt leviora mihi.
Tartareusque canis, superas extractus ad auras,
   Venit et extimuit meque meamque manum,
Et Furiae infernae me cognovere furentem,
   Et mirata meum dira Chimaera caput.
225 Sed si morte mea coelestia regna darentur,
   Illa secunda mihi, non mihi grata forent.
Non repetam quae dicta prius, sed nulla viarum
   Quas cecini, nostrae causa salutis erit.
Haec commenta abeant, quae non fecere beatos,
230   Aeternam quae non perdocuere domum.
Tunc genus humanum fusca sub nube latebant
   Misteria, et clara luce carebat idem.
Sumpsisti postquam nostro de stamine pellem
   Et Deus ex diva Virgine natus homo es,
235 Occultae patuere fores et gloria coeli,
   Et, quae ignota prius, nunc manifesta via est.

And as a man, now an old man, will be faithful to you always.
I know this man, and you, who prefer that he guide
   Your whole empire over the whole world, know him better.
He dwells in Rome, him a whole troop of kings and warlords
   And the Cesarean head worship with suppliant voice.   210
If I've said much to be quiet about, and kept quiet about much
   That needed saying, I do say things you know should be
      omitted.
Why do I mention the punishment, than which none known
   Could have been given more harsh and cruel?
If I am not to be resurrected, having glimpsed your divinity,   215
   Nothing beneath the earth could be more cruel to me.
I have seen the lower kingdoms and the gods of Tartarus
   And what they do: the whole troop was near me.
I make nothing of what is to be feared under the earth;
   Such things are more tolerable than the whips I'm used to.   220
Dragged to the upper air, the hound of Tartarus
   Came and terrified me and my hand.
The Furies of Hell have known me in my madness,
   And the dread Chimera was bewildered by my head.
But if the heavenly realms are given me at death,   225
   Those things would be secondary, unpleasing to me.
I will not repeat what I said before, but none of the ways
   That once I sang of will be the cause of my salvation.
Let those fictions depart, they have not made men blessed,
   Nor have they taught us about our eternal home.   230
Once, your mysteries were hidden from humankind
   Under a dark cloud, and were lacking clear light.
But after you assumed flesh with our mortal life
   And were born a God-man from the Blessed Virgin,
The doors and the glory of heaven were   235
   Opened, and the way, unknown before, was now plain.

Humanum genus exiliens praecepta redemptum est
    Sanguine, velle, cruce et morte tui Geniti.
Gutta nec effusa est pro nobis sanguinis una?
240   Sub specie humana denegor unus homo?
Quot rediere mali, cunctis tua brachia pandis;
    Qui rediere ad te, nulla repulsa datur.
Accinctus venio; deliqui, paenitet; arma
    Non aliena fero, si meliora tua.
245 Si miserere hominum libeat, si parcere lapsis
    Non pigeat, redeant si ad tua tecta velis,
O Pater omnipotens, cuius clementia fines
    Exiit et nullo limite clausa fuit,
Contrito da corde meos plorare reatus,
250   Exaudi fundo, quas sine fine, preces;
Da spatium vitae quod crimina deleat et quo
    Me pudeat sceleris; me iuvet atque mori.
Oro post tantas ne mors suprema sequatur;
    Quam mereor noli plectere morte virum.
255 Si moriar, spes nulla meae nec causa salutis:
    Fata sinunt homines ire, redire negant.
Mors mea iusta quidem; non est mea causa querelae
    Iusta quidem; nec ob id iustior esse potes.
Noli obitum horrendum nostrae mortemque animai;
260   Intereant nulla membra caduca nece.
Non est artificis partes coniungere et illas
    Frangere et eiusdem rumpere facta manus.

Humankind, responding to your teachings, has been redeemed
    By the blood, will, cross, and death of your Son.
Has not one drop of that blood been shed for me?
    Am I the one man denied membership in the human race? 240
You hold out your arms to as many sinners who return;
    No rebuff is offered to those who have come back.
I come ready; I have sinned, I repent; I bear
    No foreign arms, if yours are better.
If you would take pity on mankind, if you do not scorn 245
    To spare the fallen, if you will they return to your roof,
O Father omnipotent, whose mercy passes all bounds
    And who is constrained by no limit,
Allow me to weep for my offenses with a contrite heart,
    Listen to the prayers I pour out without end; 250
Give me the time to wipe away my sins and be ashamed
    Of my wickedness; time will also help me to die.
After such sufferings, I beg that the final death not follow;
    Do not punish this man with the death I deserve.
If I should die now, I have no hope or ground of salvation: 255
    The Fates let men depart, but say no to their return.
My death is just; the grounds of my complaint unjust;
    Nor on this account can you be more than just.
Do not will the fearful passing and the death of my soul;
    Do not let my limbs die a fallen death. 260
It is not an artist's way to break up what he has joined;
    It is not right for the same hand both to make and destroy.

: XXXI :

Marrasii Siculi oratio exaudita
et modus curationis ad sanctissimum dominum nostrum
Nicolaum papam V feliciter incipit.

Annuit Omnipotens; vox exaudita precesque,
    Et dixit tenui talia verba sono:
'Archigenes Terrana, veni; praebeto salutem:
    Marrasium nulla morte perire volo.'
5 Archigenes, tacto pulsu ac urina revisa,
    Praecipit: 'Abstineas, ne moriare, cave.
Intensa est febris, diffusum cauma per omne
    Corpus, et in noctem nulla futura quies.
Incidenda epatis vena est, ut sanguis acutus
10   Exiliat, febris bulliat utque minus.
Hordea cocta cibus, sint lympha et zuccara potus;
    Sit medio horarum quattuor acta mora.'
Haec mihi, cognatis et cunctis sanguine iunctis
    Et toti populo quam manifesta facit.
15 Postquam abiit, famuli praecingunt se ordine dicto;
    Non ventosa ferunt hordea cocta mihi.
Nescius aeger erat famulus purique Falerni
    Praecupidus, farris nullius estor erat.
Interea dum hausturus eram mea pocula, iunxit
20   Et risit rauce verba tacenda loquens:
'Archigenes aufert iumentis hordea, nobis
    Donat; amatque merum, vix mihi praestat aquam.
Dulcia vina bibit, succos propinat amaros;
    Estque cibos suaves, praebet inesibiles.'
25 Arguit aegrotus medicos, bene rectus ab illis

: XXXI :

A poem telling how Marrasio Siculo's prayer was heard,
and the manner of his cure, addressed to our most holy lord,
Pope Nicholas V, begins auspiciously.

The Almighty One approved, my voice and prayers were heard,
    And he spoke words such as these in a quiet voice:
"Archigenes Terrana, come: bring him health:
    It is not my will that Marrasio perish from any kind of death."
The Archigenes, having felt my pulse and inspected my urine,   5
    Advised: "You must fast or — take care — you may die.
Your fever is acute, the heat has spread through your
    Whole body, and you will have no rest at night.
A vein of your liver must be cut open, so that the acrid
    Blood may spurt out and your fever boil less.   10
Your food must be cooked barley, your drink water and sugar;
    You should wait four hours between meals."
He made these instructions as plain as possible to me, my in-
    laws,
    My blood relatives, and to the whole parish.
After he left, my servants readied themselves to follow his orders.   15
    They brought me light barley that had been cooked.
I have a sickly, ignorant servant who was over-fond
    Of unmixed Falernian wine and who never ate grain.
When I was about to drain my drinking cup, he joined me
    And laughing gratingly, spoke words that shouldn't be said: 20
"The head doctor carts off loads of barley, giving some
    To us; he likes strong wine, but hardly offers water to me.
He drinks sweet wines, but prescribes bitter drinks;
    He has tasty food, but gives inedible stuff to us."
The sickly man blamed the doctors, quite rightly,   25

Si non concedant quae nocitura forent.
Archigenes praecepta dabit: parere necesse est;
    Nolenti mors aut tarda futura salus.
Reiciunt doctos quibus est gula tota voluptas;
30   Cessuros votis saepe vocare solent.
Ille inter medicos solitus ditescere, qui scit
    Blandiri aegrotis et dare grata suis.
Sancte pater, ride; delectant carmina risu
    Digna; prius risit verba legenda Deus,
35 Et pepulit mortem instantem vitaeque pepercit:
    Pulsa febre fuit reddita prima salus.

: XXXII :

Marrasii Siculi elegia
ad sanctissimum dominum nostrum Nicolaum papam V:
Quot mala pestis et quartana habent.

Quam timui fugiendo putans evadere mortem,
    Interrupit iter pestis iniqua meum;
Pessima me ad canos et multa pericula traxit,
    Mille meis oculis obtulit illa neces;
5 Praestabatque mori quam vitam saepe tueri
    Mortibus innumeris pestiferisque modis.
Nupta ter octavos nondum compleverat annos
    Et prima infelix peste perempta fuit.
Postridie eiusdem media sub nocte sepultus
10   Indolis egregiae frater amatus humi.
Hausit putrem animam, dum viveret ille, sororis;
    Se comitem vita praebuit atque nece.
Expulsus subito ipse fui patriaque domoque;

If they don't give up things that would be harmful.
A physician will give orders: one has to obey them;
    If you don't, it's either death or a slow recovery.
Those whose whole pleasure is in their gullet reject doctors,
    But when they're dying they implore them with prayers.   30
The doctor who usually gets rich is the one who knows
    How to soothe and comfort his patients.
Laugh, Holy Father; poems worth a laugh are a delight;
    A while ago God laughed reading these words,
And he banished my imminent death and spared my life;   35
    My fever was cast out and my former health restored.

: XXXII :

An elegy of Marrasio Siculo
to our most holy lord, Pope Nicholas V:
How numerous are the evils of plague and quartan fever.

Thinking by flight to avoid the death I feared,
    The hostile plague interrupted my journey.
Worst of plagues, it dragged me to old age and many dangers;
    And brought before my eyes a thousand deaths.
And to die seemed better than to be ever guarding one's life   5
    Against countless deaths and pestilent ends.
My bride had not yet completed her twenty-fourth year,
    When the unhappy girl was the first killed by the plague.
Her beloved brother of exceptional gifts was buried
    In the ground, the next day, in the middle of the night.   10
While he lived, he inhaled his sister's contagious breath
    And made himself her companion in death as in life.
I was suddenly driven from my homeland and my house;

Oppida cuncta suis me pepulere focis.
15 Vix itur in campis, ubi templum sorte repertum est,
Grata quies: nullum mel sine felle fuit.
Mortua nata mihi caruit cruce, morte sacerdos
Nullus, sed servis est tumulata meis.
Et famuli extincti veluti iumenta per agros;
20   Alterius moriens triste cadaver humat.
Maurus, quem nigro pinxit natura colore,
Alterius comitis guttura nigra secat.
Disparibus causis nostra periere ruina:
Perditus iste nece, perditus ille fuga.
25 Rumor it, incursat plebs convicina repente:
Armati expellunt meque meamque domum.
Hic morbus sanos facit insanire, timentes
Audaces, mitem belligerumque facit.
Nam mihi poscenti nummos panemque roganti
30   Et quae vera sitis postulat atque fames
Ostendunt latices, lapides pro pane rotundos
Iactant ut ficus castaneasque pira;
Saxa volant et saxa legunt et saxa ministrant:
Qui salebrosus erat fit via plana locus.
35 Cornipedis levitas mihi grata et calcar amicum
Et fuga pervolucris vita cibusque fuit.
Praesentantque oculis adversa haec omnia mortes
Mille, nec occidunt, sed cruciare volunt.
†Vita fatigata est homines peritura cadentes:†
40   Aut dormire velis aut vigilare velis.
Somnus, si quis erat (nam nos dormire necesse est),
Somnia, si qua aderant, plena timoris erant;
Et quota pars noctis fessos submittit ocellos,
Digna quies odio facta labore meo est.
45 Non mirum: timui. Sed quis non ista timeret?

Every town expelled me from its hearth fires.
A hard trip to the countryside, where a church by chance was   15
    found;
    The peace was welcome, but there's no honey without gall.
My daughter died and was freed of torment, but at her death
    There was no priest, and she was buried by my servants.
The household servants perished like beasts in the fields.
    One dying man buries the grim corpse of another.   20
Another, a Moor, whom nature has painted black,
    Cuts the black throat of another companion.
They perished from causes different from my destruction:
    This one dies by murder, that one by flight.
A rumor spreads; people from nearby rush suddenly in: 25
    Armed men drive me and my household out.
This sickness makes the sane insane,
    The fearful bold, the mild belligerent.
When I beg for money and ask for bread
    And what real thirst and hunger demand,   30
They offer water; instead of bread they toss out
    Stones, shaped like figs or chestnuts and pears.
They throw stones, they gather stones, they serve stones:
    An area, which was once rough, becomes a level road.
The welcome mobility of a horse, the kindly spur,   35
    And swift flight were life and sustenance to me.
All these adversities presented a thousand deaths
    To my eyes; they didn't kill, but wanted to torture me.
A life on the point of death exhausts men of fading powers:
    Either you want to sleep or you want to keep awake.   40
Sleep, if any was possible (for we have to sleep),
    And dreams, if any occurred, were full of fear.
And whatever bit of the night made my tired eyes droop,
    Was odious rest, created only by my suffering.
No wonder: I was afraid. But who would not have been?   45

Sed timor ille minor, credere quippe mori.
Cetera praetereo, quae sanctis dura fuissent;
Si ad mentem redeunt, concutit ossa tremor.
Quicquid erat, discrimen erat: mea vita periclum,
50   Vivere supplitium delitiaeque mori.
Nam me per geminos ⟨febres⟩ habuere decembres:
His quartana malis addita pigra fuit.
Si deses, si tarda venit, si denique fallax,
Vicini insultus praevia signa gerit.
55 Incurvare solet quae primo brachia tendit,
Verberat et dorsum fractio longa meum.
Concutit inde tremor nostros sine viribus artus
Atque molas strepitus fortis in arma vocat
Dentatasque acies curvatis cornibus ambas
60   Alteram in alterutram bella movere facit.
Irruit ima cohors superamque impellere visa
Dentem unum ex superis in duo frusta scidit.
Nec tantum posset crepitare ciconia rostro
Ad nidum, teneras quando salutat aves,
65 Quantum ego, concussis geminas dum saepe per horas
Dentibus infringor, vexor et inde, meis.
Nonne vides? Febris littoribus haec dominatur;
Tortores tantos nulla tyrannis habet.
Somnus hebes, clamosa sitis vomitusque, labores
70   In somnisque tremor me cruciando premunt;
Me quacumque die quarta afflixere: per horas
Quadraginta latex non datur atque cibus.
Nonne alios longe melius curare fuisset?
Nam mihi nunc auro plena crumena foret.
75 Scire quid est morbus medicos iuvat et cibat; omnes
Morbum ferre nocet, carne cibatur egri.
Adde quod insanis nec delectaris amico
Eloquio ut quando, sed taciturnus abis;

Yet that fear—the belief one is dying—was less serious.
I omit other things that would have tried even the saints.
    But if I remember them, trembling strikes my bones.
Whatever it was, it was a crisis; my life was a peril;
    To live was a punishment, to die delicious.   50
For I was gripped by fevers for two Decembers
    And to these evils was added the torpid quartan fever.
If it comes lazily, if slowly, and in a word, deceptively,
    It gives advance notice of an attack to come.
Its habit is to twist arms when they first stretch out,   55
    And a long tearing pain beats upon my back.
Then trembling shakes my powerless limbs
    And a great rattling summons my molars to battle
And causes a pair of sharp-toothed battle lines
    With incurving flanks to make war upon each other,   60
The lower troop rushes in and seems to strike the upper one
    Cutting one of the upper teeth into two pieces.
A stork could not clack its bill near its nest,
    When it greets its nestlings as much as I do.
I'm worn down and vexed by my chattering teeth,   65
    Often for two whole hours at a time.
Do you not see? This fever rules the land;
    No tyranny has such powerful torturers.
Weak sleep, a demanding thirst, and vomiting, pains,
    And shivering in my sleep crush and torture me.   70
Every fourth day they afflict me; for forty hours
    Neither food nor water is given me.
Would it not have been far better to cure others?
    For by now my purse would be filled with gold.
To know what sickness is benefits and feeds doctors;   75
    To endure an illness harms everyone, but the doctor is fed
By the sick man's flesh. Moreover, you're raving and
    Don't enjoy friendly talk as before, but go off in silence;

Adde quod insanis et sunt odiosa petenti
80   Cuncta tibi et nullae complacuere dapes,
Optatumque merum veniens ex montibus, altis
    Vallibus? Aut imis respuis atque fugis.
Altilis ova mihi meliora recentia sunto,
    Quae vetula et pinguis parturit atque cubat,
85   Quam superincumbens commotis fortiter alis
    Calcasti pedibus, galle marite, tuis.
Dura nocent quocumque modo, sed mollia prosunt,
    Sive patella coquat seu coquat ardor aquae.
Ambrosiae succo atque aliis bene olentibus herbis
90   Mixta nihil sapiunt foeda sapore meo.
Dulcis fastidit me Ponticus acus acutus:
    Insipidus, salsus, pinguis, amarus obest.
Mortua nunc virtus, ablata potentia edendi,
    Quae placidos etiam respuit ore cibos.
95   Quadrupede et bipede est melioris carnis edendae
    Francolina volans, sed mihi grata parum.
Assa nocent nec frixa iuvant, sed cocta lebete
    Profectura mihi sumere lingua timet.
Si qua tenella caro peditantis sive volantis,
100   Si qua natat pelago, flumine sive lacu,
Sive ubicumque velis mixtim terraque marique,
    Mixta sapore alio sive sapore suo,
Crate, veru aut patina vel si bene cocta lebete,
    Si prodesse mihi, nulla placere potest.
105   Fercula nulla salem possunt sufferre nec ulla
    Iura, sed evomito sorpta vitella sale.
Quo placuit condire epulas terrebar aceto
    Et quo non poterat mensa vacare mea.
Putet munda Ceres, terret me Bacchus in auro
110   Aut vitro et necubi posse videre datur.

Plus you're raving and everything you ask for is odious,
    Your food gives you no pleasure, 80
And that wine you ordered, coming from the mountains,
    High valleys or low? You spit it out and leave it untasted.
 Let me have the best and the freshest eggs
    Which a fat old chicken laid and incubated,
Which, as you lay atop her, strongly fluttering your wings, 85
    You tread on with your feet, rooster husband.
Hard, they are harmful in every way, but soft,
    They are helpful whether cooked in a pan or in boiling water.
Mixed with ambrosial juice and other sweet-smelling herbs,
    They have no savor and are foul to my taste. 90
The sharp needlefish from the Black Sea, though sweet,
    Makes me squeamish: it strikes me as bland, salty, bitter;
My strength is now dead, gone my capacity to eat;
    I spit out of my mouth even the blandest foods.
The flying pheasant has better meat for eating 95
    Than a quadruped or biped, but it pleases me little.
Roasted they're harmful, and it doesn't help to fry them.
    Cooking in a pot is better, but my tongue won't touch them.
Even if it's the tender flesh of furry or feathered game,
    If it's anything that swims in the sea, stream, or lake, 100
Or if it's something from earth and sea combined,
    Mixed with the taste of something else or its own,
If it's been well-cooked on a rack, a spit or in a pot,
    If it's good for me, I'm unable to enjoy it.
No dishes or sauces can be seasoned with salt; 105
    I vomit up egg yolks that have salt dissolved in them.
I was afraid of the vinegar with which I once liked to season
    Dishes, and which my table couldn't do without.
Fine bread smells vile, wine whether in gilt or glass
    Terrifies me, and I can't look at it anywhere. 110

Partes quasque meas oris sensisset olentes
    Cuius odoratus debilis ille foret.
Et me pertaesum fuit olfecisse culinae
    Nidorem, quamvis fercula lauta forent.
115 Iuxta meos oculos iam scintillare videtur
    Littera; si qua trium, quattuor esse pedum.
Ipse opulentus eram, plura et maiora videbam;
    Divitias istas hostis habere queat.
Saepe procul melius vidi spectare senectam
120   Quam prope, qua melius sana iuventa videt.
Spiritus est senibus grossus paucusque videndi,
    Subtilem possunt reddere visa procul.
Quid vagor alterius citius numerando labores
    Et taceo ipse meos, quos recitare grave est?
125 Quod sibi longa dies, quod multa aboleverat aetas,
    Id mihi subtraxit morbus acerbus idem.
Alba recocta suo privantur vitra colore
    Et revoluta suo vina sapore carent.
Saepe infelicem torquebat sibilus aurae,
130   Saepe means tonitrus, saepe refluxus aquae.
Tinnitu surdaster eram noctuque dieque;
    Frigida hirundo meis auribus alta canit.
Os natura meum armavit triginta duobus
    Ossibus, officio quae caruere suo.
135 Non mordere valent nec quicquam findere morsu
    Aut molere aut ulla stringere parte cibos.
Ossa aliena meis visum est mihi ferre labellis
    Infixa; et nullum robur habere queunt.
Rectius ista leget bili percitus ab atra
140   Aut cui quarta dies febre molesta fuit.
Captus ab indomita quartana mense novembri
    Ipse fui prima praetereunte die.

Even someone whose sense of smell was weak
    Would have smelled that every part of my mouth stank.
It disgusted me to smell the fumes from the kitchen
    Even though the dishes were sumptuous.
A letter seemed now to flicker before my eyes,   115
    And what was three feet looked like four.
I had been rich; I was used to seeing more and better things.
    May my enemy be able have those riches.
I have often found old age to see better from afar
    Than close up; healthy youth sees better than old age.   120
Old men have a spirit that is thick and hard of seeing,
    Yet things seen from afar can render it subtle.
Why do I digress, counting up fast another's sufferings,
    While being silent about my own, so painful to describe?
That which length of days, that which great age takes away,   125
    Was what bitter illness took away from me.
White pieces of glass twice fired lose their color,
    And wine that has traveled lacks its proper flavor.
Often the whistling of the wind wracked this unhappy man,
    Often, too, the rolling thunder, often the turning tide.   130
I was deaf night and day from a ringing in the ears;
    The soaring swallow's song fell chill on my ears.
Nature armed my mouth with thirty-two teeth,
    Teeth which failed to discharge their duty.
They were not strong enough to grip or bite off food,   135
    Or to chew or nibble on any little morsel.
I seemed to be holding someone else's teeth planted
    With my lips, and they hadn't an ounce of strength.
Someone who has been stricken with black bile will read this
    With understanding, or a sufferer from quartan fever.   140
I myself was seized by an untamable quartan fever
    As the first day in the month of November passed by.

Expleturus erat sextam tum mensis aprilis
    Supremamque diem qua sine febre fui,
145 Quando resurrexit qui nos a morte redemit,
    Surrexi a morbo protinus ipse meo.
Me thalamo tenuisset hebes quartana iacentem
    Sex menses, totidem nos abeundo dies.
Longior hora die, iam lux extentior anno;
150   Unum habuit pestis, febris acerba duos.
Sic sterilis mea vita fuit, sic tempus inane
    Lapsum; dic melius: mortua vita fuit.
Tris hiemes avido mihi defluxere; volebam,
    Non merui, sanctos pronus adire pedes.
155 Quando erit ut possim nostros deflere reatus,
    Pontificis summi cum dabo labra pedi?
Interdicta mihi Romana est semita, Campus
    Martius, Exquiliae, numen adire tuum?
Non hiemare datur Romae, aut audire cicadas
160   Sive videre rosas, aut nova musta bibi?
Si mihi fata dabunt faciem vultumque videre
    Laeta tuum et sacros cernuus ante pedes
Oscula ferre tuos et tete audire loquentem,
    Polliceor templis munera lauta tuis.
165 Quid magis optandum? Nihil est quod gratius esset,
    Nil mihi sub coelo sanctius esse potest.

*Elegia narrat iter interruptum peste, febribus
et tandem quartana, quae multorum malorum
causa extitit.*

Then April was about to finish its sixth day,
  And my sickness' final day, when I was without fever;
When He who redeemed us from death rose again,   145
  I, too, rose forthwith from my bed of pain.
The torpid quartan fever had kept me lying on my bed
  For six months, it took as many days to leave.
An hour has become longer than a day, a day than a year;
  The plague gripped me for one year, bitter fever for two.   150
Thus my life was barren, thus my time passed in idleness;
  Let me say it better still: my life was dead.
Three winters have flowed away from me, all eager; I longed,
  But did not merit, to prostrate myself at your holy feet.
When shall I be able to weep for my offenses,   155
  When can I place my lips on the supreme pontiff's foot?
Is the path to Rome forbidden me, forbidden the Campus
      Martius,
  The Esquiline, and an audience with your Divinity?
Am I not to have a chance to winter in Rome, to hear
  The cicadas, to see the roses, to drink the new wine?   160
If the happy Fates will grant me to see your countenance
  And with bowed head before your sacred face
To place kisses on your holy feet and hear you speak,
  I vow to bestow lavish gifts upon your churches.
What more could one wish? Nothing could be more welcome;   165
  There is nothing under heaven that could bless me more.

     This elegy tells of the journey interrupted by the plague,
              fevers, and finally the quartan fever
                 that was the cause of many evils.

: XXXIII :

Marrasii Siculi transfretatio coepta Panhormi,
absoluta Puteoli, decimo Kalendas martias,
ubi continentur laudes Alfonsi regis Magni.

Regia me postquam suscepit celsa triremis,
    Cui bellaturae Lipparis arma tulit
(Quae tunc est nostrum vectura in proelia regem,
    Cum petet Eoos regna beata Syros;
5 Quam superare potest, dum pandit carbasa ventis,
    Qua melius pelagus nulla carina secat),
Quam primum ascendi, venti adventare furentes
    Adversi et pellunt aequor ad astra maris.
Pons mihi securus fuit irretitus eundo
10   Et clausere meum pontus et Eurus iter;
Circius et boreas vastas fregere procellas,
    Et cum saxa sonant, unda refracta cadit;
Circumsaepta fremit quam multa grandine et imbri,
    Et tonitru et nimbis regio plena manet;
15 Qui virides cingunt, veluti sua pergama, montes
    Urbem, sunt tecti nocte sequente nive.
Excelsi montes faciunt nos frendere, namque
    Algentes sufflant frigora magna nives.
Frigore vexati magnos percingimus ignes
20   Et colimus sacros quaeque caterva Lares.
Africus atque Notus sunt nisi evertere pontum
    Et salsas dulces efficit imber aquas.
Concitus atque ictus crebris conflictibus aer
    Mugit; adhuc resonant concava saxa metu.
25 Interea optabam pulsis tot flatibus Austrum,

: XXXIII :

Marrasio Siculo's sea voyage, begun in Palermo,
finished at Pozzuoli on February 20,
wherein also is praise for King Alfonso the Great.

After the lofty royal trireme took me on, a ship going to war
    And onto which the men of Lipari loaded arms,
(A ship which then would carry our king into battle,
    When he heads for the Holy Realms of Syria in the East;
A ship which no craft can beat when it spreads canvas to the   5
    wind,
    A keel that slices through the seas better than any other).
As soon as I boarded, raging adverse winds sprang up
    And drove the waters of the sea up toward the stars.
The safe deck was involved in netting for me as I went,
    And the sea and the east wind enclosed my journey.   10
The northwest and north winds broke out in great storms;
    The rocks resounded while the waves fell with a crash,
The place, girt round with pouring hail and rain,
    Raged, full of thunder and black rain clouds.
The green mountains, that ring the city like a citadel   15
    Were covered by darkness and following snow.
The lofty mountains make our teeth chatter,
    For freezing snow blew down on us great, cold blasts.
Harried by the cold, we surrounded ourselves with large fires
    And each group prayed to its own household gods.   20
The southwest and south winds strove to overturn the sea
    And the rains turn the salt waters sweet.
The air, shaken and stricken with frequent blasts,
    Moans; still the hollow rocks resound with fear.
Meanwhile, I was wishing for the south wind and calm seas   25

Ut rectum et tutum prora secaret iter.
Pulverea accumulat nimia caligine nubes;
    Expansis alis praecipitatus adest,
Qui mare, qui terras, qui totas turbidus undas
30   Vertit, et e fundo saltat arena salo;
Irruit et duros nimio stridore rudentes
    Concutit, et titubat tota triremis aqua.
Hanc tamen in portu si navita crederet Austro,
    Vidisset superos versa carina deos.
35 Sed postquam vires furibundus perdidit Auster
    Atque abiit pelago saevior ira sui,
Fit mare tranquillum, sunt venti circumeuntes,
    Nulla quibus dubiis est adhibenda fides.
Pacatum ventis magnum sulcavimus aequor
40   Et velo et remis magna carina volat.
Ustica nos tenuit, dum fit combustio Phoebes;
    Per geminos Pisces Luna trahebat equos.
Nocte sequente Africus nos est comitatus euntes
    Et pariter validus nocte dieque Notus,
45 Ingentesque maris montes transnavimus; inde
    Cumaeos portus docta Sibylla tulit,
Et retulit foliis, veluti mos unicus illi est:
    'Credite, Lipparei, prima triremis erit;
Neptuno et ventis haec praeceptura videtur,
50   Quum fuerit regis pondere pressa sui;
Illa sibi fluctus remis supponet eunti
    Et velo, reges supprimet alta reos.
Quaestor adest, nummos potuit quot ferre ministrat,
    Nec dubitat saevas mille subire neces;
55 Desus adest, Graffaeus item, qui puppe gubernant,
    Qui vitam ventis opposuere suam,
Ut maiestati sacrae servire deoque
    Possint et numen iam coluere suum.

So that the ship might steer a safe course and true.
But the south wind accumulates dark and dusty clouds,
    Driven headlong on outspread wings, it comes
And violently overturns the sea and land, and all the waves,
    And sand from the deep does a whirling dance;   30
Then it rushes in and rattles the tough rigging with a roar
    And the ship rocks, awash with water.
If the pilot had entrusted the ship to the south wind in port,
    The hull, upside down, would have seen the gods above.
But after furious Auster lost its strength,   35
    And its anger, more savage than the sea, departed,
The sea became calm, there were winds all around,
    Though no trust could be placed in their doubtful force.
We plowed the great sea, now undisturbed by winds,
    And the great ship flies by sail and by oar.   40
We stopped at Ustica, while yet the sun was glowing;
    The moon drew her chariot past the twin Pisces.
The following night Africus escorted us on our way
    And Notus, equally strong, day and night.
We sailed through huge mountains of sea; from there   45
    The wise Sibyl brought us to the Cumaean port,
And read from her leaves, as was her special custom:
    "Believe me, Liparians, yours will be the first trireme;
It seems it is going to instruct Neptune and the winds,
    When it is pressed down with the weight of its king.   50
It will subdue the waves for him on his way, with oars
    And sail; it will bring down from on high guilty kings.
The treasurer is here, he supplies as much coin as he could carry,
    And does not hesitate to incur a thousand cruel deaths;
Desus is here, and Graffeus, too, who pilot the ship   55
    And who have exposed their lives to the winds,
In order to be able to serve their Sacred Majesty
    And God, and they have now worshipped his power.

Sed si forte alia maiora oracla velitis,
60   Quae ponto et terris exiget iste deus,
Si quota pars orbis pedibus subiecta futura
    Scire libet, primo sacra piate Deo.'

Finis transfretationis
et Sibyllae Cumaeae oraculi.
Decimo Kalendas martias 1451.

: XXXIV :

Lucretiae Parthenopaeae puellae fortunatissimae laudes
per Marrasium Siculum pro
Alfonso rege Magno.

Sanguinea sese Lucretia morte peremit
    Et meruit casti corporis esse ducem.
Caesaris Alfonsi si praegustasset amores,
    Nulla cruore suo permaduisset humus;
5   Nec tibi Tarquinio peregrina taberna fuisset
    Hospitium, patria nec caruisset eris.
Pulchrior haec illa meliore a sanguine nata,
    Quo primore fuit Caesare amata meo.
Pulchra placet, sed casta iuvat, quantoque pudica
10   Tanto crevit amor, principe digna suo.
Ingenii vis magna sui, quam vincere reges
    Non potuere: suo victus amore fuit.
Non minus hac dignus quam digna Lucretia nostro
    Rege fuit, nec eo dignior esse potest.
15 Felicem voluere suam per saecula vitam
    Fata, voluptates tot voluere suas.

But if by chance you should want other and greater oracles,
    Which that God requires on sea and land,   60
If you wish to know how great a part of the world will lie
    Under his feet, perform acts of expiation to God first."

Here ends the tale of the sea voyage
and the oracles of the Cumaean Sibyl.
February 20, 1451.

: XXXIV :

Praise for Lucrezia of Naples, the most fortunate of young
women, by Marrasio Siculo on behalf of
King Alfonso the Great.

By a bloody death Lucretia made away with herself
    And deserved to become a leader in chastity.
If she had tasted the loves of Caesar Alfonso beforehand,
    The earth would not have been dampened with her blood.
No foreign inn would have been your lodging, Tarquin,   5
    Nor would your country have been free of masters.
This Lucrezia, lovelier and born of nobler blood,
    Was loved by my Caesar, her superior in rank.
He loves her beauty, chaste as it is, and worthy of her prince,
    His love grew in proportion to her virtue.   10
The power of his character is great, other kings could not
    Conquer it: but he has been conquered by his love.
He was no less worthy of this Lucretia than she was
    Of our king, nor can she be more worthy of him.
The Fates have willed them a happy life in this world,   15
    And have wished them as many pleasures as may be.

Quid magis optandum? Quid plus concedere possent?
    Fortunam pedibus supposuere suis.
Diva puella, vale, magno et sub Caesare laeta
20   Degas; sint vitae stamina longa tuae.

Neapoli pridie Kalendas martias 1451.

: XXXV :

Marrasii Siculi ad Alfonsum regem magnum.

Regibus Odrysii munuscula ferre solebant;
    Odrysiis reges munera magna dabant.
Unusquisque suas partes habuere decentes:
    Magna decent parvos parvula dona deos.
5 Alanum donare canem qui vult, dare mavult
    Non obscuri animi signa decora sui.
Alanum si dono canem tibi, tradere malo
    Ipse animi ingenui pignora tuta mei.
Saetigeros siquando sues hic dentibus ardens
10   Traxerit, esto memor pignoris ipse mei.

Neapoli xv Kalendas apriles 1451.

What more can one wish for? What more could they grant?
    The Fates have placed Fortune at the lovers' feet.
Divine maiden, fare well, and live happily under the care
    Of great Caesar; may the threads of your life be long.   20

Naples, February 28, 1451.

: XXXV :

From Marrasio Siculo to King Alfonso the Great

The Odrysians were wont to bring small gifts to their kings;
    Their kings would give large gifts to the Odrysians.
Each one played his proper part:
    Great gifts befit the gods, small gifts befit small men.
A man who wants to give a Scythian dog prefers to give   5
    Fitting marks of his noble spirit.
If I give a Scythian dog to you, I prefer to hand over
    Secure tokens of my gentlemanly spirit.
Whenever this eager beast drags boars with his teeth,
    Be mindful, sire, of my pledge.   10

Naples, March 21, 1451.

: XXXVI :

Grassiae Hispani strenuissimi equitis infausta mors.

Montibus Hispanis Romam descendit et, omni
    Deleta macula corporis atque animae,
Grassias validus Siculas discurrit ad oras;
    Cui non fere frui, Fata videre sinunt,
5 Praesulis Alfonsi frater dilectior inter
    Quattuor et tali dignus amore fuit.
Laetos quinque dies voluit Fortuna videre
    Atque omnes maestos pessima morte dies.
Venatu leporum lustrata est vallis; ovantes
10   Divertit cunctos sus ferus atque fugit.
Cornipedem stimulat, quassans venabula dextra,
    Primus Grassias insequiturque suem.
Intrepidus pungebat equum, quo more solebat
    Per medias acies ferro aperire vias.
15 Fortis eques sonipesque prius cecidere ruentes
    Saxa super lati fluminis alta parum.
Stratus humi sonipes confractis dentibus ictu
    Contremuit nequiens inde movere pedes.
Ille repente cadit subitoque infringitur illi
20   Sinciput et lympha est sanguine rubra suo.
Illum illum excipiunt famuli lacrimasque dolentes
    Germano effundunt; cogitat unus opem.
Solicitus praeses Regalis Montis in urbem
    Cursores agiles ipse volare facit:
25 Praecipites veniant medici qui vulnera curent,
    Docta manus quibus est ossa secare loco,
Expertusque senex, quo non prudentior alter,

: XXXVI :

The unfortunate death of that most strenuous knight,
Garcia the Spaniard.

Garcia came down to Rome from the Spanish mountains,
    And with every stain of body and soul removed,
Set off in good health for the shores of Sicily.
    He was the brother of Archbishop Alfonso, most beloved
Of his four brothers, and well worthy of such love,   5
    Whom the Fates allowed to see but seldom enjoy.
Fortune willed that he see five happy days,
    And every one a day of mourning through his terrible death.
They were crossing a valley, hunting rabbits; a wild boar
    Diverted all the shouting hunters and fled.   10
Garcia in the lead spurs his horse and, brandishing a spear
    In his right hand, rushes upon the boar.
Fearlessly he pricks his horse, the way he used to
    When clearing a path through the ranks with his sword.
The brave knight fell and his horse before him,   15
    Collapsing too hard on the deep rocks of a wide river.
Stretched on the ground, his teeth broken by the blow,
    The horse trembled, unable to move his feet further.
The man falls suddenly and immediately his skull
    Is broken and the waters turn red with his blood.   20
Him, him! the servants pick up with aching hearts, shedding
    Tears for the brother; one thinks to call for help.
Anxiously the archbishop of Monreale himself orders
    Swift runners to race to the city:
Let doctors come swiftly who can heal his wounds,   25
    Doctors whose hands are skilled at cutting bones.
There was an experienced old man, wiser than all the rest,

Natura et iuvenis primus in arte fuit.
Hi pellem cum carne secant atque ungue latentes
30   Fissuras nudant, ut resecare queant.
Serra rotunda suos ubi fecerat undique gyros,
    Ossibus extractis facta fenestra fuit,
Quae vomuit calidam ferventis sanguinis undam
    Foedantem vultus, tempora et ora, suos.
35 Panniculi duri facies est visa nigella,
    Quae numquam roseo melle reducta fuit.
Hoc animadverso atque aliis sine nube revisis,
    Ex medicis primus talia verba tulit:
'Assidua cum febre rigor stridorque molaris,
40   Mollities lateris panniculusque niger
Vulneribus magnis capitis, sua cruda labella
    Cum fuerint, refero proxima signa neci.
Hactenus occului germani fratris amati
    Mortem, nec volui flere reflere tuum.
45 Non opus est medicis sed pallinctoribus atris:
    Haec tibi sint curae sacra, colossus honos.
Septima lux clari germani claudet ocellos,
    Extinctura suos, gaudia et arma, iocos.'
Praecipit exsequias, fraternum funus honorat
50   Alfonsus magnis sumptibus et precibus.
Ardent innumerae taedae, stant lumina circum
    Cerea, quae magno principe digna forent.
Et luctu et planctu cuncti flevere gementes
    Et veras lacrimas fundere quisque potest.
55 Illi morte nihil, vita nil defuit illi;
    Defuit hoc unum, vivere, morte sua.
Magnificus sumptus medicis non defuit atque
    Magna sepulturae gloria honorque fuit.
Eripuit validam mors immatura iuventam;
60   Coelum animam, corpus regia busta tenent.

And a young man, first in skill from Nature's gifts.
They cut back the skin along with the flesh and lay bare
    Hidden fissures with their nails, so as to cut them off.   30
After the saw has made its round cuts on all sides,
    A burr hole was made by extracting bits of bone;
From the vent poured out a hot wave of seething blood,
    Befouling his face, his temples, and mouth.
The appearance of the inner membrane seemed rather dark,   35
    Which never was reduced by rosy hydromel.
This being observed, when other things were clearly seen,
    The first of the doctors spoke these words:
"Since there is stiffness, grinding of teeth with constant fever,
    Softness on the flanks, and the inner membrane is black   40
Owing to his great head wounds, bloody on the edges,
    I deduce the signs of approaching death.
Till now I have concealed the death of your dear brother
    Nor did I want to weep in response to your weeping.
There is no need for doctors, only pallbearers in black: 45
    These rites must be your concern, this colossal duty.
The seventh day will close your noble brother's eyes,
    It will extinguish his pleasures, arms and jests."
Alfonso gives instructions for the funeral and honors
    His brother's rites with great expense and many prayers.   50
Innumerable torches burn, waxen lights which would be
    Worthy of a great prince stand all around.
All the mourners weep with grief and lamentations
    And whoever is able to pour out true tears.
Lacking nothing in life, he lacked nothing in death.   55
    Through his death he lacked just one thing—living.
No expense was spared on his doctors' fees,
    And great glory and honor attended his burial.
Premature death carried off a strong young man:
    Heaven holds his soul, a royal tomb his flesh.   60

: XXXVII :

Ad praestantissimum virum dominum Alfonsum
Montis Regalis praesulem.

Desidia affectum non me culpare licebit;
  Quartana oppressum dicere quisque potest.
Desidia affectum non me admirabere, namque
  Causa mei reditus tardior ipsa fuit.
5 Me thalamo tenuisset hebes quartana iacentem
  Sex menses, totidem nos adeundo dies.
Nunc ego praecipiti veniam, sine tempora, penna,
  Nam velo et remis nostra carina volat.
Grassiae infaustam volui describere mortem,
10 Ut tibi pergratum collibitumque fuit,
Interitumque suum placuit flevisse; triumphum
  Scribere spero tuum et si qua trophaea manent.

: XXXVIII :

Grassiae Hispani strenuissimi equitis epitaphium.

Montibus Hispanis Romam descendit et, omni
  Deleta macula corporis atque animae,
Grassias validus Siculas discurrit ad oras:
  Germanum et sedem Fata videre sinunt.
5 Quinque dies risit Fortuna, invidit honori:
  Cornipedis casu fortis ad ima ruit.
Scissa fronte suum plures videre cerebrum,
  Unde obiit, vita nunc meliore fruens.

: XXXVII :

To that most excellent of men, Lord Alfonso,
Archbishop of Monreale.

It's not right to blame me for being overcome with sloth,
    Anyone can say he was laid low by quartan fever.
You shouldn't wonder that I've been overcome with sloth,
    For that *was* the reason my return was rather slow.
A protracted quartan fever kept me lying in bed   5
    For six months, by coming to me for as many days.
Now I will come on swift wings; allow me time,
    For my ship is flying with both sail and oars.
I wanted to describe the unlucky death of Garcia,
    An offering most welcome and pleasing to you,   10
And it made you happy to weep for his passing; I hope
    To write of your triumph and whatever trophies await you.

: XXXVIII :

An epitaph for that most vigorous knight, Garcia of Spain.

Garcia came down to Rome from the Spanish mountains,
    And with every stain of body and soul removed,
Set off in good health for the shores of Sicily.
    The Fates allow him to see his brother and his palace.
For five days Fortune smiled, envying his glory: 5
    The brave man fell to the depths from a riding accident.
With his forehead smashed, many saw his brain.
    It caused his death; now he enjoys a better life.

: XXXIX :

Epitaphium eiusdem.

Romae habita venia, Siculis allabitur oris
    Grassias; fratrem fata videre sinunt.
Impavidus stimulavit equum, quo more solebat
    Per medios hostes ferro aperire vias,
5 Insequiturque suem quassans venabula dextra
    Et sonipes cecidit et cadit altus eques.
Eripuit validam mors immatura iuventam;
    Coelum animam, corpus regia busta tenent.

: XL :

Epitaphium eiusdem.

Grassiam Hispanum mors accelerata vocavit:
    Praesulis Alfonsi frater amatus erat.
Romae habita venia, Siculis allabitur oris;
    Germanum et sedem fata videre sinunt.
5 Intrepidus stimulavit equum, quo more solebat
    Per medias acies ferro aperire vias.
Fortis eques sonipesque prius cecidere ruentes;
    Coelum animam, corpus regia busta tenent.

⁚ XXXIX ⁚

An epitaph for the same man.

Having obtained pardon in Rome, Garcia sails to the shores
    Of Sicily; the Fates allow him to see his brother.
Fearlessly he pricks his horse, the way he used to
    When clearing a path through the ranks with his sword.
He follows hard on the boar, brandishing a spear in his hand,   5
    The horse fell and the lofty knight falls also.
Premature death carried off a strong young man:
    Heaven holds his soul, a royal tomb his flesh.

⁚ XL ⁚

An epitaph for the same man.

A precipitate death has summoned Garcia of Spain:
    He was the beloved brother of our king Alfonso.
Having been pardoned in Rome, he sails for Sicilian shores;
    The fates allow him to see his brother and his palace.
Fearlessly he pricks his horse, the way he used to   5
    When clearing a path through the ranks with his sword.
The brave knight fell and his horse before him.
    Heaven holds his soul, a royal tomb his flesh.

: XLI :

Epigramma pro Gallina nostro ex Cosinano fonte.

Pauca licet numero, dum sint victura per annos
    Innumeros, certe carmina multa facis;
Carmina nulla facis, quamvis tot milia fingas,
    Si sint ad paucos interitura dies.

: XLII :

Epitaphium domini Nicolai Tudisci
Panhormi antistitis, iuris pontificii principis.

Morte tua canon, leges et iura Quiritum
    Occubuere: tibi contumulata iacent.
Tu Nicolaus eras Tudisco a sanguine natus,
    Panhormi antistes, sed Cathinensis eras.
5 Eugenio et Basilea concordi lite ruebat
    Nostra fides; steterat, te duce, concilium.
Nominis et tituli cumulos et laudis adeptus,
    Unde tuum texit rubra tiara caput.

: XLI :

An epigram for our Gallina from the Cosinano fountain.

Although they are few in number, you surely are creating
    Many poems, since they will live for countless years.
You are writing no poems, although you fashion thousands,
    If they are going to perish in a few days.

: XLII :

An epitaph for Lord Niccolò de' Tudeschi,
Archbishop of Palermo, foremost in papal law.

With your death the canon, laws, and rights of the Quirites
    Go to the grave; they all lie buried with you.
You were Niccolò, born of the blood of the Tudeschi,
    Archbishop of Palermo, though you were from Catania.
Our faith was collapsing in quarrels between Eugene and   5
    Basel; under your leadership the Council stood firm.
You amassed a mountain of fame, renown, and praise;
    Hence the red biretta crowned your head.

: XLIII :

Tetrasticon ad Marcum de Grandis.

Marce, tuum tristi praesta de Tristibus, oro,
   Nasonem; titulo nam mihi compar opus.
Lectio iocunda est et quicquid continet aptum
   Et faciem atque oculos exhilarare meos.

: XLIV :

Subitus interitus Pinae
puellae pudicissimae.

Pina, prothomedici coniunx et filia, morte
   Interii subita, fulminis icta foco.
Non me combussit, membris sed flamma pepercit:
   Ista pudicitiae signa fuere meae.
5   Petro Alisandro cum sim disiuncta marito,
   Non doleo, vita cum meliore fruar.
Te, pater Antoni, peto; vir natique valete
   Quattuor; ex utero nata puella vale.

⁖ XLIII ⁖

A quatrain to Marco de' Grandi.

Marco, please, lend your copy of Ovid's *Tristia* to someone sad:
    For, by its title, the work will make me a fine companion.
Reading it over is delightful; everything is neatly said;
    And it makes glad my countenance and cheers my eyes.

⁖ XLIV ⁖

On the sudden death of Pina,
purest of young women.

I, Pina, wife and daughter of the Protomedico died
    A sudden death, struck by a bolt of lightning.
The flame did not burn me up, but spared my limbs:
    Those were the emblems of my chastity.
Although I've been severed from Pietro Alixandro my husband,   5
    I do not grieve, for I enjoy a better life.
I am seeking you, my father Antonio; goodbye, my husband
    And four sons; farewell, daughter of my womb.

: XLV :

Ad Avanellam.

Tris concede, precor, fuerant hi quinque, libellos;
    Quartana oppressus quaerito namque iocos.
Ut cibus in longo placidus fastidit edentem
    Usu, sic rarus saepe placere solet.

: XLVI :

Ad sanctissimum dominum nostrum Nicolaum Papam V.

Edita quae teneris, sed non limata, vetustis
    Annis non puduit scribere nostra manum,
Haec sunt, ut videas quando ingrata otia serpunt
    Aut cum te fessum seria multa tenent.
5 Ferrea vis nulli, nulli est sua ferrea cura;
    Saepe etiam vincit ferrea cuncta labor.
Si prodesse negant, se delectare fatentur
    Atque animo lasso gaudia ferre tuo.
Orbis habet quaecumque queunt prodesse volenti
10 Et mala, quae invito grandia saepe nocent.
Quis poterit cunctos animi vitare labores?
    Quis poterit nutu volvere cuncta suo?
Utile laetitiam, pariunt nocumenta dolores
    Maestitiamque simul nocte dieque suam.
15 Hos auferre potest festivus sermo; iocosum
    Eloquium et si qua est lingua faceta valet.

: XLV :

To Avanella.

Please let me have the three little books (there *were* five of
    them!).
    I'm laid up with quartan fever and am looking for some fun.
Just the way plain food, with long use, disgusts the eater,
    So exquisite foods are often wont to please.

: XLVI :

To our most holy lord, Pope Nicholas V.

These poems of mine, published long ago in my tender years,
    But never polished, did not shame my hand to write.
Look at them when unwelcome idleness drags on,
    Or when you're tired and need distraction from serious affairs.
None of them is hard to master, none presents hard cares,   5
    Often work defeats all things hard too.
If they deny their usefulness, they claim to delight,
    And to bring joy to your weary mind.
The world contains everything that can benefit the willing
    And evils, great ones, that often harm the unwilling.   10
Who could avoid all wear and tear of spirit?
    Who could direct everything according to his own will?
The useful gives birth to happiness, and pain to harms
    And to its companion, gloom, by night and day.
Such things gay speech can take away; a well-told joke   15
    And a witty tongue, if you have one, can do so too.

Dixero pace sua, non omnia seria coelo;
    Saepe etenim iocos gaudet habere deos.
Utile quid coelo citharae resonantis amoenum
20   Permodulare sonum et thura Sabaea dare?
Quid prosint etiam fumosi thuris honores,
    Pallia texta auro et murice tincta Deo?
Delectant pia thura focis levioribus usta
    Et quae circumdat plurima gemma togam.
25 Sed tu, qui superos omnis veneraris et ornas
    Templa Dei et cunctis antelocanda iubes,
Cum te primum habeat divini cultus honoris,
    More suo placeat dicta iocosa cani.
Psalterio aut cithara si quando propheta canebat,
30   Nonne Deus dixit: 'Fila canora placent'?
Frangitur interdum, qui semper tenditur, arcus;
    Dextera tendentis fessa reperta fuit.
Interdum requie ac interdum lassa labore
    Perniciosa suis membra fuere viris.
35 Utitur alterno motu requieque decenti,
    Qui sua sana modo pectora habere cupit.
Laetatur luditque sua perdice, sed alter
    Bellatorem Opici scalpere Muris ovat.
Plurima habere petas, quae te iocunda salutant,
40   Cum solus curas totius orbis habes;
Hinc †mutetat† tuos, illinc Perusina labores
    Laetitia expellet, quando molesta subis.
Hinc tua vis primo poterit compescere fluctus;
    Quid mea, quam nullum robur habere puto?
45 Diversas epulas gustusque oculusque requirunt;
    Saepe novella placent, saepe vetusta placent.
Mitia poma solent prius immatura placere;
    Dulcia vina probant, Pontica saepe probant.
Cum variare ‹velis›, quae possunt tollere causas

I'll say it, by your grace: in heaven not everything is serious,
    And indeed even the gods enjoy jokes.
Why is it useful to heaven to play delightful music
    Of the tuneful lyre or to offer incense from Saba?   20
How are gifts of smoking incense, cloaks woven with gold
    And dyed with purple profitable to God?
The gods delight in incense burned piously on less serious altars.
    And in a mass of gems that borders a toga.
But you who adore all the gods above and adorn   25
    God's churches and bid them be valued before all else,
Though the worship of God may claim your first loyalty,
    May you enjoy too in its way the joking talk of an old man.
Whenever the prophet would sing with psaltery or lyre,
    Hasn't God said, "Tuneful strings please me"?   30
Sometimes the bow that is always stretched breaks;
    The hand of the bowman was found to be tired.
Limbs sometimes grow lax from rest, sometimes with toil,
    And those lax limbs proved destructive for men.
The man who wants now to have a sound heart   35
    Alternates appropriately between motion and rest.
One man delights in and plays with his partridge, but another
    Celebrates with his burin a warrior of the Oscan Mus.
May you seek out many pleasures that will keep you well,
    Since you alone hold the cares of the whole world.   40
On this side the joy of [. . .], on that, of Perugia
    Will dispel your cares when you suffer distress.
On this side your vigor will be able first to check its flow.
    What about mine, which I think to have no force?
The taste and the eye require different dishes;   45
    New fare often pleases, but often too does old.
Sweet fruits are wont to please before those unripe;
    Sweet wines win approval, but so often do Pontine crus.
When you want variation that can dispel the causes

50   Langoris, nugas experiare meas.
Ut cibus in longo placidus fastidit edentem
    Usu, sic rarus saepe placere solet.
Quandoque in pretio est lauta inter fercula blitus;
    Dulcius efficiunt altera vitra merum.

Romae decimo septimo Kalendas iunias 1452.

⋮ XLVII ⋮

Marrasii Siculi doctrina carminum et versuum,
qui tali nomine nuncupari merentur,
ad sanctissimum dominum nostrum Nicolaum papam V.

Accipe primitias et delibamina quaedam
    Temporis adversi quae meus annus habet.
Insomnis intus febres agitare solebam
    Carmina, quae somnum surripuere meum;
5   Surreptumque suis sic infixere medullis,
    Ut dormire magis quam vigilare velint.
Si somno careant aegri, si languida volvunt
    Membra thoro et fessis vix datur ulla quies,
Carmina, quae tali sunt evigilata cubili,
10   Nescio si versus nomen habere queant;
Si non illud habent, ea somnolenta vocentur,
    Donec eis dabitur pervigilare nimis.
Luciferi ante ortus experrectura cubantes
    Carmina si fuerint, vivere posse puta;
15   Si nequeunt vigilare neque expergiscitur ullus
    Sensus acutus, hebes sed gravat illa sopor,
Torpida ad interitum ibunt perniciemque latentem

Of weariness, give my trifles a try.   50
Just the way plain food, with long use, disgusts the eater,
    So exquisite foods are often wont to please.
Sometimes amid sumptuous courses it's spinach that's prized;
    Other glasses makes unmixed wine all the sweeter.

                        Rome, May 15, 1452.

                        : XLVII :

The teaching of Marrasio Siculo to our most holy lord,
Nicholas V, about poems and verses
that deserve to be called by such a name.

Please accept some firstfruits and foretastes
    Which my year retains from a time of adversity.
From within my sleepless fevers I used to work out
    Poems, and these would steal away my sleep.
And they so drove the stolen sleep into their marrow   5
    That they would prefer to sleep rather than stay awake.
If the sick lack sleep, if they roll their weary limbs
    Upon their bed and get no rest in their weakness,
I don't know if poems composed in the night watches
    On such a bed can truly have the name of verse;   10
If not verses, let them be called "drowsies"
    Until they're allowed to stay up too late at night.
If poems are able to awaken those who lie sleeping
    Before the daystar rises, believe that they can live on;
If they can't stay awake and no sharp feeling   15
    Awakens them, but dull stupor weighs them down,
They will go sluggish to their deaths and are going to suffer

Sunt habitura, crocum aut dilacerata tegent.
Carminibus cunctis non sat vigilare, sed illa
20   Morte silente decet sollicitare viros.
Alliciant cantu pueros iuvenesque senesque,
    Nec pigeat cithara detenuisse deum.
Taedeat illa tamen si non surrexerit ullus
    Ante diem et mentem sollicitarit ovans.
25 Talia ni fuerint, tinea rodentur et inde
    Iam sunt ad paucos interitura dies.
Illis vigilia est opus et mihi claudere ocellos,
    Si quod honoratum nomen habere volunt.
Lapsibus oppositis nos aegrotare videmur:
30   Haec perimit somnus, me vigilare nimis.
Et pretiosa mihi medicina est morbus eorum;
    Qui mihi morbus obest est sibi tota salus.
Una ope tu poteris binis succurrere morbis:
    Aufer eis somnos, quos mihi cede, precor.
35 Si mihi, dive Pater, dulcem quietumque somnum
    Aut si oculis nostris otia tuta dabis,
Incolumis qui te colit et tua numina adorat,
    Ingenium et mores integra semper erunt.
Grata quies oculos poterit submittere nostros,
40   Versibus unde queat nomen adesse suum.
Tunc potero cantare tuas per saecula laudes,
    Et memor et gratus muneris ipse tui.

Hidden destruction, or be ripped up to wrap saffron.
It is not enough for all poems just to be awake,
    But it becomes them to wake men from silent death.   20
Let them lure boys, youths, and old men by their song,
    Nor let it displease them to entertain a god with the lyre.
Yet let it bore them if no one has risen
    Before dawn, and, exulting, roused his mind.
If they aren't like that, they will be nibbled by the worm   25
    And they will then die a few days after.
If they want to have some respectable name,
    Their job is to stay awake; mine to close my eyes.
By opposite weaknesses, it seems, we get sick:
    Sleep kills these poems, and sleeplessness me.   30
Their sickness to me is precious medicine:
    The illness that harms me is full health to them.
With one act of aid you can relieve twin diseases:
    Please take sleep from them and give it to me.
If, Holy Father, you give me sweet sleep and quiet   35
    Or if you grant secure rest to my eyes,
I shall survive to venerate you and your divine spirit;
    Your mind and your mores shall ever be whole.
Welcome rest will be able to close my eyes
    So that their own fame may be able to support my verses.   40
Then shall I be able to sing your praise forever,
    Both mindful and grateful for your generous gift.

APPENDIX I

: I :

Ad Carolum Regem Francorum.

Sis licet invictus multaque in proelia victor,
Carole Gallorum rex inclite, sit licet ingens
gloria gestorum; turmas ductante puella
fregeris et duces, qui te regnumque petebant,
5   ista tamen longos non est mansura per annos
fama, pium si non invenerit ipsa poetam.
Desinat Eacides, qui vicerat Hectora Trohem,
nomen honorati dudum labatur Ulixis,
ni quibus in rebus fuerint scripsisset Homerus.
10 Egregius pereat, Musa reticente Maronis,
Troius Aeneas, pietate insignis et armis.
Omnia nata cadunt, nata omnia surripit aetas,
nascimur ad mortem tacitisque senescimus horis.
Carmina sola necem possunt depellere: magnos
15 eripuere viros a mortis dente Camene.
Nulla potest vires effringere carminis aetas:
immortalis erit, nullis obscurus in annis,
qui sua facta dabit numeris cantanda poetum.
Ergo tibi et sancte gestorum consule fame:

APPENDIX I

ILLUSTRATIVE TEXTS

: I :

Poem of Enea Silvio Piccolomini to Charles VII of France
urging him to appoint a poet laureate
and praising Marrasio
[July 1429][1]

To Charles, King of the French.

Even if you are invincible and the victor in many battles,
O Charles, illustrious king of the French, even if great
Is the glory of your deeds; and if, with the guidance of a girl,[2]
You scatter the troops and warlords who menace your kingdom,
Nevertheless, this fame of yours will not last   5
Through the long years if it does not find a devoted poet.
Achilles, who beat Trojan Hector would have been forgotten,
The name of honored Ulysses would have disappeared long ago,
If Homer had not written of their deeds.
Trojan Aeneas, famous for piety and courage,   10
Would have perished had Vergil's Muse remained silent.
All that is born dies, time takes away all things,
We are born to die and grow old in the silent hours.
Only poetry can drive off death: the Muses snatch
Great men from the teeth of Death.   15
No passage of time can break the power of poetry:
Whoever entrusts his deeds to be sung in the poets' verse
Will be immortal, and his fame will never grow dark.
Therefore care for yourself and for the holy fame of your deeds:

20 quere tuas aliquem valeat qui scribere laudes
    eximias, nomenque tuum claramque tuorum
    et gentem et stirpem, Troiano a sanguine cretam.
    Est opere precium belli cognoscere quales
    scribentes habeat virtus spectata domique,
25 indigno et gracili non committenda poetae.
    Prestat ames aliquos, qui munus Apolline dignum
    efficiant, studioque petant Helicona virentem,
    assiduo et tenui deducta poemata filo
    reddere promittant, et vatibus addere calcar.
30 Hos vocites, et egere vetes, et carmina cogas
    edere, vel priscis non aspernanda Latinis.
    Quis tamen has tantas audebit sumere curas?
    Quis dabit ingenium vivax et ad omnia tutum,
    ut possit patulas implere legentibus aures?
35 Sunt qui magna canunt dominorum bella ducumque
    aeternamque valent homini concedere vitam.
    Qualis ad Italiam Siculis Antonius oris
    venit ut illustris perstringeret acta Philippi;
    Marrasiusque simul, cui non vetuere paterne
40 Sicelides Musae pretendere ad ubera guttur.
    Quin etiam Vegius, quem divae aluere sorores
    Pieriae, missus caelesti munere nobis;
    atque alii, quorum sunt nomina nota leporque
    dicendi: hos tecum conducere sit tibi curae,
45 hortari ut scribant, concedere multa laborum
    praemia: te aeternum facient caeloque locabunt.

Seek out someone who is able to write praises   20
Of your glory, your reputation and illustrious family and
Your ancestors, descended of Trojan blood.
It is worth recognizing the kind of writers whom
Your virtue, conspicuous in war and peace, should have;
It should not be entrusted to a weak and worthless poet.   25
It is better that you love those who write things worthy of
      Apollo,
And with constant effort seek out the shade of Helicon,
And promise to yield poetry that is polished and refined,
And it's better that you spur your poets on.
Summon them, don't let them feel want, and make them write   30
Poems that the ancient Latin writers would not despise.
But who will dare take on such great responsibilities?
Who has a lively intelligence, reliable for every task,
That can fill the gaping ears of his readers?
There are poets who sing the great wars of lords and generals   35
And are able to grant eternal life to men.
Poets like Antonio,[3] who came to Italy from Sicilian shores
To collect the deeds of the illustrious Filippo,
And at the same time Marrasio, whose throat the paternal
Muses of Sicily did not refuse to suck at their breasts.   40
Or Vegio,[4] whom the divine Pierian sisters nurtured,
Sent to us as a gift of the gods;
And others, whose names and verbal grace are known.
These you should make it your concern to have with you,
Encourage them to write, give great rewards for their labors: 45
They can make you live forever and raise you to the stars.

: II :

Marrasius Siciliensis Antonio Panhormitae
poetae clarissimo s.p.d.

1 Sarcinulas tuas antequam e Senis discederem ad te misi; molestum
mihi quidem est te non habuisse. Eas enim, ut rem a principio
audies, Francius Ianuam misit. Literas quibus significabam sarci-
nulas tibi assignandas esse Francius una cum sarcinulis non misit.
Mercator Ianuensis illas Pisas remisit, et nunc vero per Paulum
tuum Castagnolum ad te venient. Scripsi Francio, ut eas Paulo
daret; item Augustino nostro, ut Francium certiorem redderet, ut
Pauli nomine cuidam de Borromeis Pisis traderet. Augustinus
hactenus silentium agit. Rescripsi per Sabinum nostrum. Dabitur
opera et diligentia per Paulum tuum Castagnolum ut ad te ve-
niant.

2 Is te colit et vehementer amat; is fortunas tuas mihi aperuit:
numquam ipse ego dubius fui quin te Dux magnificaret atque
amaret. Evades, credo equidem, talis vir qualem te optat Marra-
sius: dignitas enim maxima et honorum cumulus non tibi defutu-
rus est.

3 Postremo te oro, per immortalem animum tuum et amicitiam
nostram, ut semel ad me scribas eo pacto et ea lege ut non 'quam
raptim' ad me scribas. Omnes enim epistolae tuae plenae atque
imbutae sunt et 'quam raptim' et 'quam raptissime.' Misi ad te ob-
trectatorum versus; non respondes? Te oro non obtumescas, ne

: II :

Marrasio's first letter to Panormita in Padua
12 March [1430]⁵

Marrasio Siculo sends warm greetings to the most
renowned poet Antonio Panormita.

Before I left Siena I sent you your packages; it annoys me that you   1
don't have them. To go back to the beginning, Francia⁶ sent them
to Genoa. He did not send with them the letter in which I said
that the packages were your packages. The Genoese merchant sent
them back to Pisa, and now those things will come to you through
your friend Paolo Castagnolo.⁷ I wrote Francia that they be given
to Paolo; similarly to our friend Agostino that he inform Francia
that they should be handed over in Paul's name to a certain repre-
sentative of the Borromei at Pisa.⁸ So far Agostino has kept silent.
I wrote again through our friend Sabino. A careful effort will be
made so that they will get to you through your friend Paolo Cast-
agnoli.

The latter cherishes you and loves you dearly; he revealed your   2
good fortune to me.⁹ I was never in doubt that the duke would
prize you and care for you. I truly believe you will end up the very
sort of man Marrasius wishes you will be, and that the highest
rank and a heap of honors will be yours.

Lastly, I beg you, by your immortal soul and our friendship,   3
that you write just once to me, under this arrangement and rule,
that you not write to me "very quickly." All your letters are full,
indeed drenched, both with "very quick" and "very, very quick." I
sent you some verses written by your detractors; why don't you
answer? I beg you not to get swollen up, lest I waste away and
starve out of hunger for your letters. I am sending some verses to

tuarum literarum inedia tabescam atque esuriam. Mitto aliquot versus Maffeo Veggio, quos emenda eique tua lima tornatos da.

4   Vale et Ergotilem nostrum salvum facias meis verbis. Karolus Arretinus hesterna die ostendit mihi trecentos versus ab se traslatos ex Homero de ranarum et murum acerrimo bello et quidem elegantes, et nisi Paulus ad te volarat misissem. Versus promissos ab te mihi hactenus sentio esse rariores corvis albis et cignis nigris.

Vale et me ama. Ex Florentia XIII martii.

: III :

Andreoccius Petruccius Senensis Barnabae suo salutem.

1 Quod Marrasius Siculus, amicus et familiaris meus, Senam iverit et incolumnis quidem, vehementer gaudeo et eo vehementius quod eum salvum venisse meis verbis illi fueris congratulatus. Marrasium videre cupio in mirum modum, cupio colloqui, amplecti denique et id quidem ad satietatem, si fieri possit, verum id quom nequit, saltem ad lassitudinem. Vellem hinc mihi discedere liceret, perreptarem totam urbem uti illum convenirem, perreptarem — inquam — etiam, si opus esset, ad multam noctem, quoad desiderium illius quod me tenet explerem. Attamen me hinc abire edictum prohibet, quod nosti quam minax sit; itaque convenire illum, si vellem, meus non est arbitratus.

Maffeo Vegio, which when they are returned, please correct and polish with your skill.[10]

Goodbye and greet my friend Ergotiles for me.[11] Yesterday 4 Carlo Aretino showed me 300 very elegant lines which he had translated from Homer about a ferocious battle between frogs and mice, and I would love to have sent them to you except that Paolo was in a rush.[12] At this point I believe that verses from you to me are rarer than white crows or black swans.

Goodbye and love me. From Florence, March 12.

: III :

Andreoccio Petrucci to Barnaba Pannilini,
A letter discussing Marrasio
(14 May 1430)[13]

Andreoccio Petrucci sends greetings to his Barnaba of Siena.

I'm delighted that Marrasio Siculo, my friend and companion, has 1 gone to Siena, and in safety too, the more so as you will convey my congratulations to him on his safe arrival. I have a wonderful desire to see Marrasio, I want to converse with him and finally to embrace him to the point of satiety, if possible — but since it's not possible, at least embrace him to the point of exhaustion. I wish I might leave this place, creep around the whole city to meet him — creep around, I say, if necessary, even late into the night, so as to satisfy the desire for him that obsesses me. However, an edict prohibits me from leaving here, and you know how menacing it is; so I've decided it's not possible, if I wished to, to meet him.

2   Quare, si vis mihi gratum facere, si vis omnia erga me studia tua atque offitia gratiora esse—quanquam sint gratissima—effice ut Marrasium, plus quam animi dimidium mei, videre possim.

Vale, suavissime atque requies mea. Quam raptim, pridie Idus maias.

<h2 style="text-align:center">: IV :</h2>

Marrasius Siciliensis Antonio Panhormitae s.p.d.

1   Vellem abs te intelligere quid illud est, quod tuo me ex animo obliteravit. Quamquam enim ad te frequentissimas mittam, tu eas videris nihili facere; quid istoc sit ignarus sum. Fortunas tuas mihi aperias; ego medius fidius ita his laetor veluti meis. Tu omnem vitam taciturnitate consumis, me perdis atque enecas. Rem omnem a principio insinues: quam vitam ducis et quo sub caelo vivis et quo lare quove principe scribis; nec me tuarum voluntatum expertem facias.

2   Indicium mihi est sempiternum silentium in carminibus tuis, ita ut videar bellum tecum habuisse. Si me amas, ut te ego ipse et

Hence, if you would do me a favor, if you would have all your 2
goodwill and good services to me be still more appreciated — although they are extremely appreciated — arrange it that I can see
Marrasio, who is more than half of my mind.[14]

Farewell, sweetest of men and my repose. As quickly as possible, May 14.

∶ IV ∶

Marrasio's second letter to Panormita, written from Padua
[late 1430/July 1432][15]

Marrasius the Sicilian sends warm greetings to Antonio Panormita.

I would like to know from you what it is that has effaced me from 1
your soul. For, although I send letters to you very often, you seem
to do nothing about them; I don't know why that is so. You might
explain your good fortune to me; so help me God I would delight
in it as if it were mine. You eat up all my life with your silence, you
ruin and destroy me. Introduce me to everything from the beginning — what life you are leading, under what sky you are living, in
whose household and for what prince you are writing — don't shut
me out of your plans and desires.

The everlasting silence in your poetry is a sign that I seem to 2
have had a war with you. If you love me, as I myself extol you and

nomen tuum apud omnes celebro, abrumpas mores tuos in scribendo et me soleris carminibus tuis. Patavium urbem spurcissimam et civitatum faecem habito; hoc ad mearum infelicitatum cumulum accessit. Postremo ego ⟨a⟩ te vellem meis verbis salvum facias ⟨Vegium et⟩ domino Catoni viro praestantissimo me committas.

Vale et me ama.

: V :

Aurispa Marrasio.

Non me germani, patriae nec dulcis amores
Sollicitant; me solus habes, mea pectora versas
Solus et ante oculos noctuque dieque pererras.

: VI :

Leonardus A⟨rretinus?⟩ Marrasio Siculo s.d.

1 Vix dici posset quam litterae tuae gratissimae fuerint, praesertim longo sane intervallo ad nos scriptae. Avidus quippe cognoscendi eram quis esset status rerum tuarum quaeve fortuna post discessum a nobis tuum consecuta fuisset. Quod et per litteras tuas et

your name with everyone, break out of your accustomed way by writing and comfort me with your poems. I am living in Padua, the filthiest of towns and the shit of city-states; it only adds to the heap of my unhappiness. Lastly, I wish you would send my greetings to Vegio and that you would put me in contact with that most excellent man, Master Cato.[16]

Goodbye and love me.

: V :

Aurispa to Marrasio
[after 1437?][17]

My brethren, my homelands,[18] my sweet amours
Do not move me; you alone possess me, you alone stir
My heart, and pass endlessly before my eyes day and night.

: VI :

Undated letter to Marrasio,
dubiously ascribed to Leonardo Bruni
[1442/44][19]

Leonardo [of Arezzo?] sends greetings to Marrasio Siculo.

One can scarcely say how very pleasing your letters have been to me, most especially because they were written after such a long time. Indeed, I was eager to know how things stood with you and what luck attended you after your leaving us. Now both through your letters and through a long conversation about you with my

per longa colloquia de te cum M. nostro habita intellexi. Ea nempe tibi adesse puto in ipsa patria tua, quibus alius quidem libentissime acquiesceret; te autem politioribus studiis ac moribus, ut ita dixerim, elegantioribus assuetum ingens desiderium tenet primarum conversationum amicorum ac familiarium tuorum, nec sane immerito tales te viri nobiles ac tam egregii per Italiam amaverunt. Sed, ut inquit ille sapiens, contentum esse rebus suis maximae sunt certissimaeque divitiae et apud Graecos usurpatur illa sententia: 'Sparta tibi patria contigit, eam conserva.' Nec eo ista ut, si quid melius et honorabilius tibi oblatum sit, non accipias, sed ut, dum in patria manes, non moleste degas.

2   Nostra autem hic talia sunt ut, praesens si esses, non difficulter, ut opinor, te promoveremus. Tu enim praesentia tua nos plurimum adiuvares; absentem vero vocare ad aliquos honoris gradus difficillimum esset. De quibus multa cum M. egimus, ut uberius ex illo audire poteris.

Vale. Flor⟨entiae⟩. Vale iucundissime Marrasi.

friend M. I have come to know what has been happening. Of course I think that you have advantages in your very own country in which another might very easily take comfort; still a great yearning possesses you, accustomed as you are to more refined studies and more elegant manners, as it were, to hold converse with your earliest friends and acquaintances, and noble and very famous men throughout Italy have loved you, and quite rightly. But, as the wise man says, to be content with one's own life is the greatest and surest wealth,[20] and among the Greeks this maxim is frequently heard: "As homeland, Sparta is your lot, take care of her."[21] Not that you should not accept something better and more estimable if it is offered you, but that while you live in your homeland, you should live without distress.

In addition, our affairs here are such that, if you lived among us, we might advance you, so I believe, with no difficulty. You would help us greatly by your presence; absent, it is really extremely difficult to summon you to some position of honor. I have done much with M. about those things, which you can hear from him more fully.

Goodbye from Florence. Goodbye, most delightful Marrasio.

2

: VII :

Ad Marrasium.

En tibi mille, canam vatis tibi carmina mille
    Exsopi, si vis, carmina mille canam.
Traducam, quot sunt, eius monumenta relicta,
    Traducam et faciam cuncta latina sonent,
5 Dummodo non reprobes que iam vigilavimus hisce
    Noctibus, alterno facta latina pede,
Vel non displiceant tibi soli, o maxime vatum
    Marrasi, o animae dimidiumque meae!
Vale.

Τέλος καλός [*sic*].

: VIII :

Marrasii Siculi vatis epigramma ad Hieronymum.

Hieronime, altiloquos inter numerande poetas,
    Qui facis Aonia carmina digna lira,
Quor sinis ingenium diro torpere veterno,
    Despicis et nomen tollere ad astra tuum?
Armisonae refugis caelestia dona Minervae,
    Quae iubet extremo te procul esse rogo.

: VII :

Leonardo Dati's liminal poem to Marrasio
added to his translation of Aesop
[ca. 1443][22]

To Marrasio.

Look! I shall sing a thousand, thousand songs to you,
　　Songs of the bard Aesop, if you wish, I shall sing.
I shall translate his literary remains, as many as they be,
　　I shall translate and make them all sing in Latin,
So long as you will not condemn what has kept me awake
　　These last nights, poems in Latin elegiac verse,
Or so long as you alone like them, O greatest of bards,
　　Marrasio, O half of my soul![23]
　　Farewell.

A pretty ending.

: VIII :

An epigram of Marrasio for Girolamo Forti[24]

An epigram of the bard Marrasio of Sicily to Girolamo.

Girolamo, who will be counted among poets in the high style,[25]
　　You who write poems worthy of the Aeonian lyre,
Why do you abandon your mind to gloomy torpor,
　　And disdain to elevate your name to the stars?
You flee the celestial gifts of Minerva of the resounding arms,
　　Who orders you to keep yourself far from the funeral pyre.[26]

Incipe, Cyrraei plenus iam numine Phoebi,
    Martia Pieriis bella tonare modis;
Tristibus aut elegis teneros deflebis amores:
    Nam Citherea favet laudibus alma suis.
Est in te velox patriae facundia linguae,
    Dulcior ambrosia defluit ore lepos.
Excubat ante fores vivax tibi Fama superbas:
    Huic licet hospicii debita iura dare.
Sume fidem calamoque leves laurumque virentem,
    Qua tibi flaventes cingat Apollo comas.
Clare puer, Latiae decus immortale Camenae,
    Da mihi grata, precor, munera Pegasidum.

Finis.

Now inspired by Cirrhaean Apollo,[27] begin
    To chant the wars of Mars to the Muses' modes;
Or to weep for the loves of youth in sad elegies:
    For fond Venus favors those who praise her.
You possess the swift eloquence of your native tongue,
    A charm sweeter than ambrosia flows from your lips.
A living Fame keeps watch for you before her proud gates:
    Hers it is to grant the rights of hospitality you deserve.
Take up the lyre, the reed pipe and the green laurel
    Which Apollo may use to bind your flowing blond hair.
Illustrious boy, immortal ornament of Latin poetry,
    Give me, I pray, the welcome gifts of the Muses.

The end.

APPENDIX II

∴ I ∴

De ortu et vita larvarum poema ac
confutatio confutationis.

1 [1] *Larvati dicunt:* Expositio histrionum. Faciem Thespis primus faece perunxit ne agnosceretur, ut, dum scenae comediis aliisque gesticulationibus operam daret, sine rubore aptius et promptius persona exprimeretur. Post hunc venit Haeschylus, qui faecem amovit et larvam invenit. Post primam faeceam, invitati ut lautius per non faeceam res ageretur; hoc modo poetae, ut populo placerent, fabulas recitabant. Mortuis comicis poetis et quia scenae vacabant, larva prima poetarum mortua atque extincta fuit.

2 Ea vero quoque nostri temporis ex desidiosa Venere orta et nata est. Iuvenes enim negotiorum expertes, opibus abundantes et voluptatibus, gustui et tactui vitam suam dedicantes, hanc nostri temporis larvam parturierunt atque hoc novum genus aucupii enixi sunt, ut puellas sine rubore adire possint et vino, affatu, cantu aliisque provocationibus ad eorum animi voluptatem explendam aditum faciliorem haberent. Eam larvam me obscuris verbis

APPENDIX II

MARRASIO'S MASQUE IN FERRARA
(1433)

: I :

Marrasio's Commentary on
Carmina Varia XVII

A poem on the rise and life of masques,[1] and
a refutation of the refutation.[2]

[1] *The maskers speak:* Exposition of the actors. Thespis first 1
smeared the face with lees [of wine] so as not to be recognized, so
that, when devoting effort in a scene to comedic and other gesticu-
lations, the character might be expressed more fittingly and readily
without shame. After him came Aeschylus, who got rid of the lees
and invented the mask. After the first wine-stained one, [poets]
were urged to conduct matters with more refinement using masks
without stains; in this way poets used to recite their plays so as to
please the people. Once the comic poets died off and stages were
empty, the first masks of the poets died too and became extinct.[3]

But the masques of our time rose also and were born of an idle 2
Venus. For youths experienced in affairs, abounding in wealth and
pleasures, devoted to taste and touch, gave birth to the masque in
our time, and exerted themselves in this new genre of the chase, so
that they could approach girls without shame, and with wine, con-
versation, song and other provocations have easier access in order
to satisfy their desire to take their pleasure of them. They say I
had described this masque in obscure words. Beseeched by certain

descripsisse aiunt. Adolescentibus quibusdam me orantibus, promptam et claram larvam efficere institui; et cum poeticae artis finis delectare aut prodesse aut utrumque ⟨sit⟩, delectabilem primo, secundo utilem expositionem subnectam.

3   Venio itaque ad textum ubi obscurus esse videtur.

[1] *Larvati* nostri temporis, cum venereis dediti sint, patre carent sive etiam paterno consensu; solam Venerem imperatricem pro parente et matre habent: ideo [3] *nulli coniuncta marito parens*; Venus [4] *lucida*: quae, quamvis faciem eorum larva velavit, cum larvatis omnia videre in luce permisit et eis tribuit [5] *quaternos oculos* et eos [3–4] *uno partu parturiit*; plures simul et tempore uno larva velantur.

[4] *Nocte caeca*: obscura aut caeca. Occurreret alia expositio: larvati venereis dediti *nocte caeca* nati sunt ⟨quia⟩ caecum Cupidinem facieque velatum poetae describunt, nam caeci omnes amatores sunt.

[4] *Parens lucida* est, scilicet Venus, cum nihil aliud eis reluceat quam Venus ipsa, quam in parentem et matrem mitem assumpserunt, noctuque dieque eam semper ante oculos habent.

[3] *Uno partu*: plures perditissime amant puellam unam quae unica visione allicit et hoc uno partu parit plures amatores.

[3] *Nulli marito coniuncta*: puella quae nulli viro coniuncta fuit, intacta et illibata; hae enim fortius trahunt pluresque capiunt.

[5] *Geminas facies*: non unam faciem fovent, sed variatur vultus: aliquando quidem maestum, aliquando hylarem habent, variabilem quidem ad maesticiam seu iocunditatem puellae amantis.

young men, I planned to bring off a quick and famous masque, and since the goal of the poetic art is to delight or to benefit or both,[4] I may append an exposition that is, first, delightful and second, useful.

I come therefore to the text, where it seems to be obscure.   3

[1] *The maskers* of our time, since they are devoted to matters erotic, lack a father or even fatherly assent; in the place of a parent or mother they have only Venus the empress; hence [3] *parent, not joined to any husband*; Venus [4] is *shining*: and although she veils their face with a mask, she allows the maskers to see everything in her light [5] and gives them *quadruple eyes* and [3–4] *brings* them *forth in a single birth*; many are disguised by the mask together at the same moment.

[4] *In the blindness of night*: blindness or darkness. Another reading suggests itself: the maskers devoted to matters erotic are born *in the blindness of night* [because] the poets describe Cupid as blind and with his face veiled, for all lovers are blind.

[4] *Shining parent*, that is, Venus, since nothing else shines upon them except Venus herself, whom they accept as their parent and gentle mother, and they have her always before their eyes day and night.

[3] *In a single birth*: many of them love a single girl desperately who ensnares them in a single vision [i.e. at first sight], and this brings forth many lovers from a single birth.

[3] *Not joined to any husband*: a girl who is attached to no man, untouched and perfect; these girls exercise a stronger attraction and captivate many men.

[5] *Twin faces*: they cherish no single face, but their countenance varies: sometimes sad, sometimes joyful, variable in relation to the sadness or happiness of the girl they love.[5]

[6] *Composuit* Venus *celeri manu*: visio fit instanti, ad solam visionem quasi instantaneam amantes capiuntur.

[5] *Quaternos oculos* larvati habent: cum enim in amando caeci sunt, in discutiendo vias et modos quibus puellas fallere possint, non solum quatuor oculos habent sed Argo similes fuerint.

4   [15] *Sat mensibus unis* dictum est et non mensem unum; larvatorum vita extenditur, cum diebus festis larvati vivant, non quidem mensem unum continuum, sed ex intervallis in tribus mensibus, a Decembri mense usque ad Quadragesimam; hi enim dies festi vix mensem complent. Ille itaque mensis unus est in pluribus mensibus et ideo *mensibus unis*, mense uno in mensibus non continuato, sed interrupto.

Alia clara sunt; ex omnibus his liquet quod de larvatis videbatur obscurum. Lege feliciter. Vale.

: II :

Nicolaus Luscus Francisco Lusco s.p.d.

1   Quoniam te semper omnis antiquitatis amatorem fuisse certe scio, frater optime, et eos non solum in iocundis artibus quibusdam, verum etiam in rebus quae possunt gloriam parere quibusque nomen immortale comparatur, imitari voluisse—quod tibi non parum fuerit ad virtutem adiumento et auxilio—praeterea, cum nuper Ferrariae autore vate Marrasio actum sit antiquitatis aliquid, non te id fugere, quantum in me esset, aequum existimavi; quam-

[6] *With a swift hand* Venus *shaped:* the vision appears for an instant, lovers are captivated with respect to a single, almost instantaneous sight.

[5] The maskers have *four eyes:* since they are blind in their loving, in discussing ways and means whereby they may deceive girls, they not only have four eyes but will be like Argus.[6]

[15] *Let single months be enough* is said and not "one month": the   4
life of the masker is extended, since maskers live on feast days; [they live], not for one month continuously, but at intervals in three months, from December to Lent; for these feast days scarcely fill out a month. Thus this one month is in several months, hence *single months*, not for one month continuously, but interruptedly over [several] months.

Other words [in the poem] are clear. From all this it is made manifest what seemed to be dark about the maskers. Read with good fortune. Farewell.

:   II   :

A letter of Niccolò Loschi describing Marrasio's masque[7]

Niccolò Loschi sends warm greetings to Francesco Loschi.

Since I know very well that you have always been a lover of antiq-   1
uity, best of brothers, and have desired to imitate [the ancients] not only in certain pleasant matters, but also in matters which can yield glory and in which an immortal name may be won — a thing that for you was of no small assistance in acquiring virtue — and moreover, since something of the antique was enacted recently at Ferrara, authored by the poet Marrasio, I reckoned it was right that this not escape you, as far as in me lay, although you might

vis eam non possis ex meis capere iocunditatem litteris, quam si oculis vidisses, nam

> Segnius irritant animos demissa per aurem
> Quam quae sunt oculis subiecta fidelibus et quae
> Ipse sibi tradit spectator.

Sed hoc pacto cognovisse tamen iuvabit.

2   Festus fuit hic dies, quo in principis aula choreae celebratae sunt magnifice. Ut nunc res et tempus expostulat, larvati saltantes aderant; nec tamen quicquam novi, quo plus hominum mentes oblectarentur, erit. Interea res iocunda et memoratu digna divini Marrasii ingenii conspecta est. In Salvatoris locum accedere nunc superorum et inferorum cernes ordines. Procedebat ante alios radiis Apollo refulgens; aurata usque ad calcem palla satis erat ipsi deo conveniens: denique ut Apollinem cerneres. Inde nutante Bacchus gradu, ut

> Nec pes nec manus suum satis faceret officium,

quemadmodum ait comicus, longis cornibus tyrsum manu retinens veniebat: hanc aiunt Marrasium formam suscepisse. Paulo post cana barba Aesculapius gradum ferebat. Inde erat operae pretium Martem furibundum stricto gladio armis fulgentibus respicere cum Bellona pariter incedere. Post hos Mercurius immisis ad pedes alis. Cunctae Priapo accedente aves pavidae aufugerant; fixa erat canna capiti; inde qualem secum matrimonium adduceret comitemve [. . .].* Nec Venus aberat speciosa admodum forma, aurato malo adveniens; matrem Cupido sequebatur, nec aliter quidem erat ac eum poetae fingunt, tela plumbea pariter et aurata iactans. Insanae praeterea Furiae, ut nonnullis terrorem immitte-

---

* _illeg. (Sabbadini)._

not take from my literary description the same pleasure you would have had if you had seen it with your own eyes, since

Minds are stirred less vigorously by aural report
Than by what falls beneath faithful eyes and what
The spectator reports to himself.[8]

Yet it will be pleasant to have experienced it in this [literary] way [too].

The festival fell on the day when choral performances were magnificently celebrated in the prince's hall. As time and circumstance now demand, masked dancers were present; yet there will not be anything modern than which the human mind may be more delighted.[9] Amid these festivities, there was a pleasant and memorable spectacle created by the divine wit of Marrasio. In place of the Savior you see ranks of higher and lower [gods]. Before the rest there proceeded Apollo with gleaming rays; his cloak was gilded down to the heel in a manner suitable to that god, so you would identify him as Apollo. Then came Bacchus with unsteady tread, so that

Neither his foot nor his hand were adequate to their office,[10]

(as the comic poet says), with long horns, holding the thyrsus in his hand: they say that Marrasio played this part. Shortly thereafter, in walked Aesculapius with a white beard. After that, it was worth looking at a furious Mars, in gleaming armor and drawn sword, walking in step with Bellona. After them came Mercury with wings on his feet. All the birds fled in panic as Priapus approached. He had a Panpipe affixed to his head; then he brought along with him like marriage [a matron?] or a companion [. . .].[11] There was present too a very beautiful Venus, approaching with a gilded apple; Cupid followed his mother, exactly like the poets imagine him, firing off leaden and golden arrows. In addition there were raving Furies who terrified some [of the onlookers]. Then

rent. Inde Clotho Lachesis Atropos, quae, si credere dignum est, vitam hominum nent, accedebant. Nec non Hercules, leonis indutus pellem clavamque manu retinens, Cerberum triplici collo habebat. Ac multi quidem erant alii, quos dicere otiosum est.

3   Multus fuit hominum plausus pariter ac admiratio. Post vero ibi saltando paulum fuere; et inde aliqua a Marrasio edita carmina Cupido ille apud Ferrariae principem egit. Quibus pro illustri marchione carminibus Guarinus optimus praeceptor meus responsum reddidit; quae omnia ad te mitto, ut nullius rei expers sis.

Clotho, Lachesis and Atropos approached, who know the life of men (if you believe that). Also Hercules, dressed in his lion pelt and holding a key in his hand, was holding Cerberus with his triple neck. There were many others too whom it's unnecessary to describe.

The people applauded and admired this a great deal. Afterward 3 there was dancing, and then the Cupid delivered some poems published by Marrasio before the prince of Ferrara. To these my excellent teacher Guarino[12] gave a response on behalf of the illustrious marquis. I send all this to you so that you may know it all.

Note on the Texts

The Latin texts collected in this volume, with six exceptions, are based on the critical edition of Gianvito Resta, *Johannis Marrasii Angelinetum et carmina varia* (Palermo: Centro di studi filologici e linguistici siciliani, 1976). In some cases the punctuation and capitalization of Resta's text have been silently altered.

Four texts have been added to Resta's Appendix (= Appendix I in this edition). We have also included a second appendix, Appendix II, containing two texts illustrating Marrasio's masque of 1433. The sources from which we have taken these additional texts are indicated in the relevant place.

For the *Carmina Varia*, we have preserved the sequence of texts found in Resta's edition since it reflects in part Marrasio's own intentions as witnessed by the earliest manuscripts. In general, the poems of the *Carmina Varia* fall into four parts or stages, corresponding to periods of Marrasio's life:

Part I: Paratexts relating to the *Angelinetum* (1429–30). A–E and I–III.
Part II: Marrasio in Siena and Florence (1420/24–1430). IV–XIII and
    XXI–XXIII
Part III: Marrasio in Ferrara (1432–42). XIV–XX and F
Part IV: Marrasio in the Aragonese Kingdom of Naples (1442–52).
    XXIV–XLVII.[1]

The classical parallels indicated in the Notes to the Translations are for the most part based on those found in Resta's apparatus, but all references have been verified and in some cases corrected. We have pruned away some of the more tenuous parallels while adding a few sources overlooked or excluded by Resta's method. The Notes to the Translations, the notes in the Appendices, and the Bibliography were compiled by James Hankins with the assistance of Dr. Ariane Schwartz.

The following changes have been made to the texts as printed by Resta. Many were suggested in reviews of Resta by Scevola Mariotti, Guido Martellotti, and Alfonso Traina, whose works are cited in the Bibliography.

A II.5. Perhaps *carminum nervi* should be read.

A V.8. The revised punctuation is Martellotti's suggestion.

A VI.6. In *Poeti latini* Monti Sabia, following different MSS, prints *niveas* for Resta's *Niveos*, a change we have accepted.

CV I.37. The correction of *neu* to *ne* and the change in punctuation was proposed by Mariotti; the latter made also a second, less attractive suggestion: *Et (neu frigescant vires) mihi micte Thaliam*; the latter is preferred by Martellotti.

CV I.38, *CV* II.46. Mariotti prefers the rare Lucretianism *noenu* to the unmetrical *numquam* of the MSS, a rather recherché emendation (endorsed also by Traina[2]) but unlikely, given that Marrasio could not have known the text of Lucretius at this date.[3] *anne* is a conjecture of J. Hankins.

CV E.4. *id (scil. hoc opusculum)* emended from Resta's *eum* (suggested by Luke Roman).

CV III.17. Martellotti corrects *canentem* to *canentes* and *Borborophontes* to *-phontem*.

CV III.40. The conjecture of *hederas . . . comae* for Resta's *hederis . . . comas* is Martellotti's (the MSS read *hederas* or *hedera*).

CV III.76. *Maenalio* corrected from *Maeonio* (by J. Hankins); see ps. Vergil, *Copa*, 9.

CV XV.42. Martellotti corrects *venti* to *ventis*.

CV XX.35. The conjecture *pace* for the MSS's *pacis* comes from Traina.

CV XXVIII. The transposition of Resta's lines 9–10 to after lines 11–12 is Martellotti's correction.

CV XXVIII.66. The unmetrical *Concretum est lac* has been changed to *Est lac concretum*, following a suggestion of Mariotti recorded in Resta's apparatus.

CV XXX.263. We follow Martellotti's suggestion to restore the *manus* of the MSS against Mariotti's unnecessary conjecture *manu*.

CV XXXI.25. One is tempted to read *ad illos* for *ab illis*.

CV XXXI.30. J. Hankins conjectures *Cessuri* for *Cessuros*.

CV XXXII.15. We follow a suggestion of Luke Roman and read *itur* for *iter*

CV XXXII.29. Reading *nummos* for *nummis* (suggested by Luke Roman).

CV XXXII.148. Reading *abeundo* for *adeundo* (J. Hankins).

CV XXXIII. The false transposition of lines 32 and 33 in Resta's text, noted by Martellotti, has been corrected.

CV XXXIV.6. Resta rightly obelizes the MS reading *armis*; we accept the suggestion *eris* from his apparatus.

CV XXXVI.4. We have preferred the *fere* of the MS to Mariotti's conjecture *fratre*, recorded in Resta's apparatus. Mariotti's conjecture seems to have been suggested by the parallel texts at XXXVIII.4 and XXXIX.2, but is unnecessary.

CV XXXVI.15. The unmetrical *primus* has been emended to *prius*, following a suggestion of Mariotti recorded in Resta's apparatus (and endorsed by Traina).

CV XL.7. As in the identical line above, XXXVI.15, we have replaced *primus* with *prius*.

CV XLVI.18. We follow the suggestion in Resta's apparatus to substitute *iocos* for *minimos*, taking *gaudet* as impersonal (see *OLD* s.v. 2).

CV XLVII.35. We follow Mariotti's conjecture of *dive* for *dulce*.
In addition, the following may be noted:

A VIII.42. Traina prefers *Thomase* to *Thomasi* (*metri causa*).

CV III.40. Mariotti suggests *nectat* in place of *vincat*; but Martellotti's repair (above) is preferable.

CV XXVIII. Traina conjectures *ac illa* for *illaque* (*metri causa*).

CV XXXI.6. Traina conjectures *urinaque* for *ac urina* (*metri causa*).

J. H.

NOTES

1. See Resta, 93–98, and Tramontana in *DBI* on the four main *stadi* (or strata) revealed by the manuscript evidence for the text.

2. In his review of Resta. However, in a review of *Poeti latini* in *Maia* n.s. 19 (1967): 281, discussing the same line, Traina says that he would prefer to take the second syllable of *numquam* as short rather than emend.

3. For the history of Lucretius' manuscript circulation in Italy, see Ada Palmer, *Reading Lucretius in the Renaissance* (Cambridge, MA, 2014), 36–41.

Notes to the Translations

𐰋𐰃𐰋

ABBREVIATIONS

A   *Angelinetum*

CV   *Carmina Varia*

DBI   *Dizionario biografico degli italiani* (Rome: Treccani, 1960–),
          and online at www.treccani.it.

Manetti   *Iannotii Manetti De vita ac gestis Nicolai Quinti summi pontificis,*
          ed. A. Modigliani (Rome, 2005).

OLD   *Oxford Latin Dictionary*, ed. P. G. W. Glare (Oxford, 1982).

Poeti latini   *Poeti latini del Quattrocento*, ed. F. Arnaldi, L. Gualdo Rosa,
          and L. Monti Sabia (Milan-Naples, 1954).

Resta   *Iohannis Marrasii Angelinetum et carmina varia*, ed. G. Resta
          (Palermo, 1976).

ANGELINETUM

I

The word *Angelinetum* combines *Angelina*, the diminutive of Marrasio's beloved Angela, with the suffix *-etum*, "formed mainly from names of plants to denote the place where they grow (*arboretum, quercetum, rosetum*)" according to *OLD*; so "the place where Angel(in)a is cultivated" or "the place where Angel(in)a flourishes." Leonardo Bruni, the greatest humanist of Marrasio's day, though a naturalized Florentine citizen, was born in Arezzo and in Latin was usually known by his toponymic, as *Leonardus Arretinus*. On him see J. Hankins, "Bruni, Leonardo," in *Encyclopedia of the Renaissance* (New York: Scribner's, 1999), 1:301–6.

4. *quicquid . . . fuit*: Ovid, *Ars Amatoria* 1.56; *Fasti* 1.284, 494.

5. our ancestors] the Romans.

6. Marrasio uses the ancient spelling of *Arretinus*, with two *r*s, as Bruni preferred, rather than the form more common in his day, *Aretinus*.

7–8. Referring to Bruni's renown as a historian. By 1429 he had published lives of Cicero and Aristotle, a three-book account of the Punic Wars based on Polybius, and the first six books of his *History of the Florentine People.* "Superabundant majesty" refers to Bruni's prose style.

9–16. Bruni had won equal renown as a translator of Greek literature into Latin, including works of Plutarch, Demosthenes, and Plato as well as the moral philosophy of Aristotle. By 1429 Bruni had translated the *Nicomachean Ethics* and the pseudo-Aristotelian *Economics* into Latin; his version of the *Politics,* however, would not be published until 1438.

13–14. The humanists since Petrarch had claimed, on Cicero's authority, that the original writings of Aristotle had been written eloquently in Greek, but their elegance had been destroyed by the clumsy literal versions of the scholastics.

16. King Cicero] Something of a joke: Bruni, a famous defender of Florence's republican government, had written in his biography of Cicero, the *Cicero novus* (1413), that Cicero was descended from Tullus Attius, king of the Volscians. His source, Plutarch, had reported this information with greater skepticism.

17–18. Bruni had also numerous written works of his own in Latin, including orations; treatises and dialogues on education, civic knighthood, and the art of translation; as well as a panegyric of Florence and an introduction to moral philosophy.

19. *Italiae lumen:* Silius Italicus 6.130.

21. *indulgere . . . furoris:* Ovid, *Metamorphoses* 9.512; Statius, *Thebaid* 5.670. *Furor* is also the word Bruni used to translate μανία, the Platonic word for divine madness, in his partial Latin version of the *Phaedrus,* alluded to in Bruni's response to the dedication of the *Angelinetum* to him. See also A I.73 and CV D.3, below.

24. wrapping for incense] That is, whether the paper it is written on should be recycled. The motif is a common one in ancient Latin poetry; see, for example, Horace, *Epistles* 2.1.264–70.

27. sketches (*tabellis*)] A *tabella* in antiquity was a wax-coated tablet intended for taking notes or making drafts, which in final form would be

written down on paper. The word emphasizes that Marrasio is ready to modify his poems in light of Bruni's critical comments.

II

2. The ancient house of the Piccolomini was among the most noble in Siena, according to the highly interested testimony of Enea Silvio Piccolomini, later Pope Pius II, in his *Commentarii* 1.1 (ed. Meserve and Simonetta [Cambridge, MA: Harvard University Press, 2003], 1:7). Marrasio was friends with Enea Silvio as well as with Tommaso Piccolomini. Enea Silvio also praised Marrasio in a poem dedicated to Charles VII of France; see Appendix I.1

5. *carmina nervi:* perhaps *carminum nervi* should be read.

15. *sideribus . . . oculos:* Ovid, *Amores* 2.16.44; *Metamorphoses* 1.499.

18. *signa . . . dabis:* Ovid, *Metamorphoses* 5.468; Lucan 2.2; Statius, *Thebaid* 3.43.

III

3. *fusus in herbas:* Ovid, *Metamorphoses* 3.438.

3–4. On the proverbial bitterness of Sardinian herbs, see Erasmus, *Adages* 2401 ("Risus Sardonius"); Vergil, *Eclogues* 7.41.

6. *et Tartara . . . vident:* Ovid, *Metamorphoses* 10.20–21.

16. The black Falernian] A wine traditionally considered the finest wine of ancient Rome; see Pliny the Elder, *Natural History* 23.20.

IV

11. *non quaerenda . . . gloria:* Cicero, *De officiis* 2.42; Vergil, *Aeneid* 9.278.

17. *vincit Amor:* Vergil, *Eclogues* 10.69; Ovid, *Amores* 3.2.46, 3.11.34, *Heroides* 9.26, *Metamorphoses* 10.26.

17. *tela Cupido:* Tibullus 2.5.107; Ovid, *Metamorphoses* 5.366, 10.311.

20. *Mars ferus:* Ovid, *Heroides* 7.160.

20. I saw Jove wearing horns] That is, Jove in the form of a bull, who carried off Europa according to the myth. See Ovid, *Fasti* 5.606.

27–28. Marrasio uses the language of the business contract: since I have given you my love, you owe ungrudging payment of a reciprocal love. See Statius, *Silvae* 2.1.207; and Horace, *Satires* 2.2.125.

V

Johannes Pratensis] Probably the jurist Giovanni Ceparelli of Prato mentioned in Poggio's letters, who taught in the Studio of Siena in the years 1428–29 and later worked as a papal *scriptor* under Martin V (Resta).

4. Vergil did not write elegies, as Marrasio knew well, so *Virgilios* must refer back to *versus* in line 2.

25. *quod . . . ut*: Ovid, *Metamorphoses* 10.135.

27. *thure Sabaeo*: Vergil, *Aeneid* 1.416–17, *Georgics* 1.57.

VI

3–4. *semper . . . gramine*: Vergil, *Georgics* 2.219.

4. *solibus . . . riget*: Ovid, *Heroides* 5.112.

VII

1. *numquam . . . dolores*: Propertius 1.16.25

4. *deque . . . eant*: Ovid, *Heroides* 8.62.

9. *obscuro . . . natus*: Statius, *Silvae* 5.3.116.

21. The fountain] The Fonte Gaia, for which see the Introduction.

22. your own mirror] Angela's window in the Piccolomini palace overlooked the Campo and had a direct view of the Fonte Gaia.

25. *marmoribus funebria carmina ponam*: compare Horace, *Odes* 4.1.20. Like Propertius 2.1.78, Marrasio dictates the epitaph to be incised on his tomb, as Martellotti points out.

VIII

Marrasio imagines his own unburied corpse arriving in the Underworld.

5. *ad infernas . . . umbras*: Vergil, *Aeneid* 7.770–71.

13. *rabidissima . . . leonum:* Horace, *Ars Poetica* 393.

20. be unable] Because the corpse has been so mutilated by animals and monsters.

20. *funera flere:* Ovid, *Epistulae ex Ponto* 1.9.17, *Ibis* 16; Lucan 2.118–19.

22. Corsican crowd] Marrasio's view of Corsicans reflects that of Seneca, who was exiled there in 41–49 CE. See especially the pseudo-Senecan *Epigrammata.*

37. *Stigiam . . . paludem:* Vergil, *Aeneid* 6.369, *Georgics* 4.503; Statius, *Silvae* 3.2.67.

IX

5. a poet] For Bruni as a poet, see Hankins, "The Latin Poetry of Leonardo Bruni."

17. publish] *Edo* was the contemporary word for publish, that is, turn an author's writings over to a bookstore for copying by professional scribes.

20. Horace, *Epistles* 2.1.269–70; and Catullus 95.8.

CARMINA VARIA

A

Antonio Beccadelli (1394–1471), called "il Panormita" from his birthplace in Palermo. He studied law in Siena with the famous Sicilian jurist Niccolò de' Tudeschi (also, confusingly, known as *Panormitanus*), where he probably met Marrasio. He was made court poet to the Visconti dukes of Milan on December 10, 1429, and after 1434 held various offices in the court of Alfonso V of Aragon. His most famous, or notorious, work was the ribald *Hermaphroditus* (1425), published in this I Tatti library (no. 42, 2010), with a translation by Holt Parker. This work was censured by various moral and religious authorities. Later, Panormita became a more respectable figure, serving as a minister in the government of King Alfonso "the Magnanimous" of Aragon. Resta dates the present poem to late 1429 or early 1430, shortly after the publication of the *Angelinetum.*

1. *tela Cupido:* Compare *A* IV.17.

5. what I don't say] The figure of *praeteritio*, a not-saying that allows one to say the unsayable.

7. lap of Venus] Or "from Venus' affection."

B

Maffeo Vegio (1407–1458), a Latin poet and humanist born in Lodi in Lombardy. He studied and later taught at the University of Pavia before entering papal service under Eugene IV in the later 1430s. His most famous work was his continuation of Vergil's *Aeneid* (1427), published with other short epics in this I Tatti library (no. 15, 2004), with an introduction and translation by Michael C. J. Putnam. Resta dates this poem to before March 13, 1430.

2. *pulcher Apollo:* Vergil, *Aeneid* 3.119.

5. Antonio] Antonio Beccadelli, for whom see the headnote to *CV* A.

8. *pignus amoris:* Ovid, *Ars amatoria* 2.248, *Heroides* 4.100, 11.113, *Metamorphoses* 3.283, 8.92.

10. protected by his name] That is, Cato's name, synonymous with moral probity. Vegio warns the Muse not to allow indecency in Marrasio's poetry, a warning famously violated in the poetry of Beccadelli. Vegio, by contrast, wrote poetry of a more pious stamp. The question of decency in poetry was a subject of frequent debate in the Renaissance.

C

Date: Around March 1430. An imaginary response on the part of Angelina to *A* VII and VIII, reminiscent of Ovid's *Heroides*.

13. *tenero . . . amore:* Ovid, *Amores* 2.18.4, 2.18.19, *Ars amatoria* 1.7.

24. *sanguine . . . humus:* Ovid, *Heroides* 1.54.

26. *me . . . amor:* Terence, *Hecyra* 404; Horace, *Epodes* 11.24.

27. *quae . . . mentem:* Vergil, *Aeneid* 4.595.

31. *dii . . . fecere:* Horace, *Satires* 1.4.17.

35. faithful lovers] Pyramis and Thisbe, whose tale is told in Ovid's *Metamorphoses* 4.55–166. The story is also related in Boccaccio's *Famous Women*, XIII, published in this I Tatti library (no. 1, 2001), translated by

Virginia Brown. The gods change the white berries of the mulberry tree to crimson in honor of their love.

55. *sua . . . Cupido:* Ovid, *Amores* 1.9.1.

57. *truculentior ursis:* Ovid, *Metamorphoses* 13.803.

59. *de . . . nata:* Ovid, *Metamorphoses* 7.32, 9.613.

72. quiver-bearing god] Cupid or Amor.

73. Godly power, etc.] Vegio alludes to the theory of the poet's divine inspiration, probably derived from Leonardo Bruni's partial translation of Plato's *Phaedrus* (1424). See Hankins, *Plato in the Italian Renaissance*, 1:70–72, and text D, below.

81. what lies hidden under love] That is, the poets understand that the apparently lascivious stories about love found in the poets have a deeper, spiritual meaning.

89. *Gallo . . . Lycoris:* Ovid, *Amores* 1.15.30.

96. jurisdiction] Perhaps a playful reference to Marrasio's status as a law student, as also at 100, "you possess all rights over my welfare."

I

The poem responds to *CV* C, above, though lines 25 and 31 seem to refer back to the Cato of *CV* B.10. The poem was sent to Vegio via Panormita, accompanied by a letter of March 12, 1430 (see Appendix I.2), in which Marrasio asked Panormita to correct and polish it. Both Vegio and Panormita at that time were in Pavia.

7. *nivea . . . veste:* Ovid, *Metamorphoses* 10.432.

18. *Sicilis . . . volo:* Ovid, *Heroides* 15.52.

19. *persona,* character] In classical Latin, *persona* usually means "mask" or "a character played by an actor." Marrasio's meaning seems to be that the truth of the sentiment had won out over the fictive nature of the poem.

25, 31. Cato] See note at *CV* B.10. It seems less likely that Marrasio is referring to the jurist Catone Sacco, as Resta says (p. 142 n. 1), than that he is once again alluding to the moral severity of true poetry.

29. *lascive Properti:* Martial 8.73.5.

D

Bruni's letter to Marrasio stands first in Book 6 of his epistolary and is dated to October 7, 1429, in a number of manuscripts. The Aretine draws, sometimes word for word, on the partial translation of the *Phaedrus* he had made in 1424.

1. a certain spring] The fountain of youth.

1. stories and pictures] There are innumerable sources for this legend, going back at least to Herodotus (3.23); popular medieval sources of the story were the *Letter of Prester John* and the French *Roman d'Alexandre*, both texts of the twelfth century. The fountain was also a popular subject in late medieval, especially Gothic, art; see R. van Marle, *Iconographie de l'Art profane*, 2 vols. (La Haye, 1932), 2:432–45.

3. Plato] *Phaedrus* 265a–b.

4. Vergil] *Aeneid* 6.11–12.

6. For "sober poets," see Horace, *Ars poetica* 296.

6. whence do you bid me go?] Statius, *Thebaid* 1.3–4.

6. Vergil] *Aeneid* 7.41–45.

9. *vates*] That is, inspired bard. The word perhaps descends from the Gaulish root *wat-*, meaning seer or prophet.

9. as Plato said] *Phaedrus* 250d.

13. Themistocles] Plutarch, *Life of Themistocles* 21.4, which Bruni could have known in the Greek original or in the translation of Guarino Veronese.

13. *sed . . . illis:* Vergil, *Eclogues* 9.34.

II

The poem responds to the previous text.

1. Scythian] It is not clear why Marrasio identifies the source of the fountain of youth as Scythia. In ancient texts Scythia is a barbarous land lying to the north of the Black Sea, anywhere from northeastern Greece to Georgia. In following a subterranean pathway to Siena, the fountain's water resembles the river Alpheios in Arcadia, which ran under the sea to resurface in Ortygia (Sicily).

11. *Nestoreos . . . annos*: Ovid, *Fasti* 3.533; Martial 11.56.13.

22. her offspring] Cupid or Amor.

37. the Gorgonian spring] That is, the fountain of Hippocrene, created when Pegasus stamped his hoof on Mount Helicon. The blow released the river Helicon, sacred to the Muses, which filled with poetical power any poet who drank of its waters.

46. *fefellit amor*: Ovid, *Amores* 3.4.20.

E

Carlo Aretino is better known as Carlo Marsuppini (1398–1454), a Latin poet; a professor of poetry, rhetoric, and Greek at the University of Florence; and Leonardo Bruni's successor as chancellor of Florence. He left few works, among them a partial translation of Homer's *Iliad* and a Latin version of the pseudo-Homeric *Batrachomyomachia* (1429), his most famous work, dedicated to Marrasio. See the article of Paolo Viti in *DBI* 71 (2008). This letter was written before March 12, 1430 (see Appendix I.2).

1. *Ac si repente . . . poeta prodirem*: an echo of Persius, prol.1–3. The transformation of a raven into a poet is perhaps meant to recall Aesop's fable, the Raven and the Swan (Perry 398); in Greek myth the swan was known for its power of song.

2. Plutarch] Marsuppini's source here and in §3 is the pseudo-Plutarchan *Life of Homer* translated by his teacher Guarino Veronese.

2. *Margites . . . Hymns*] Works that circulated in antiquity under the name of Homer.

2. *Culex . . . Copa*] That is, "The Gnat" . . . "The Barmaid." These are now considered spurious works of Vergil.

2. Homer in this work] That is, the *Batrachomyomachia*.

2. that he might sing of shepherds, fields and dreadful wars] An echo of the second line of the celebrated inscription on the tomb of Vergil: *cecini pascua rura duces*: "I sang of pastures, fields and military leaders," that is, he composed the *Eclogues*, *Georgics*, and *Aeneid*.

2. *non sum animi . . . honorem*: Vergil, *Georgics* 3.289–90.

2. *in tenui labor . . . gloria*: Vergil, *Georgics* 4.6.

3. On the birthplace of Homer, see the pseudo-Plutarchan life mentioned above and Plutarch's genuine *Life of Sertorius* 1.3, a work that had been translated by Leonardo Bruni around 1410.

III

Marrasio's reply to Marsuppini, written around the beginning of 1430.

2. uneven sound] That is, in elegiac couplets.

14. *ornabat . . . manus*: Propertius 3.6.12.

19. Meridarpaga Borborophontes] "Broken-meat-eater" (Μεριδάρπαξ) and "Mud-sleeper" (Βορθοροκοίτης), two warriors in the *Batrachomyomachia*. Marrasio, following Marsuppini, confuses and conflates the two names. Martellotti suggests that the Greek word was contaminated owing to its similarity to *Bellerophontes*.

32. *quom testudineam . . . liram*: Tibullus 3.8.22.

54. gave to the leaves] That is, wrote upon the leaves; see Vergil, *Aeneid* 6.74.

62. nag's wave] Pegasus; a blow from his foot created the spring of Hippocrene on Mount Helicon.

72. Niccolò] Niccolò Niccoli (ca. 1364–1437), the famous Florentine humanist and book collector, whom Marsuppini regarded as a friend and second father.

75. *eia agites*: Vergil, *Aeneid* 4.569.

75. Maenalian cave] A cave beneath Mount Maenalus in Arcadia, sacred to Pan.

75–76. That is, you have translated a minor Homeric work, the *Batrachomyomachia*, now translate the *Odyssey!* (Antiphates and Cyclops are characters in the *Odyssey*). Marsuppini began his translation of Homer's *Iliad* shortly thereafter.

93–94. There were no complete Latin translations of the *Iliad* or the *Odyssey* before the fifteenth century. To have one made was a desideratum of the humanist movement since the time of Petrarch.

IV

Written on the occasion of a pestilence. Resta suggests it was the major outbreak of plague in 1424. Cornelio is unidentified, and the Angelina mentioned here cannot be identified with the Angela Piccolomini of the *Angelinetum*.

V

Nothing is known of Sabino Siculo apart from a brief reference to him in a letter from Marrasio to Panormita (see Appendix I.2). Poems IV–XII appear all to be from Marrasio's Sienese period and constitute almost, as Resta remarks, a *canzoniere* within a *canzoniere*.

VI

Neither Margara, Fabrizio, nor Grifo Siculo can be identified.

VII

Eva has not been identified.

2. *pectora . . . forent:* Ovid, *Epistulae ex Ponto* 3.4.33–34.

5. *ignibus Aetnaeis:* Vergil, *Aeneid* 7.786; Statius, *Thebaid* 11.68; Silius Italicus 8.653.

IX

Petrus Victorinus (Piero Vettori?) has not been identified.

6. *aeternam . . . tenent:* Vergil, *Aeneid* 6.235.

14. A reminisce of Horace, *Art of Poetry* 268–69.

X

Barnaba, sometimes called "Barnaba Senese," has been identified by Pertici (*Tra politica e cultura*, 9f.) as Barnaba Pannilini (1399–before 1465), a major figure in early Sienese humanism and in Siena's political life as well. On him see Pertici's article in *DBI* 80 (2014). His letters have been edited by Giacomo Ferraù, *Barnaba Senese: Epistolario* (Palermo: "Il Vespro," 1979). Resta dates this poem to 1426/29.

1. charming letter] The letter does not seem to survive, though an extensive correspondence existed between the two men, some of it found in Ferraù's edition, cited above.

4. Petrucci] Andreozzo or Andreoccio di Rinaldo Petrucci (d. 1449), Sienese humanist, diplomat, and statesman, who exchanged letters with many well-known humanists of the day, including Bruni, Aurispa, Filelfo, Panormita, and Enea Silvio Piccolomini. On him see Pertici, *Tra politica e cultura*; and also Petrucci's letter to Barnaba Pannilini in Appendix I.3.

7–9. Hippolytus . . . Phaedra] Marrasio would have known the tale from the younger Seneca's tragedy *Phaedra*, as the use of the word *immitis* to describe Hippolytus suggests.

9–10. Phalaris] Phalaris, the tyrant of Akragas (Agrigento), who tortured his victims in a bronze bull beneath which a fire had been lit. There are many sources for the story, used often by philosophers as a test case for the Stoic doctrine that the wise man is always blessed.

15–27. The story equates Barnaba with the poor man, a "free rider" who thinks, because others labor to provide crops, that he can live off their labors. Similarly, when Barnaba was young, there were no teachers of rhetoric; now there are an abundance, but he abandons his efforts to learn eloquence, the defining skill of the *studia humanitatis*. Not to take advantage of his opportunities is a crime.

20. *excepi . . . poma*: Ovid, *Metamorphoses* 10.649–50.

XI

According to Resta, pp. 168–69nn, Maurizio Luti belonged to a noble Sienese family and took an active part in the city's public life.

10. *spargo . . . rosas*: Ovid, *Amores* 1.2.40.

14. *candidiorque nive*: compare A III.20.

XII

Enea Silvio Piccolomini (1405–64), Siena's most famous literary man, later a diplomat, bishop, cardinal archbishop, and finally Pope Pius II (1458–64). His memoirs, the *Commentaries*, are published in this I Tatti Library, translated by Margaret Meserve. Enea Silvio had praised Marrasio in an elegy dedicated to Charles VII of France (Appendix I.1), dated July 1429, and this poem of Marrasio's may be a response to that act of generosity. If so, it would be datable to the second half of 1429.

4. wrapping pepper, etc.] See above, I.24.

8. madness (*furor*)] See above, I.21.

10. Picula] Presumably the name of Enea Silvio's literary mistress; "Picula" ought to mean something like "little pitch," that is, little love torch (torches in antiquity were commonly smeared with pitch).

XIII

Nothing is known of the Venetian girl mentioned in line 2 of the poem. Resta speculates that she may belong to Marrasio's Ferrarese period (1432–42). Unlike Resta or Altamura, we have printed this poem in six-line stanzas, to emphasize its experimental relationship with the volgare *sestina* and its use of a two-line refrain, unusual in Neo-Latin poetry.

21. *astrictum . . . geluque*: Ovid, *Tristia ex Ponto* 2.1.196.

22. by oar or by foot (*pede*)] Seemingly, an odd form of marine propulsion, but Marrasio might be thinking of horse-drawn canal boats in the system of canals and *navigli* between Ferrara and the Po.

30. disarmed by my soul] The activity of the soul in the body maintains the latter's formal characteristics, according to the standard Aristotelian psychology of the time.

XIV

Nothing is known of Francesco Tallone; internal evidence shows him to be a cultivated friend, perhaps a patron, who wrote verse and appreciated Latin poetry. Resta dates the poem to between the autumn of 1432 and the spring of 1433, during Marrasio's Ferrarese period. This is the first of seven "Ferrarese" poems in the collection (XIV–XX).

6–8. Marrasio refers to his medical studies in Padua. (Pseudo) Hippocrates' *Aphorisms* and the works of Avicenna ("the royal Arab") were staples of the medical curriculum.

33–34. *vultuque . . . rideat*: Ovid, *Tristia* 1.5.27.

41. Marrasio once again alludes to his need for love as an inspiration for *carmina docta*. It is not clear whether he wants Tallone to provide him with a real or merely a literary mistress. Marrasio seems to imagine a woman whose behavior will supply him with the usual themes of elegiac poetry.

XV

"Medusa," mentioned also at XIV.35, has not been identified. Resta dates this poem to spring 1433.

2. *laqueo . . . ligas*: Ovid, *Epistulae ex Ponto* 1.6.39.

10. the dog] Cerberus.

12. *caesaries aurea*: Vergil, *Aeneid* 8.659.

28. with an even hand] That is, with consistency, so that he will remain unaltered.

75. *Iuppiter . . . amantum*: Ovid, *Ars amatoria* 1.633.

81–82. "As many eyes"] Possibly the first words of a magic spell. In lines 83 to 96 the speaker employs magic arts to subdue her to his will.

94. her blacksmith husband] Vulcan.

XVI

Leonello d'Este (1407–50), illegitimate son of Niccolò d'Este III, was Marquis of Ferrara from December 1441 until his death. A pupil of the great humanist educator Guarino Veronese, he was an important patron of the humanities, the arts, and music. As a statesman, he acquired a reputation for avoiding war with his quarrelsome neighbors. Several phrases in the poem and the general tone (no events from Leonello's own reign are mentioned) suggest that the work was written to celebrate the inauguration of his reign.

17. Fierce enemies from a western race] Referring to a famous duel between two Aragonese knights, scheduled to be held in Ferrara in 1432, that was settled without combat thanks to the intervention of Leonello's father, Niccolò.

30. Fruitful peace] The Peace of Ferrara, April 26, 1433, wherein Niccolò d'Este acted as peacemaker between the warring powers of Milan, Florence, and Venice.

30. snake-bearing duke] The duke of Milan, Filippo Maria Visconti, whose arms bore the image of a snake.

45–46. it has seemed sweet . . . I've loved] Marrasio was coming to the end of his sojourn in Ferrara.

64. If they do anything] Presumably, a euphemistic expression.

XVII

According to Resta, the poem was composed by Marrasio in 1433 for a mythological masque that he had organized at court, probably on the occasion of the Peace of Ferrara (see CV XVI.30). From a letter of Niccolò Loschi (Appendix II.2) we learn that the masque won great applause and that Marrasio himself probably played the role of the god Bacchus. Sozzino Benzi, himself a well-known doctor, was the son of the famous professor of medicine Ugo Benzi. According to D. P. Lockwood's study, *Ugo Benzi, Medieval Philosopher and Physician* (Chicago, 1951), confirmed by CV F, below, Sozzino played the principal role, that of Cupid. In answer to critics of the poem's obscurity, Marrasio composed a short commentary (see Appendix II.1).

3. Our brilliant parent] Venus.

15. single months] In the commentary (Appendix II.1.4) the plural is explained: it refers to the duration of the festivities. They occur in multiple, different months from December to Lent, but add up to a single month in number of days; hence "month" is at once singular and plural.

25. *spatium . . . breve*: Ovid, *Metamorphoses* 3.124.

35. *nil . . . erat*: Ovid, *Fasti* 5.126. *nil . . . habetur*: Ovid, *Tristia ex Ponto* 2.1.38.

40. happy deaths] No doubt with the double entendre of "death" in the tradition of courtly love.

47–56. Marrasio offers his services as court poet to Niccolò d'Este; his offer to celebrate the house of Este includes Niccolò's son and designated successor, Leonello (50).

52. Probably a reference to Niccolò d'Este's troubled relationships with women. He was married three times, had five legitimate and eleven illegitimate children, including Leonello. Niccolò had his second wife, Parisina, executed for an alleged affair with his illegitimate son Ugo, who was also executed.

Explicit . . . legeris] Another manuscript has: *Ferrariae Kal. Febr.* ("Ferrara, February 1").

F

Guarino Veronese (1374–1460), Leonello d'Este's former tutor, was one of the leading humanist educators of the Renaissance and a major figure at the court of the Este and the University of Ferrara. On Sozzino Benzi, see the headnote to CV XVII, above. Marrasio took Guarino's sketch of dramatic history, based on Horace, as an implicit criticism of his own failure to do so, and answered both in CV XVIII and in the anonymous commentary (Appendix II.1) plausibly attributed to him by Resta. Guarino was also a strict moralist, and certain lines in the poem hint at disapproval, for example, 14–16 and 23–24; 41–54 invoke the conventional principle that while a certain license is allowed to youth, age and religion should eventually impose a more serious view of life.

7–8. a better origin] Perhaps a slighting reference to Sozzino's and Marrasio's family origins is intended, although on the surface Guarino seems to be referring to the ancient origins of drama, relying, as does Marrasio in his commentary, on Horace, *Ars poetica* 275–88.

25. great father, Ugo] Ugo Benzi the physician; see CV XVII, headnote.

38. only Minerva is spared] Only the goddess of wisdom is too prudent to fall victim to love's fires.

45. the harsh queen] Proserpina, queen of the dead.

57. So that he may then be readier] An allusion to the Renaissance educator's doctrine that the purpose of play was to relax one to undertake more serious studies.

XVIII

Dated by Resta to 1433.

9. You translate the histories that Plutarch wrote] Guarino translated Plutarch's biographies of Coriolanus (before 1414), Themistocles (1417), Pelopidas and Marcellus (1437, both dedicated to Leonello d'Este), Philopoemen (1416/18), Flamininus (1411), Lysander and Sulla (1435, both dedicated to Leonello d'Este), Eumenes (1416/18), and Alexander and Caesar (ca. 1414). See Marianne Pade, *The Reception of Plutarch's Lives in Fifteenth-Century Italy*, 2 vols. (Copenhagen, 2000).

11–22. In answer to Guarino's implied criticism, Marrasio states he was not writing about the masks used in ancient Greek theater, but the modern genre of the court masque. If he had been writing about the ancient masked drama, he too would have taken Horace's *Ars poetica* for his starting point. Marrasio scores a point by drawing attention to Guarino's failure to mention Thespis first in his account of the origins of drama.

23–36. Marrasio insists on the difference between the ancient masked drama Guarino describes and the modern play he himself has written, and he proposes a hybrid, "monstrous" form, which will combine the two traditions, ancient and modern.

24. *arma canis*: Vergil, *Aeneid* 1.1.

26–28. Perhaps: the actor changes but the part endures?

37–38. Marrasio, perhaps fearing that his response to Guarino might be taken as too sharp, dismisses it as a joke suitable to the days of festival.

The *explicit*, referring back to the title of XVII, encourages the reader to take XVII, F, and XVIII as a unit.

XIX

Cyriac of Ancona, one of the great travelers of the Renaissance, was also a humanist, diplomat, and antiquarian; some credit him with founding classical archeology because of his notebooks full of inscriptions and drawings collected in Italy, Greece, and the Eastern Mediterranean. See the two volumes of his writings in this I Tatti series: *Life and Early Travels*, ed. Charles Mitchell, Edward W. Bodnar, and Clive Foss (2015), and *Later Travels*, ed. Edward W. Bodnar with Clive Foss (2003). Resta dates this epigram to 1433. Cyriac was in Ferrara for the peace celebrations and in his *Itinerarium* notes being given the epigram by Marrasio.

XX

The Holy Roman Emperor Sigismund (1368–1437) stopped in Ferrara between September 9 and 16, 1433, on his way back to Germany from Rome, where he had been crowned by Pope Eugene IV.

20. any Otho] Any medieval German emperor.

31–32. Marrasio offers his services as court poet to Sigismund, who like Charles VII of France, Niccolò III d'Este, Leonello d'Este, and perhaps others, did not take advantage of his offer. Sigismund had bestowed the laurel crown on Marrasio's friendly rival Panormita at Parma in May of 1432. A few years later, in 1442, his Sienese contemporary and friend Enea Silvio Piccolomini was also crowned poet laureate, by the Holy Roman Emperor Frederick III.

32. matching verse] That is, epic verse, dactylic hexameter.

XXI

On Panormita see *CV* A. Marrasio's poem, unusually for him, is very much in the Panormitan manner, though it draws too on the collection of anonymous Latin poems known as *Priapea*. The poem is dated only "Siena, November 19"; Resta establishes the year as 1429.

2. *alma Venus:* Lucretius 1.2; Horace, *Odes* 4.15.31–32; Ovid, *Metamorphoses* 10.230.

16. from her band] But the word *coetus*, as *OLD* (s.v.) delicately points out, "is not distinguishable [from *coitus*] in some senses."

XXII

Resta states that the poem "is certainly from [Marrasio's] Sienese period." Antonino, the diminutive of Antonio, probably refers to his compatriot Panormita.

3. The hill of Alveria] The hill upon which rose the ancient site of Noto in Sicily, Marrasio's birthplace.

XXIII

The epitaph of the poet, promised in *A* VII.25–26. Probably also from the Sienese period.

2. Marrasio plays with the conventional language of the epitaph, in which the body would typically lie "beneath" (*sub*) the stone, and the stone would "cover" (*tegit*) his bones. Thanks to this epigram however, not his body but his soul is made known, not covered, by the sculpted word.

XXIV

The first poem in the last part of the *Carmina Varia*, containing verse from Marrasio's last decade in the Kingdom of Aragon, begins with what looks like a dedicatory poem to the greatest patron of humanists in the mid-Quattrocento, Pope Nicholas V (pope, 1447–55), born Tommaso Parentucelli. As we learn from *CV* XXVII, Marrasio had met Parentucelli twenty years before in Bologna, and perhaps hoped to build on that connection to find patronage at the papal court. But his long illness, described below, kept him from going to Rome for a number of years (see especially *CV* XXXII.148–60, below). He finally made the journey from Palermo to Rome in April 1452, and most of the poems addressed to Nicholas V in the *CV* (XXIV–XXXII and XLVI–XLVII) must come from that period. Whether the Aragonese poems (XXXIII–XLV) were also to have been part of the collection dedicated to Nicholas is open to doubt. In any case, Resta supposes from the numerous instances of clumsy, obscure, ungrammatical, and unmetrical expression that the twenty-three poems in this final section of the *CV* were left in an unfinished state. That hypothesis is given weight by the circumstances of transmission: all the poems in the last part of the *CV* are preserved only in a single manuscript of the late fifteenth century (Parma, Biblioteca Palatina MS Parm. 283, siglum *Pm* in Resta's edition).

5–21. For Parentucelli's studies of natural philosophy, see Manetti, 17–18; for his theological studies, including both ancient and modern theologians, see ibid., 19–24.

5. human mortality] The precise nature of human immortality was a major source of disagreement in Renaissance, as in medieval, theology.

11. *vias . . . labores:* Vergil, *Georgics* 2.477–78.

11. *lunaeque labores:* compare Vergil, *Aeneid* 1.742.

13–14. Compare Sacrobosco, *De sphaera,* cap. 4.

15. That is, whatever Nature's powers are, whether in potency or act. Marrasio struggles to express technical terms of Aristotelian physics in the poetical idiom of classical Latin.

17–28. Marrasio praises Nicholas for the extensive program he organized to translate the literary heritage of the Greeks, pagan and Christian, into Latin. This included scientific treatises (*artes*), works of rhetoric and oratory (including history), and theology. See Manetti, 53–67.

30. the man from Syracuse] Archimedes. As a Sicilian himself, Marrasio is happy to draw attention to Sicilian scientific achievements. At 41 he speaks as a representative of the Sicilian Muses.

32. Bryson] An ancient Greek mathematician whose work on squaring the circle was known from Aristotle, *Posterior Analytics* 1.9, 75b, and *Sophistical Elenchus* 2.11, 171b, and 172a. He is mentioned in Dante, *Paradiso* 13.125.

33. Antiphon] Antiphon the Sophist (fl. 420–400 BCE), a mathematician who tried to calculate the value of pi by inscribing a circle within a series of polygons. Marrasio probably knows him via Aristotle, *Physics* 1.2, 185a.

36. The meaning is obscure, but Marrasio may intend to allude to Zeno's paradox of the arrow, known presumably from Aristotle, *Physics* 6.9, 129b.

39. Jacopo di San Cassiano of Cremona, here identified with Mantua, probably owing to his association with his teacher Vittorino da Feltre: from 1446 to 1449 he took Vittorino's place in Mantua after the great schoolmaster's death. Jacopo translated Archimedes for Nicholas V. Archimedes worked in the Greek city of Syracuse in Sicily, whose language was Doric Greek. The reason why Mantua is blamed for its neglect of the Syracusan Muses may only be guessed at: did the Gonzaga too refuse Marrasio their patronage?

41. *Sicelides Musae*: Vergil, *Eclogues* 4.1.1.

51. Theodore Gaza (ca. 1415–ca. 1476), another translator in Nicholas' court, was famous for his translations of Greek scientific texts into humanist Latin, including Theophrastus' *De plantis*.

54–62. Marrasio's plea for a Latin Homer soon bore fruit when Nicholas commissioned his old friend Carlo Marsuppini to translate the *Iliad* in 1452. Marrasio reuses some phrases from *CV* III.

68. Marrasio alludes to the splendid reception accorded Frederick III from March 9 to 21, 1452, during the latter's visit to Rome to be crowned Holy Roman Emperor.

71. *a te principium*: Vergil, *Eclogues* 8.11.

71. *nostri . . . auctor*: Ovid, *Metamorphoses* 13.142.

XXV

1–2. Referring to the pope's supposed "power of the keys" (Matthew 16:13), the power to decide who may be a member of the Church and therefore gain entry to heaven or be condemned to Hell, on the principle *nulla salus extra ecclesiam.*

XXVI

The poem was most likely written by Marrasio himself rather than by the pope.

1. For Nicholas V's birth in Sarzana, see Manetti, 5n. Giannozzo Manetti in his biography of Nicholas claimed, dubiously, that he had been born in Pisa.

XXVII

See the headnote to CV XXIV.

5–7. Marrasio is recalling Nicholas' skill in scholastic disputation.

11. Neither Tiresias' nor Apollo's shrine] Neither human nor divine prophetic powers.

XXVIII

4–24. Marrasio praises Nicholas for his very real achievement in securing the dissolution of the schismatic Council of Basel and the abdication of its antipope, Felix V, in April 1449; see Manetti, 41–45.

25. Great Pardon] In thanksgiving for the restoration of church unity, Nicholas proclaimed a Jubilee for the year 1450, which brought many thousands of pilgrims to Rome to seek pardon for their sins. See Manetti, 48–53.

34. *Ploeripedes*: Apparently a coinage of Marrasio, from *pl(o)erus* and *pes*.

37. each chanting *Miserere*] Marrasio seems to be referring to the chant *Miserere* (Have mercy on me, o Lord), a psalm text of the Divine Office particularly associated with penitence and atonement, and therefore highly appropriate to the Jubilee and the Great Pardon.

42. Parrhasis] An epithet for the nymph Callisto, who according to myth was transformed into the constellation Ursa Major; Ovid, *Metamorphoses* 2.405–531 and *Fasti* 2.155–92, would have been the versions of the myth most readily available to Marrasio. Marrasio's meaning in these lines is obscure, but he likely is continuing the thought of the preceding lines referring to the difficulties of attending the Jubilee from afar. Callisto, standing for the constellation Ursa Major (and by extension, for inhabitants of the northern hemisphere?), had difficulty attending "burdened by her own weight": that is, because of her pregnancy (Ovid: *uteri manifesta tumore / proditur indicio ponderis ipsa suo*). In punishment for her pregnancy, Artemis or Juno changed her into a bear, and Jupiter then translated her to the remote northern heavens.

43–70. The story of the envoy from India, whom Marrasio calls an abbot, seems to be a literary fiction whose details are based on passages in

Isidore's *Etymologies* and in Pliny the Elder; see Resta's detailed source notes. There is no mention of such an episode in Manetti (q.v.).

64. How greater and smaller things do not much differ] The thought is again obscure (and the syntax unclassical), but Marrasio is perhaps playing on the much-used phrase from Vergil's *Eclogues* 1.23, "thus am I wont to compare great things with small." Unlike Vergil's simple shepherd, the Indian abbot does not have a sense of proportion in comparing the wonders of India with those of Rome.

66. *lac concretum*: Vergil, *Georgics* 3.463.

79–84. I said] Marrasio here begins to speak in his own person as one of the Sicilians. It now appears that the abbot-envoy from the unnamed Indian prince is a diplomat from the Christian kingdom of Prester John, the legendary ruler imagined to reside in India (or Central Asia or Africa); according to medieval fantasy he was a rich and mighty warrior who might well come to the aid of European Christians beleaguered by the Turks.

91. The abbot is now identified as a member, possibly the head, of the mythical order of St. Anthony the Abbot, supposedly founded by Prester John. St. Anthony the Abbot (ca. 251–356 CE) was the founder of Western monasticism.

95–105. The poet reproves himself for his exotic digression and bids his own spirit return, with the speed of thought, to address the state of Italy.

109. The pope is (deservedly) praised for his leadership in bringing peace to Italy: in 1447 he ratified a peace agreement with Alfonso of Aragon; in 1448 he signed a concordat with Frederick III regarding the rights of the church in Germany; he wisely acquiesced in Francesco Sforza's efforts to make himself duke of Milan in 1450; he laid much of the groundwork for the Peace of Lodi in 1455. See Manetti, Book 2, passim.

116–18. If ever the standards of God] If ever a crusade against the Turks should be organized; the latter was a goal of many Renaissance popes. See *CV* XXIX.

129–30. *sectaris . . . pacem:* 2 Timothy 2:22.

139–40. tottering churches . . . better churches] The lines refer to Nicholas' extensive program to rebuild Rome, particularly its churches, for which see Manetti, Book 2.

XXIX

Exhortations to launch a crusade against the Turks were a staple of humanist literature in the 1400s, especially after the fall of Constantinople in May 1453. See James Hankins, "Renaissance Crusaders: Humanist Crusade Literature in the Age of Mehmed II," in idem, *Humanism and Platonism in the Italian Renaissance*, vol. 1 (Rome: Edizioni di storia e letteratura, 2003), 293–424. Resta dates this poem to 1452, which seems plausible, given the absence of any reference to the fall of Constantinople. Jerusalem in this period was under the control of the Mamluk Sultans of Egypt, not the Syrians; Marrasio's "Syrians" is a literary name for the traditional enemies of crusading armies, based on older crusading literature, not on contemporary circumstances.

1. he] Nicholas V

2. Augustus] For a comparison between Nicholas V and Augustus in a funerary epigram composed by Maffeo Vegio, see Manetti, XVIn. Anna Modigliani, ibid., remarks on the use of Suetonius' *Life of Augustus* as Manetti's model in his life of Nicholas.

4. sovereign and independent] As Nicholas effectively did with Bologna at the start of his reign.

5. Holy walls] That is, the walls of Jerusalem.

13. *eia . . . moras:* Vergil, *Aeneid* 4.569.

18. warlords] *Condottieri*, who tended to rule small mountain principalities in Italy, contrasted with great transalpine monarchs, such as Charles VII of France and Henry VI of England.

30. *pari pede*] That is, in hexameters, the meter of epic poetry.

XXX

The next three poems describe in rather too much self-pitying detail several maladies that afflicted Marrasio in his last years, beginning with a fall from the back of a mule (XXX.86 and 136ff.), followed by bouts of plague and quartan fever (or malaria). These maladies lasted from approximately the summer of 1447 to April of 1450. According to Resta the three poems are arranged in chronological order and were composed "not much later than April 1450," after Marrasio regained his health. *CV* XLVII, the last poem in the Parma collection (see *CV* XXIV), seems to have been written as a dedication to this group of poems.

18. Referring to the common scholastic debating-point about the limits of God's power, which here is said to be limited only by the principle of noncontradiction, a radical position not accepted by Thomists.

24. do not help] Mere assent to principles of faith does not lead to conviction or moral reformation.

25–26. some people hold] The Epicureans believed that nothing survived the dissolution of the body.

26–30. Other positions on life after death: that the soul survives the body (Platonist); that a physical body will rise again with its soul (Aristotelian-Thomist); that the soul dies with the body (Epicurean). Marrasio states (29) that only the Aristotelian-Thomist position is consistent with the Catholic faith.

38. *Luciferi . . . decidit:* Isaiah 14:12.

43–44. The story of David, Bathsheba, and Uriah the Hittite, told in 2 Samuel 11.

45–46. The story of Moses and the Egyptian soldier, from Exodus 2:12.

47–72. The story of Jonah from the eponymous Old Testament book.

50. *carpit . . . remige:* Ovid, *Tristia ex Ponto* 1.10.4.

73. Did it keep me] "It" is the mercy of God, symbolized by the ivy plant. Marrasio now begins his complaint to God, comparing his own treatment at God's hands with that of Jonah. He makes full use of the Old Testament prophet's freedom to argue and haggle with God. That Marrasio intends his one-sided argument with God to be witty is suggested by XXXI.34.

78. *stomacho . . . meo:* Ovid, *Remedia amoris* 356.

79. monster] Literally, turtle (*testudo*).

86. slip first] See headnote.

92. I shall find shade] A common humanist image for finding a patron.

113–16. *consueram . . . meis*: compare CV XV.71–74.

134. the bull of brass is a light penalty] by comparison: Marrasio refers to the famous bronze bull built by the tyrant Phalaris of Agrigento. Victims were placed inside the bull, then a fire was lit under it.

171. one seed of the Sun] Phaethon; see Ovid, *Metamorphoses* 1.751.

198. The thought is obscure. The line may be corrupt or simply unpolished.

203–4. useless arts / And barbarous kingdoms] Does God think he is rebellious because he is holding on to pagan classical culture, useless for salvation? See 226, below.

207. this man] An abrupt shift of subject; "this man" must now be Nicholas V.

210. the Cesarean head] Frederick III, the Holy Roman Emperor, crowned by Nicholas in 1452.

214. the punishment] Presumably, condemnation to Hell.

215. If I am not to be raised] The thought seems to be: "My punishment is meaningless unless it is to purify the soul and atone for sin, so that I may have salvation." Possibly also: "Given the hellish sufferings I've endured, I deserve to escape Hell, which can offer nothing worse."

226. Those things] Again, the thought is far from clear, but Marrasio may mean here the "useless arts" of his youth, that is, love poetry, or perhaps classical studies in general. He admits they do nothing to bring men to salvation, in 227–30.

228. *causa . . . erit*: compare CV C.48.

244. No foreign arms] The literary arts of the pagans.

260. a fallen death] Do not let me die in a state of sin, without grace.

XXXI

3. Archigenes Terrana] This person, a Sicilian doctor it would seem, has not been identified. The words do not sound like a proper name; in a

manner reminiscent of Boccaccio's bogus Greek, Marrasio may have wanted *Archigenes* to mean something like *protomedico* (see CV XLIV, below), or "head doctor."

18. unmixed Falernian wine] Not a contemporary *cru*, but a wine famous and expensive in antiquity, known from Pliny and other sources. Since ancient diners drank their wine mixed with water, for a servant to drink "unmixed Falernian" means that he is both a drunkard and a wastrel, and probably a thief as well.

XXXII

1–2. The dangling modifier is in the original.

39. The translation is a guess at the meaning of an ungrammatical sentence. Perhaps *fabricata*: "Life on the point of death manufactures men of fading powers."

43. *fessos . . . ocellos:* Ovid, *Amores* 3.5.1.

46. was less serious] Fear of death was less than my other sufferings.

52. quartan fever] A form of malaria, among whose symptoms are physical paroxysms at three- or four-day intervals.

58. Marrasio compares the chattering of his teeth to a battle.

63. *crepitare . . . rostro:* Ovid, *Metamorphoses* 6.97.

74. It will be remembered that Marrasio himself practiced medicine in Palermo, having obtained a degree in that subject in Ferrara in 1433.

119–20. Referring to the phenomenon of farsightedness in the old.

125–26. In other words, he was old before his time. Marrasio was only about fifty when these sufferings overtook him.

128. Traveled: *revoluta*. Wine barrels were transported from place to place by rolling them onto carts and ships.

144–45. The date of Easter in 1450 was April 5th; the next time it fell on April 6th was in 1455, after Marrasio's death. Resta suggests that *sextam* may modify an understood *partem*, so that "April was finishing its sixth part," that is, its fifth day. This may be to credit Marrasio's poem with too much calendrical precision.

159–60. That is, to pass the four seasons at Rome, to spend a year in Rome.

160. *nova . . . bibi*: Ovid, *Ars amatoria* 2.695.

XXXIII

Marrasio's voyage from Palermo to Pozzuoli, near Naples, is described. Resta says that the voyage was undertaken shortly after he recovered from his illnesses (a reasonable conjecture given the date of the poem, February 20, 1451) and that he was probably seeking a benefice from Alfonso of Aragon, then in Naples. He took passage aboard a galleass from Alfonso of Aragon's fleet that was preparing to go on Crusade to the East. Alfonso's initial objective was not Syria, however, as Marrasio says (see the headnote to *CV* XXIX) but probably Albania, where he was going to reinforce his ally Scanderbeg against the Turks. See Alan Ryder, *Alfonso the Magnanimous, King of Aragon, Naples and Sicily, 1396–1458* (Oxford, 1990), chapter 7.

2. Lipari is an island north of the Sicilian coast, possibly a staging area for Alfonso's naval adventures; or perhaps the boat's crew were simply sailors from Lipari.

27. south wind accumulates dark and dusty clouds] The Sirocco, a hot, dusty wind from the Sahara desert that can reach hurricane speeds.

41. Ustica] A small island north of Sicily, 155 kilometers west of Lipari. Either the ship had been blown far off its course or the pilot had stood far out to the west to catch the southwest wind into the Bay of Naples.

43–44. Africus] The southwest wind and the south wind, working in tandem.

46. the Cumaean port] The port of Puteoli, next to the Lake of Avernus, where the Cumaean Sibyl dwelt.

48–62. Believe me, *etc.*] The Cumaean Sibyl foretells the future in a typically gnomic manner.

53. the treasurer] Probably the condottiere Iñigo d'Avalos, appointed Gran Camerlengo in 1449, also a patron of humanists; Pisanello struck a portrait medal in his honor in 1449. The Aragonese Parliament had

voted a huge subsidy for the crusade, most of which was diverted into a war with Venice against Francesco Sforza.

55. Desus and Graffeus] Not identified; presumably Aragonese naval officers.

XXXIV

The subject of Marrasio's poem is Lucrezia d'Alagno (ca. 1430–79), a woman of noble birth and King Alfonso's lover. Their love was the theme of other humanist poems, including verses by Panormita, Filelfo, Giovanni Pontano, Porcellio, and Pietro Odo da Montopoli.

1. By a bloody death Lucretia] That is, Lucretia (d. ca. 510 BCE), the wife of Lucius Tarquinius Collatinus, whose rape by the son of the last Roman king, Tarquin the Proud, and subsequent suicide was the spark that led to the founding of the Roman republic. Her story is told in Livy 1.57–58; Ovid, *Fasti* 2.721–852; Dionysius Halicarnassus 4.64–85 (which Marrasio is unlikely to have known); and in Boccaccio's *Famous Women*, XLVIII.

3. Caesar Alfonso] Perhaps Marrasio is encouraging Alfonso to claim the imperial title, as others at the time hoped he would; or perhaps the name is used merely in reference to Alfonso's military successes. In any case, using the name allows Marrasio to draw the contrast between the love of a virtuous monarch, Alfonso, and a vicious rape by the tyrant Tarquin.

7. This Lucrezia] Lucrezia d'Alagno.

10. A play on Ovid's *quoque minor spes est, hoc magis ille cupit* ("and the less his hope [of seduction], the more he wanted her"). The implied contrast continues: Tarquin and Lucretia were opposites in the scale of human virtue; Lucrezia and Alfonso are equals.

XXXV

This poem seems to have accompanied the gift of a hunting dog to Alfonso.

1. Odrysians] A people of Thrace. The Odrysian gift-giving customs may be a garbled version of Thucydides 2.97. The lines are an oblique

comment on the asymmetrical exchange of gifts between Marrasio and King Alfonso: a hunting dog for a benefice.

4. The chiastic word order is unusual, but this must be the sense.

XXXVI

Garcia di Cuevasruvias was the brother of Alfonso, archbishop of Monreale, a diocese just south of Marrasio's Palermo. The poem describes his death in a hunting accident in Sicily after going on pilgrimage to Rome. Resta dates the poem to after April of 1450. The next five poems, CV XXXVI–XL, form a group. The first two were possibly intended for presentation to Archbishop Alfonso. The last three read like three drafts of the same epitaph, reusing materials from the much longer poem, XXXVI.

10. *Divertit:* sc. *Devertit.*

11. *quassans . . . dextra:* Ovid, *Metamorphoses* 8.404.

21. Him, him!] Marrasio imitates the speech pattern of the servants as they realize just who has fallen, an obscure rhetorical scheme called *conduplicatio* (*Rhetorica ad Herrenium* 4.38), designed to heighten pathos.

29. Marrasio describes the medieval surgical technique of trepanning with his usual excess of detail.

39. Marrasio imitates the professional patter of the medieval doctor.

XXXVII

Resta dates this elegy to early 1451, just before Marrasio's departure for Naples to seek an audience with King Alfonso. Marrasio apologizes for the delay in paying his respects to Archbishop Alfonso following the death of his brother.

XXXVIII

Resta dates the poem to after April 1450. The first three verses are a variant of XXXVI.1–3.

XXXIX

Presumably, written around the same time as XXXVI and XXXVIII. Verses 3–4 repeat 13–14 of XXXVI; 5 repeats part of II; and 7–8 repeat 59–60.

XL

The poem is mostly woven of elements from the preceding poems and must have been written around the same time.

XLI

Resta identifies Gallina as Tolomeo Gallina, an astrologer born in Catania near Marrasio's home town of Noto. Gallina lived in Naples and was the author of a treatise entitled *On Matters Astrological*. He was one of Pontano's teachers; the latter dedicated a short poem to him. According again to Resta, the poem was probably written during Marrasio's sojourn in Naples in 1451. The *fons Cosinanus* has not been identified.

XLII

Niccolò de' Tudeschi (1389–1445), who had been a professor of canon law at Siena from 1419 to 1430 during the period when Marrasio was studying there, was appointed archbishop of Palermo in 1435, a position he held until his death on February 24, 1445. He was Alfonso V of Aragon's representative at the Council of Basel, where he upheld a strong pro-conciliar line against Pope Eugene IV. The date of this poem is presumably shortly after de' Tudeschi's death.

1. Quirites] A name for the citizens of ancient Rome.

8. the red biretta] The council's antipope Felix V named de' Tudeschi a cardinal in 1440.

XLIII

Marco de'Grandi was a poet and statesman who lived in Syracuse. Of a noble family, he was made senator in 1425 and 1432 and served as secretary of the Camera Regionale from 1437 to 1465. He was the author of a sacred drama, the *Resurrectio Christi*, in Sicilian dialect (1414/34).

1. *Tristia*] Ovid's five-book collection of letters in elegiac couplets, written during his exile in Pontus.

4. makes glad] The language is biblical: see Psalms 104:15 and Proverbs 15:13.

XLIV

Pina was the daughter of Antonio Alessandro, the *protomedico* of Sicily. She married Antonio's successor in this position, a certain Pietro Alixandrano (here called Alixandro), who died young in 1452; the poem must then have been composed at some earlier date. A *protomedico* in Aragonese Sicily was a court official who oversaw medical services in a given area and licensed medical practitioners.

XLV

Nothing is known of the poem's recipient, Avanella. If the poem was actually written during Marrasio's bout of quartan fever, its date would be 1449 or 1450.

1. the three little books] Ovid's *Amores*, his first book of poetry, in elegiac couplets. For the three book/five book conceit, see the playful epigram introducing Ovid's work:

> Qui modo Nasonis fueramus quinque libelli,
> > Tres sumus; hoc illi praetulit auctor opus.
> Ut iam nulla tibi nos sit legisse voluptas,
> > At levior demptis poena duobus erit.

> We who once were five little books of Ovid,
> > Are three now; the author liked this version better.
> So now, if you take no pleasure in reading us,
> > The punishment is lighter with two books less.

XLVI

Another verse dedication of his poems for Nicholas V. Compare *CV* XXIV, above. The date of May 15, 1452, was shortly after Marrasio's arrival in Rome, but after *CV* XXIV, dated April 26 of the same year. This poem is more preoccupied with justifying the moral status of light verse, a traditional concern of Christian neoclassical poetry.

6. *vincit . . . labor*: Vergil, *Georgics* 1.145.

7. A play on Horace's advice in *Ars Poetica* 343 to mix the useful with the sweet, and to give advice and please the reader in equal measure.

20. *thura Sabaea*: Vergil, *Aeneid* 1.416–17.

25. you] Nicholas V. For his program to restore the churches of Rome, see Manetti, Book 2, and above, *CV XXIV*.

38. warrior of the Oscan Mus] Something of a pun, taken together with "partridge" in the previous line; *mus* is Latin for "mouse." The Decii Mures were an ancient plebeian clan of Oscan descent; two consuls called Publius Decius Mus distinguished themselves in battle during the wars of the fourth century BCE. See Livy 8.9–10, 9.40–41.

41. The line is corrupt. The couplet is unlikely to contain veiled references to courtesans, although it was common to refer to courtesans by their place of origin. But given Nicholas' reputation for holiness and the general unlikelihood that Marrasio could allude to such a subject in a poem addressed to the pope, the suggestion must be put aside. In any case, the great age of papal courtesans lay three decades in the future. The following couplet is equally obscure and possibly admits of a *sensus obscoenus*.

48. Pontine crus] Ovid famously complained about the frozen, acidic wine of Pontus, his place of exile.

51–52. Repeated from *CV XLV*.3–4.

XLVII

See the headnote to *CV XXX*. If this poem was written as an introduction to XXX, XXXI, and XXXII, just after Marrasio's recovery, it should be dated to 1450.

7–8. *languida . . . thoro*: Ovid, *Epistulae ex Ponto* 3.3.8.

9–12. Marrasio plays with the ancient convention that the best poetry is polished to a high sheen during the vigils of the night. The wider conceit is that poems conceived during his late bouts of fever are "sleepy" but that he cannot rest until the pope accepts them. Papal acceptance will allow the poems to "wake up" and survive, while he will be able to sleep and allow his poems to make their own reputation.

15–16. Perhaps referring to the *aubade*, a morning love song.

16. The daystar (*Lucifer*)] Venus.

18. wrap saffron] See *A* I.24 and *CV* 12.4.

APPENDIX I

1. From *Poeti latini*, 136–39 (no. XLIV). Our notes are based on those of the editor, Lucia Gualdo Rosa. The translation is by J. Hankins.

2. Joan of Arc.

3. Antonio Beccadelli, called "il Panormita," a Sicilian like Marrasio, who served Filippo Maria Visconti as his court poet in the late 1420s and 1430s; see the headnote to *CV* A.

4. Maffeo Vegio, for whom see the headnote to *CV* B.

5. Resta, 253–55. On Panormita, see the headnote to *CV* A.

6. A professional copyist esteemed by Enea Silvio Piccolomini, whose skills were recommended to Panormita by Giovanni Aurispa; Aurispa wrote a poem upon Francia's death in 1447.

7. Paolo Castagnoli is referred to by Panormita in another letter as "our man of business." See Resta, 254.

8. The Borromeo were a Milanese banking family with close ties to the ruling family of Milan, the Visconti.

9. Beccadelli was named court poet of Filippo Maria Visconti on December 10, 1429, with the rich stipend of four hundred gold florins per annum.

10. Almost certainly *CV* 1.

11. "Ergoteles" ("Good-at-his-work") was Panormita's disparaging nickname for Tommaso Tebaldi, a humanist-statesman from Bologna and a familiar of Filippo Maria Visconti; in 1447 he was governor of Piacenza.

12. See *CV* E.

13. Pertici, *Tra politica e cultura*, 76. On Petrucci, see *CV* X.4. Translation by J. Hankins.

14. *Animi dimidium mei* seems to be a variant (or perhaps a misremembering) of Horace's "half of my soul," *animae dimidium meae* (*Odes* 1.3.8). In Renaissance philosophy, *animus* generally means the rational part of the soul.

15. Resta, 255–56.

16. The jurist and humanist Catone Sacco (1394–1463) of the University of Pavia.

17. Resta, 257. Resta writes that the date of the poem "is perhaps after 1437, since Aurispa's father is not recorded, being already dead by that date."

18. Marrasio claimed to have two homelands, Noto and Siena. See *A* VII.28–30.

19. Resta, 256–57. The attribution to Bruni has been doubted, and the letter seems to have been "anonymized" in a manner common when familiar letters are adapted to become examples of the *ars epistolandi*. It is not known who "M." is; Resta's suggestion that he is Carlo Marsuppini *prima facie* seems unlikely, given that the latter was referred to by contemporaries (and by Marrasio himself) as Carolus Ar(r)etinus. Yet Marsuppini, given his closeness to the Medici, would have been a powerful patron, just the man to slip Marrasio into Florence's informal clientage system. As to the authenticity of the letter, nothing disqualifies it as a letter of Bruni, and the Latin style is not inconsistent with the Florentine chancellor's limpid elegance. The situation fits the state of Marrasio's career after his departure from Ferrara and return to Sicily; it would therefore have to date between 1442 and Bruni's death in March 1444.

20. Cicero, *Stoic Paradoxes* 6.51.

21. Cicero, *Letters to Atticus* 1.20.3.

22. Text from Tramontana, "Un inedito epigramma," 105n, based on Wrocław, Biblioteka Uniwersytecka, MS Rehdiger 60, ff. 116r–127r; see P. O. Kristeller, *Iter Italicum*, vol. 3 (London-Leiden, 1989), p. 428a. The poem appears at the end of Dati's translation of forty fables of Aesop,

completed around 1443. The text was previously published by O. Tacke, "Eine bisher unbekannte Aesopübersetzung aus dem 15. Jahrhundert," *Rheinische Museum für Philologie* 67 (1912): 299, but with errors, corrected by Tramontana. For Leonardo Dati (1408–72), see the entry of Renzo Ristori in *DBI* 33 (1987). Translation by J. Hankins.

23. Horace, *Odes* 1.3.8, quoted from Horace's tribute to Vergil.

24. Text from Tramontana, "Un inedito epigramma," 120, based on Paris, Bibliothèque Nationale de France, MS lat. 8413, ff. 8v–10v. The poem is undated but probably from the late 1440s or early 1450s. Girolamo Forti, a humanist born in Teramo, was Uditore della Sacra Rota and chaplain to King Ferrante in the 1460s, later an associate of Pontano's academy. A consolatory poem to him is found in Giovanni Pontano's *Eridanus* (1.41), published in this I Tatti Library, translated by Luke Roman (Cambridge, MA, 2014), 250–55. For the poetic context of this epigram, which responds to a poem by Girolamo to one Gaspare da Teramo (probably the schoolmaster Gaspare Lelli da Teramo), see ibid. Translation by J. Hankins.

25. Marrasio reuses what appears to be a coinage, *altiloquens*, in Girolamo's poem (l. 9). For later uses of the word and its derivatives, see Johann Ramminger's website, *Neulateinische Wortliste* at www.neulatein.de.

26. That is, to make yourself immortal: see Ovid, *Amores* 3.9.28 and *Epistulae ex Ponto* 3.2.32; Propertius 1.19.2.

27. That is, Delphic Apollo, the god of inspiration. Cyrrha is the port of Delphi.

APPENDIX II

1. Found in Parma, Biblioteca Palatina MS Parm. 28, ff. 36v–37r, this brief, anonymous commentary has been plausibly attributed to Marrasio himself by Resta. It was published in a footnote to his edition on pp. 185–86. Our text follows Resta's, with some adjustment of punctuation. The numbers in square brackets refer to the line numbers of CV XVII. (The English translation and notes are by J. Hankins.) The manuscript contains also the text of the poem.

2. It is not clear what "refutation" Marrasio is refuting. Here he seems to answer the charge that the poem was too obscure.

3. Compare Horace, *Ars poetica* 275–88.

4. Horace, *Ars poetica* 333–34.

5. Marrasio seems to be referring to the traditional tragic and comic masks.

6. Argus Panoptes, the hundred-eyed giant of Greek mythology.

7. Niccolò Loschi, who had been a student of Guarino's, was the son of the better-known Antonio Loschi, secretary to Filippo Maria Visconti; he writes to his brother, who is in the family's hometown of Vicenza. The text of this letter is taken from R. Sabbadini, *Biografia documentati di Giovanni Aurispa* (Noto, 1890), pp. 182–83, with slight adjustments of punctuation. The English translation and notes are by J. Hankins.

8. Horace, *Ars poetica* 180–82.

9. Loschi seems to concur with Marrasio that the modern masque differed from its ancient dramatic prototype.

10. Terence, *The Eunuch* 729, inaccurately quoted.

11. The editor, Remigio Sabbadini, found the passage illegible; perhaps *matronam* should be read for *matrimonium*.

12. On Guarino see the headnote to *CV F*.

Bibliography

꽃S꽃

EDITIONS

Altamura, Antonio. "I carmi latini di Giovanni Marrasio." *Bollettino del Centro di studi filologici e linguistici siciliani* 2 (1954): 204–44. Contains the *Angelinetum* and *CV* I–XIX only. Reviewed by Resta, "Per una edizione critica," as below.

Iohannis Marrasii Angelinetum et carmina varia. Edited by Gianvito Resta. Palermo: Centro di studi filologici e linguistici siciliani, 1976. Substantive reviews by Mariotti, Martellotti, and Traina, as below.

Poeti latini del Quattrocento. Edited by Francesco Arnaldi, Lucia Gualdo Rosa, and Lucia Monti Sabia. Milan-Naples: Ricciardi, 1954. Contains the Latin text with Italian translation of *A* I, III, IV, VI, VII; *CV* II, XIX.

STUDIES

Bisanti, Armando. "Aspetti dell'imitazione virgiliana nei carmi latini di Giovanni Marrasio." *Orpheus* 13 (1992): 33–51.

—— . "Suggestioni properziane e «descriptio pulchritudinis» nei carmi di Giovanni Marrasio." In *In memoria di Salvatore Vivona. Saggi e studi*, edited by Giuseppe Catanzaro, 143–75. Assisi, 1997.

Bottiglioni, Gino. *La lirica latina in Firenze nella seconda metà del secolo XV.* Pisa: Nistri, 1913.

Constant-Desportes, Barbara. "L'*Angelinetum* de Giovanni Marrasio: De l'inter- à la transculturalité?" *Camenulae* 6 (November 2010): 1–23 [online journal].

Coppini, Donatella. "I canzonieri latini del Quattrocento. Petrarca e l'epigramma nella strutturazione dell'opera elegiaca." In *"Liber," "fragmenta," "libellus" prima e dopo Petrarca. In ricordo di D'Arco Silvio Avalle. Seminario internazionale di studi, Bergamo, 23–25 ottobre 2003*, edited by

Francesco Lo Monaco, Luca Carlo Rossi, Niccolo Scaffai, 220–26. Florence: SISMEL, 2006.

Coppini, Donatella, and Paolo Viti. "La produzione latina dell'età umanistica." In *Storia della letteratura italiana*, vol. X: *La tradizione dei testi*, edited by Enrico Malato. Rome: Salerno, 2001.

Di Giovanni, Vincenzo. "Marrasio siciliano poeta latino del sec. XV." *Nuove effemeridi siciliane di scienze, lettere ed arti* 2.1 (1874): 317–19.

Di Lorenzo, Enrico. "Appunti sul distico elegiaco di Giovanni Marrasio." In *I Gaurico e il rinascimento meridionale*, edited by Alberto Granese et al., 311–27. Salerno: Centro Studi sull'Umanesimo Meridionale, 1992.

Fantazzi, Charles. "The Style of Quattrocento Latin Love Poetry." *International Journal of the Classical Tradition* 3 (1996): 127–46.

Galli, Roberta. "Una poesia umanistica sulla Fonte Gaia di Siena." In *Interrogativi dell'Umanesimo*, vol. I: *Essenza-persistenza-sviluppi. Atti del IX Convegno internazionale del Centro di studi umanistici, Montepulciano, Palazzo Tarugi 1972*, edited by Giovannangiola Tarugi, 81–86. Firenze: Olschki, 1976.

Gavinelli, Simona. "The Reception of Propertius in Late Antiquity and Neolatin and Renaissance Literature." In *Brill's Companion to Propertius*, edited by Hans-Christian Günther, 399–415. Leiden: Brill, 2006.

Hankins, James. "The Latin Poetry of Leonardo Bruni." *Humanistica Lovaniensia* 39 (1990): 1–39. Reprinted with corrections in idem, *Humanism and Platonism in the Italian Renaissance*, vol. I: *Humanism*, 137–75. Rome: Storia e letteratura, 2003.

——— . *Plato in the Italian Renaissance*. 2 vols. London-Leiden: Brill, 1990.

Mariotti, Scevola. "Marrasio Carmina varia 1, 37R." *Giornale italiano di filologia*, n.s. 7 (1976): 322–23. [Mariotti's conjectures and suggested repairs to the text are also found *obiter* in Resta's own apparatus.]

Martellotti, Guido. "*I carmi del Marrasio.*" In idem, *Dante e Boccaccio e altri scrittori dall'umanesimo al romanticismo*, 257–71. Florence: Olschki, 1983. [A reprint with corrections of his review in *Annali della Scuola Normale di Pisa* (1977): 1705–13.]

Parker, Holt. "Renaissance Latin Elegy." In *A Companion to Roman Love Elegy*, edited by Barbara Gold, 476–90. Malden-Oxford: Wiley-Blackwell, 2012.

Pertici, Petra, ed. *Tra politica e cultura nel primo quattrocento senese: Le epistole di Andreoccio Petrucci (1426–1443)*. Preface by Riccardo Fubini. Siena: Accademia Senese degli Intronati, 1990.

Ponte, Giovanni. "Appunti sul distico elegiaco di Giovanni Marrasio, Di Lorenzo, Enrico (review)." *La Rassegna della letteratura italiana* ser. 8, 98 (1994): 280.

Resta, Gianvito. *L'epistolario del Panormita. Studi per una edizione critica*. Messina: Università degli studi di Messina, 1954.

———. "Per una edizione critica dei carmi di Giovanni Marrasio." *Rinascimento* 5.2 (1954): 261–89.

———. "Un antico progetto editoriale dell'epistolario del Panormita." *Studi umanistici* 1 (1990): 7–67.

Sabbadini, Remigio. "L'*Angelinetum* di Giovanni Marrasio." In *La Biblioteca delle scuole italiane* 4 (1892): 193–96.

Traina, Alfonso. "Note al testo del Marrasio." *Studi e problemi di critica testuale* 16 (1978): 63–67. Reprinted in idem, *Poeti latini (e neolatini). Note e saggi filologici*, 2:163–71. Bologna: Pàtron, 1981. A review of Resta.

Tramontana, Alessandra. "Marrasio Siculo." In *Dizionario biografico degli Italiani* 70 (2008): 706–11.

———. "Un inedito epigramma di Giovanni Marrasio per Girolamo Forti." *Studi medievali e umanistici* 5–6 (2007–2008): 105–23.

Vecce, Carlo. "Il latino e le forme della poesia umanistica." In *Manuale di letteratura italiana. Storia per generi e problemi*, edited by Franco Brioschi and Costanzo Di Girolamo, 1:438–62. Torino: SEL, 1993.

Index of First Lines

Index

𝕬𝕾𝕻𝕬

Note numbers to the poems refer to line numbers of the various poems included in the Notes to the Translations. Thus, "257n79–84" indicates a note found on page 257 referring to lines 79–84 of the given poem. Headnotes have *n* immediately following the page number (e.g., "263n"). Notes to the Introduction and the Appendices are given by page and note number, e.g., "xix n3" or "268n3."

Publication of this volume has been made possible by

The Myron and Sheila Gilmore Publication Fund at I Tatti
The Robert Lehman Endowment Fund
The Jean-François Malle Scholarly Programs and Publications Fund
The Andrew W. Mellon Scholarly Publications Fund
The Craig and Barbara Smyth Fund
for Scholarly Programs and Publications
The Lila Wallace–Reader's Digest Endowment Fund
The Malcolm Wiener Fund for Scholarly Programs and Publications